T0291520

Data Protection:
Governance, Risk Management, and Compliance

David G. Hill

CRC Press
Taylor & Francis Group
Boca Raton London New York

CRC Press is an imprint of the
Taylor & Francis Group, an **informa** business

Data Protection: Governance, Risk Management, and Compliance

David G. Hill

CRC Press
Taylor & Francis Group
6000 Broken Sound Parkway NW, Suite 300
Boca Raton, FL 33487-2742

First issued in paperback 2019

ISBN-13:978-1-4398-0692-0 (hbk)
ISBN-13:978-0-367-38533-0 (pbk)

Library of Congress Cataloging-in-Publication Data
Application submitted.

**Visit the Taylor & Francis Web site at
http://www.taylorandfrancis.com**

**and the CRC Press Web site at
http://www.crcpress.com**

Dedication

To the memory of my parents,

David H. and Zona R. Hill,

For all that they did for me.

Contents

Preface

Waking up one day and finding that your enterprise has suffered from a lack of data protection would be a traumatic event. The reason might be as dramatic as a disaster such as a hurricane, earthquake, or other natural event, so that mission-vital information you thought was protected was instead lost forever. Think of the unpleasant consequences not only to your organization, but also to you personally. Or consider the serious consequences that might ensue if your organization has to admit publicly that a data breach has violated the data privacy rights of many.

Less dramatic, but still important, is what to do about a revenue-producing application being unavailable for much longer than your company can afford. Or the consequences of failing a compliance audit. Or the unexpected mind-numbing cost of having to collect, analyze, and manage huge amounts of information because of a lawsuit.

More examples are unnecessary: You get the idea. You do not want the one or more key issues about data protection in which you have a personal investment to keep you up at night.

Data protection is well-known to be a business necessity (and business here means not only for-profit business, large or small, but also nonprofit organizations and governmental agencies). Yet few agree on exactly what data protection is. You might not realize that all of the examples of a lack of data protection are really about data protection, but they are. Many different interpretations of data protection exist (and that is part of the problem). For example, the European Union equates data protection with data privacy. While data privacy is certainly an important element of data protection, data protection has much more breadth and depth.

Failure to appreciate the full dimensions of the data protection challenge can lead to poor data protection management and costly resource allocation issues as well as exposure to risks created by ineffective data protection.

The Sea Change in Data Protection

In the last several years, the landscape of data protection has changed fundamentally—there has been a true "sea change." This change has significantly affected risk management, compliance, and governance responsibilities for data protection, which is why the focus in much of this book is on a governance, risk, management, and compliance (GRC) framework. These changing requirements affect where data protection "bets" should be placed and how much should be "bet." The net result, as will be seen, is a sea change—a marked transformation.

People, processes, and technology have all been affected by this sea change. The change has not been a revolution, in that much of what already exists with regard to data protection is not likely to be thrown away, but it has definitely been a rapid evolutionary process in which change has and will continue to happen very quickly. In evolutionary terms, the sea change in data protection is a punctuated equilibrium, in which a long period of relatively little change is followed by a period of rapid evolutionary change.

This sea change in data protection raises a number of questions for which organizations must have answers. Among these questions are

- How do governance and compliance fit with risk management in presenting a broader picture of data protection than is now typically considered?
- What is the right target and what are the right objectives for a comprehensive data protection strategy?
- How are data protection infrastructure holes identified and—if any are found—how are they filled?
- How do all the existing and emerging piece of the data protection puzzle fit together to help build a roadmap for evolving the overall data protection strategy?

Who Should Read This Book

Data protection—or the lack of data protection—affects everyone. While that is true, the real question is why you should read a long and detailed book on data protection. The answer is that, if you can or should have an influence in making sure that one or more of the vital aspects of data protection are done effectively, then you should read this book.

Data protection is both a business and a technical issue. Business has to set the direction, including policies, for data protection, and suffers the consequences if data protection is not done well. But, since our focus is protection of electronic information, data protection is a technical issue in that information technology is required to carry it out.

On the technical side, anyone in whose organization data protection is carried out should read this book, including data center managers and system managers. Also, anyone who is involved with data protection in any way, such as consultants and professional service professionals, should read this book. In addition, the chief information officer (CIO) and the chief information security officer (CISO), whose organizations are responsible for ensuring the technical aspects of data protection, should give their full attention. Many members of their respective staffs, including managers and front-line professionals, should also be intimately familiar with the data protection framework.

On the business side, those who have a special knowledge and interest in at least one of the key aspects of data protection should find this book useful. This includes compliance officers, business continuity and disaster recovery specialists, risk management specialists, legal personnel involved in electronic discovery or data privacy issues, and records managers. But it also includes people with special knowledge of a particular business function—sales and marketing, order entry, human resources, finance, etc,—who are involved in a project such as for compliance or legal discovery.

Finally, C-level executives should be aware of the breadth and scope of data protection. Realistically, such executives (except for those mentioned above) are not likely to read a book on data protection, but at least one key individual on their staff should be aware of the issues and be able to summarize them. Effective data protection costs money—in people, time, and resources. With the always-competing demands for always-scarce dollars, euros, or the like, executives have to prioritize the different aspects of data protection appropriately. And executives have to have an ongoing commitment (which means that they remain firm in ensuring that the appropriate actions are carried out).

Those who interact with businesses regarding some aspect of data protection should also find the book of interest. This includes vendors who sell products or services that relate to at least one facet of data protection, professionals whose clients are businesses and who advise on one area or other that touches upon data protection, and those who need a better understanding of what can and cannot be done in data protection before proposing rules, regulations, or laws that will affect the business community.

xxii   Data Protection: Governance, Risk Management, and Compliance

In addition, academics in computer science, and their students, should understand the scope of data protection. In fact, students in a computer science program should have a comprehensive understanding of data protection.

What Should You Read

For many readers, why you should understand the broad picture will be obvious. However, although data security is pervasive, many readers have a very specific interest—say, compliance with a particular law or how to respond to a specific civil litigation event. The answer is that in the GRC framework, all the pieces of the data protection puzzle are interrelated. You need to know how they are interrelated (as well as how they are independent) so that you can better understand the context in which the aspect of data protection in which you are most interested is expressed. Even though that understanding has a technical flavor, you should still find that a non-technologist can follow along.

David G. Hill
Principal
Mesabi Group LLC
www.mesabigroup.com

Acknowledgments

I would like to thank all of the many people who helped me, either directly or indirectly, in the preparation of this book. Your knowledge, wisdom, and support have been (and are) invaluable in advancing my research. However, while I would like to identify each of you by name, I feel that I need to single out those who have been supportive and helpful over a period of years for special acknowledgment. Kudos are deserved by:

Wayne Kernochan
Charles King
Bob Moran
Paul Payack
Dan Tanner
Anyck Turgeon

And, last but not least, my very supportive wife,

Irene Hill

Acknowledgments

About the Author

David Hill is the principal of Mesabi Group LLC, which focuses on how enterprises can adopt new and improved IT processes and technologies that not only meet immediate requirements, but also help position themselves for future growth. Data protection is a key area of concentration. Prior to founding Mesabi Group, he was the vice president and founder of the Storage & Storage Management practice at the Aberdeen Group. Previously he spent many years at Data General, where, among other activities, he directed Data General's internal data centers as well as managed the introduction of new analytical tools and business systems. Later at a large storage vendor, he carried out strategic marketing, competitive analysis, sales force planning, and primary market research. He is frequently quoted in the trade press. He has an advanced degree from the Sloan School at the Massachusetts Institute of Technology.

Chapter 1

The Time Has Come for Change

1.1 What to Look for in This Chapter

- Why data protection is important
- What data protection is
- Why the right framework for data protection is necessary
- Why organizations should ride the sea change in data protection
- How to read this book

1.2 Why Data Protection Is Important

The protection of electronically stored information—in all its different expressions—should be at or near the top of the *have-to* issues for any business. First, data protection seeks to protect that information without which businesses cannot function well—if at all. Indeed, electronic information is now a primary source of many businesses' competitive advantage. The permanent physical loss of key information (such as customer account information) or the loss of confidentiality of sensitive information (such as the theft of a trade secret) could have a severe negative impact on a business (such as loss of revenue or capital value of the firm). So data protection is a cornerstone of any organization's management of risk, and risk management is now recognized as one of the fundamental tasks of any enterprise.

Moreover, businesses have other obligations to protect their data, apart from the risk of loss of usability for normal business purposes. Compliance is—or should be—at the top of consciousness for nearly every organization today. As one of the many facets of compliance, the well-known data security threat that loss of confidentiality of information through a data breach can bring, such as a loss of data privacy, is paramount. And the need for better accountability has led to the need for better governance, notably from a data protection perspective, in how to deal with information with respect to requirements for managing the civil litigation process.

Today, data protection touches a wide spectrum of business issues, including but by no means limited to:

- Backup and restore
- Disaster recovery
- Business continuity
- High availability
- Compliance
- Governance
- Data privacy
- Data security
- eDiscovery

How all these pieces of the data protection puzzle fit into a comprehensive data protection framework is the subject of this book.

1.3   What Data Protection Is

Data protection is mitigation of the risk of loss of or damage to an enterprise's data. That loss can take many forms. One is physical loss of the data itself, either temporarily or permanently. Another is the loss of confidentiality of sensitive data. Still another is loss of the ability to be able to use the data because of a loss of access to the data for any reason or a loss of responsiveness in which the data cannot be retrieved for use (even if it is technically *available*) within a reasonable period of time.

Data protection, as a *have-to* function, means that it is a cost of doing business, and not a *want-to* function, which directly carries out the mission of any organization. This means that managing the costs of data protection is important, since spending more money on data protection generates fewer profits for for-profit businesses or requires more tax dollars for governmental organizations. However, data protection can be thought about in a different way than most other cost functions.

Think of data protection as an insurance policy. In that sense, the aim of data protection is not to maximize profits or revenues, or to minimize costs, but to minimize worst-case losses. Like other insurance, data protection insurance is a necessary cost of the prudent business, and it balances the costs of unplanned outages against the costs of the insurance policy. A side effect of data protection may be more cost-effective use of information assets; but users should not require profits from their data protection solutions, any more than from their life insurance policies on key executives.

Unlike the traditional insurance markets, the data protection market offers no "third-party" insurers (with the possible exception of Lloyd's of London). Enterprises are "self-insured" today, and should expect to be self-insured tomorrow. Insurance "premiums" are paid internally, in the form of additional hardware, software, and people. One principle remains the same, however: When payment is made for data protection insurance, the goal is to minimize its cost and maximize its value.

One principle remains the same, however: When payment is made for data protection insurance, the goal is to minimize its cost and maximize its value.

As noted above, data protection seeks to ensure not only the preservation and availability of data, but also its confidentiality, privacy, and availability to regulators. This is still insurance—the legal costs of failure to protect confidentiality and privacy, or to fail to supply appropriate information to regulators, are high, as are the competitive disadvantages of leaking proprietary information.

1.4   Data Protection Has to Be Placed in the Right Framework

Businesses are actively examining how to improve the data protection function from the perspectives of people, processes, and technology. And many data protection technologies, both old and new, are vying for attention as enablers of data protection processes. Trying to sort through the myriad of choices can be difficult.

The key to choosing any of these technologies is understanding the overall context, the overall "data protection infrastructure portfolio," into which individual data protection technologies should fit. Otherwise, what appear to be individually sound decisions may not lead to the necessary levels of data protection. Among the problems that can occur are

- Failure to protect data adequately, which can lead to negative consequences, such as loss of revenue from lost customer orders.
- Making the wrong allocation decision (spending too much on areas that do not really require that level of protection and too little on areas that require greater protection)
- Straining the administrative resources assigned to data protection even further and with less results than necessary

Without the right model, enterprises cannot know where to place their longer-term data protection technology investment bets or how much they should place on each bet. And that means that any model has to take into account the changing world of data protection technology.

1.5   Evolving to the Governance, Risk Management, and Compliance Framework

Data protection means many things to many people. Yet what is data protection really, and what does it cover? The depth and breadth of data protection can be daunting. Exploration of data protection starts with defining the first principles of data protection and then expanding to get a more detailed and comprehensive view. That process starts with traditional risk management but eventually moves on to include the compliance and governance-related aspects of data protection.

Getting to an overall understanding of the breadth and depth of data protection was an evolutionary process. Finding a concept that offered a way of tying the pieces of the data puzzle together was necessary. That organizing principle would simplify thinking about data protection at the highest level and then allow a drill-down to deeper levels of understanding.

The organizing principle that eventually seemed to fit the best was built around the concepts of governance, risk management, and compliance (GRC). The most visible advocate of GRC is the Open Compliance and Ethics Group (OCEG). OCEG has promulgated the concepts of governance, risk management, and compliance from a corporate perspective. OCEG promotes what it calls *principled performance,* so it is a strong advocate of businesses operating with the highest ethical standards.

How the general concept of GRC applies to data protection has been independently derived, but hopefully the application to data protection with the overall goal of proper conduct by all organizations is consistent with the broader corporate perspective.

1.6   Ride the Sea Change in Data Protection

Change that affects the requirements for data protection is coming from several directions. One of the directions is extending and improving what is already being done. An example of this from a technology perspective is disk-to-disk backup that improves on the traditional backup/restore process.

A second direction is change in the basic way that the movement and storage of information is carried out in an organization. For example, information lifecycle management (ILM) is not only about moving information from one tier of storage to another, but also about managing stored information differently—and a major effect of the difference in information management is in better data protection. Moreover, ILM leads to an overall change in the mix of data protection technologies (e.g., data replication versus data backup) that are used within an enterprise.

A third direction of change comes about from changing business requirements. A key illustration is a new emphasis on business-governance/compliance policies, which require organizations to understand and implement new policies, processes, procedures, and practices as well as possibly new hardware and software data protection technologies.

The rest of this book examines the basic principles of data protection in light of these changing business requirements and in light of existing and emerging data protection technologies. The key takeaways that should be kept in mind are these:

1. Determine where overinvestment and underinvestment in data protection are taking place, so future investments can be directed to shore up the weak spots.

2. Determine what the effects of changing business requirements and technology advances on the data protection investment are.

3. Gain a sense of how the major categories of data protection technologies interact, so that a determination of the proper mix and delivery of the proper level of service can take place.

1.7   How to Read This Book

The starting point for understanding data protection is risk management. Chapters 2 through 6 build the story of data protection from a risk management perspective.

Chapter 2 starts off the exploration of data protection with a familiar subject—business continuity as part of risk management. Disaster recovery and operational recovery are the two key components of business continuity. A key distinction is made between logical data protection (such as protecting against data corruption) and physical data protection (such as protecting against the failure of a storage device). Chapter 3 uses a simple matrix of the disaster-operational-physical-logical first principles as a reference point in describing where key problems of data protection lie for business continuity. Chapter 4 discusses how the concept of high availability is important for data protection, but that there are three other primary objectives—preservation, confidentiality, and responsiveness—that have to be met as well. Chapter 5 introduces the need to have multiple degrees (or layers) of data protection to prevent failures from destroying the ability to protect data.

Chapter 6 introduces how information lifecycle management changes the data protection game dramatically, because ILM leads to the need for active archiving. Active archiving not only affects what data is stored where, but how different data is managed differently, such as for data retention purposes.

Chapter 7 on compliance and Chapter 8 on governance introduce the two other pillars of the GRC framework. Chapter 8 also shows how the data protection objectives match up with each of the GRC responsibilities.

Chapter 9 expands earlier mentions of data retention into the greater depth and detail that is necessary to discuss this pivotal issue in data protection.

Chapter 10 gives a data security perspective of data protection. Data security is integral to data protection. Many data protection issues are often viewed under the rubric of data security. This chapter focuses on the issues related to the loss of confidentiality for sensitive information, including data privacy and encryption, but also touches on a number of other topics, including information assurance and nation-state attacks.

Chapters 11 through Chapter 15 focus on data protection technologies, primarily from a risk management perspective. This part of the book includes Chapter 12 on traditional technologies, such as backup/restore software. Chapter 13 discusses technologies that do not perform data protection functions directly, but that support the ability of data protection to work better and more efficiently, such as data deduplication, WAN acceleration, and disaster recovery testing. Chapter 14 describes how disk and tape technologies complement and compete with each other, including virtual tape libraries. Chapter 15 covers high-availability and low (or no)-data loss technologies, including point-in-time copying, continuous data protection, and replication technologies.

Chapter 16 discusses the special technology requirements for compliance, governance, and data security, and Chapter 17 covers the importance of eDiscovery for civil litigation for the governance pillar of the GRC framework.

Chapter 18 dwells on the issues surrounding the impact of the use of third-party services in conjunction with data protection. This impact is growing in importance. Notably, cloud computing, software-as-a-service, and storage-as-a-service take center stage in this discussion.

Chapter 19 covers a number of other considerations that have to be taken into account when performing data processing. The role of tiering in data protection, from flash computing to tape, is an important consideration. So is the impact of server and storage virtualization on data protection. Interestingly, better data protection can lead to better overall information management, such as master data management, which can yield benefits derived from the ability to use information more effectively. And, of course, the role of data protection in green computing deserves attention.

Chapter 20 describes a kick-start planning model to help businesses get started in the planning process to improve their data protection as well as summing up and giving suggestions on redesigning data protection.

1.8   An Aside on Process Management

Although data protection technologies are an important part of the overall data protection picture, data protection is much more than a collection of technologies. Technology is not a *deus ex machina*. That is, users should not expect technology to fall from the sky and magically lead to the design, implementation, and ongoing carrying out of the activities that exemplify chosen data protection strategies. Instead, the 4 Ps of process management—*policy, process, procedures,* and *practices*—have to be put in place. (Technology enables the 4 Ps, but it does not replace them.) *Policy* defines a course of action but does not actually carry out the necessary actions. *Processes* are the actions that are necessary to reach the ends directed by a policy; they make the policy actionable. *Procedures* define the steps in any process. *Practices* ensure that the procedures with the processes that fulfill a policy are actually carried out.

Each of the 4 Ps requires conscious effort and thought on the part of any business for each of the pieces of data protection. Think of what needs to be done—who, what, where, how, and when—for each aspect of data protection separately and integrated as a whole. Throughout this book, think how people need to use the 4 Ps to ensure the proper use of technology.

1.9   Key Takeaways

- Protection of electronically stored information is essential for an organization, to meet not only risk management requirements, but also those of compliance and governance.
- Data protection is the self-insurance policy that an organization takes to mitigate the risk of loss (in a number of ways) of its data.

- If data protection is not set in the right framework, organizations are exposed to consequences from the failure to protect data adequately, misallocation of funds spent on data protection, and unnecessarily high costs to administer data protection.
- Change in data protection is coming about because of new business requirements, new and evolving data protection technologies to meet those business requirements, and a change in the basic way that information is moved and managed. Together the changes amount to a sea change that organizations have to align themselves with in order to avoid being swamped.

Chapter 2

Business Continuity: The First Foundation for Data Protection

2.1 What to Look for in This Chapter

- Why business continuity plays a key role in risk management
- How business continuity and data protection are interrelated
- Why business continuity, from an IT perspective, is more than disaster recovery
- What disaster recovery and operational recovery are really all about
- Why data protection must respond to both physical and logical data protection problems

2.2 Business Continuity as a Key to Risk Management

Risk management is one of the key responsibilities for any size enterprise. Business continuity is an essential subset of risk management. Business continuity is the mitigation of risk caused by interruption to normal enterprise activities and processes. Effective business continuity protects key stakeholders' interests, brand reputation, the goodwill of customers, and the value-creating activities of the enterprise. If a business continuity strategy fails, the consequences can range from undesirable or unacceptable (customer dissatisfaction or loss of productivity) to severe (economic loss of market valuation/revenue or loss of public or customer confidence), to outright catastrophic (business failure).

Even though electronically stored information (ESI) and the information technology (IT) infrastructure that supports that information is a *vital* component of business continuity, it is only a part of overall business continuity. People and non-IT physical assets are also critical components of business continuity. Still, that information and its supporting infrastructure require the utmost attention, because the word *vital* means just what it says from the perspective of existence, continuance, or well-being of the business. So focusing on business continuity from an IT and information perspective is worthy of attention.

More specifically, business continuity requires a software and hardware superstructure on top of key IT systems and networks that aims to ensure that (1) essential applications (and associated information) are available to all end users all of the time, despite failures of individual components (resiliency); and (2) when these applications are not available, the outage time is as short as possible (high availability in the sense of unplanned downtime of the order of only minutes per year). Note that in the case of a disaster these conditions may not apply. In that case, the focus is on minimizing the impact on business continuity.

For an application to work, all of its components—hardware, software, information storage, and networks—need to work. Of these, information storage is typically the most important, both because its loss can be irreparable and because, over time, it becomes the key bottleneck to recovery. Likewise, reloading an application, hot-swapping a server, or rerouting messages along a network is in practical terms a matter of minutes; reloading data may take much longer.

The key question, however, is whether the data is available to be restored at all. Replacing or restoring servers, networks, and applications is a necessary condition, but it is all for naught if the data cannot be restored to a working state. Therefore, a key task of any business continuity strategy is data protection, which means mitigating the risk of loss or damage to an enterprise's data, either temporarily or permanently. The inverse is also true: A key (although not the only) aim of data protection is business continuity. Furthermore, a business continuity strategy and architecture can serve as a good framework into which to fit data protection technologies and strategies. It is comprehensive; it ensures that the needs of other parts of the architecture, besides storage and the business as well as IT, are taken into account; and it fully recognizes the crucial role of information storage. The rest of this chapter considers how a business continuity framework can enlighten and improve a data protection strategy.

2.3   Business Continuity and Data Protection

To understand why enterprises may not be receiving the level of data protection that they think they are requires understanding that business continuity is not only about *disaster continuity* (more familiarly thought of as disaster recovery) but also about *operational continuity* (more familiarly thought of as operational recovery)—the ability to deal with day-to-day operational problems. For data protection to be effective, the right amount of attention has to be given to each—and that may not always be the case.

If IT organizations do not understand that day-to-day operations and disaster recovery planning have different requirements for both physical and logical data protection, they may not have the right technology mix—and therefore they may make the wrong investments—for data protection.

Both operational and disaster continuity require the proper level of both *physical* (storage device level) and *logical* (the data itself) data protection. Physically, a storage device, such as a hard disk drive (HDD), may fail or be destroyed, so the data on that drive may be lost. The loss will be permanent if no other copies are available. The loss will be temporary if a copy of the data has been safely preserved on a different disk or on magnetic tape. Logically, a data item may be flawed (and therefore cannot be used properly) even though the physical disk on which the data is stored is functioning perfectly. For example, a virus could corrupt data and make it unusable from a logical perspective even though the data is still physically available on a disk.

There are ways to ensure logical data protection, but the primary emphasis has traditionally been on the physical side. This can be a problem—database corruption that occurs in the middle of a vital business-intelligence query or customer order is not in the best interests of the business. Operational continuity requires an emphasis on logical data protection after the basic physical data protection requirements have been met.

2.4 Business Continuity Is Not Just Disaster Recovery

Business continuity tends to have an information technology flavor, but it is (or should be) an enterprise-wide activity that includes manual practices, processes, and procedures as well. Likewise, business continuity spans both operational continuity and disaster continuity.

On the IT side, data protection is a necessary but not a sufficient condition for business continuity (Figure 2.1).

As noted above, information (i.e., useful and usable data) is at the heart of business continuity. Depending on the level of severity, without data protection, the ability of processes and people to work successfully is jeopardized, if not impossible.

People
ex: internal application users,
IT professionals, customers,
suppliers, and partners

Networks
ex: LAN, MAN, WAN

Application Processes
ex: Web apps, supply chain,
business intelligence

Information
ex: Databases, fixed content

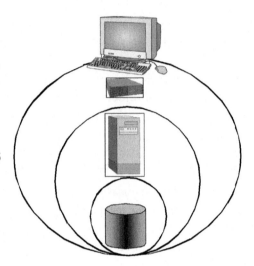

Figure 2.1   Business Continuity Is More than Data Protection

Yet data protection alone is not enough. Without the applications, processes, and networks working properly—and without people with the right skills in the right places who are able and willing to use them properly—the data cannot be accessed and used.

Likewise, IT may have responsibility for achieving high availability and resiliency of the computer systems, but business continuity involves more than this. Business continuity requires planning, so that the right people with the right skills will have the right tools and the right knowledge at the right time in order to respond to a threatened or actual negative service-level-impacting event. Thus, IT typically cannot have full responsibility for overall business continuity.

Business continuity requires planning, so that the *right* people with the *right* skills will have the *right* tools and the *right* knowledge at the *right* time in order to respond to a threatened or actual negative service-level-impacting event.

IT's responsibility for the availability of the IT infrastructure builds on two pillars: operational continuity and disaster continuity. The word *continuity* indicates that both types of strategy require proactive actions—for example, provisioning a disaster recovery facility to minimize the impact of a potential disaster (see Figure 2.2).

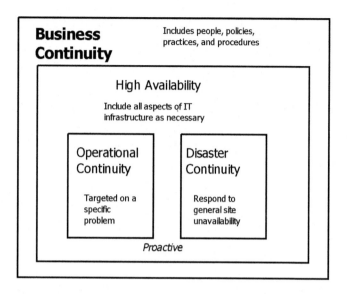

Figure 2.2   Overview of Business Continuity

Note that operational continuity focuses on targeting individual problems that it is hoped will have a limited scope, whereas disaster continuity has to focus on what would need to be done in the event that the entire IT infrastructure—including all applications and their supporting server, storage, and network services—has to be replicated at a site other than the original home of the applications.

Proactive activities of planning, provisioning, monitoring, and preventive maintenance prepare an enterprise as well as possible against the storms of service-level-threatening or devastating events. If and when such events occur, the two pillars turn into operational *recovery* and disaster *recovery* (Figure 2.3). *Reactive* actions that take place when a service-level-threatening event takes place should take advantage of previous proactive activities to better deal with the event.

Both operational recovery and disaster recovery involve danger from natural causes (including the inherent limitations in technology) and human-related causes, whether that is inadvertent human error or intent-based malignant attacks. Understanding the difference between the two types of recovery is essential for understanding the type of data protection that is best for each.

	Operational Recovery	Disaster Recovery
Time Down	• Minutes/year	• Hours to day per event
Infrastructure Threat	• Disk failure • Network congestion • Application performance degradation	• Earthquake • Blizzard • Fire • Flood
Willful Threat	• Computer viruses • Hacking	• Disgruntled employee • Terrorist attack

Figure 2.3   Business Continuity Keeps Your Business Running

2.5   Disaster Recovery: Let's Get Physical

The Storage Network Industry Association (SNIA) definition of disaster recovery (SNIA Dictionary at www.snia.org) is

> *Disaster Recovery (DR):* The recovery of data, access to data and associated processing through a comprehensive process of setting up a redundant site (equipment and work space) with recovery of operational data to continue business operations after a loss of use of all or part of a data center.

> This involves not only an essential set of data but also an essential set of all the hardware and software to continue processing of that data and business. Any disaster recovery may involve some amount of downtime.

Note that an event is considered a "disaster" only when data processing has to be moved from a primary to a secondary site and when that processing is carried out using a different set of computer hardware (including both servers and storage).

Physical data protection is properly the first focus of disaster continuity, but logical data protection needs to be taken into account (as well as, of course, reconstitution of applications, networks, and people resources). If there is a failover to a second site, that site now assumes an operational role, and so the data must not only exist physically at the second site but also must be usable immediately.

Problems that can be fixed at the primary site without requiring moving data to a second site are not a disaster in a business continuity sense. However, operational problems, such as the long-term loss of a critical database, could still be catastrophic to a business. (While IT personnel will understand the difference from a planning perspective, business management may not understand, and therefore care about, the distinction!)

Recovery from a disaster may take hours to days (if not longer). That may seem contrary to intuition to those businesses that employ a data protection technique called synchronous remote mirroring. *Mirroring* means to duplicate the data in a disk storage array on another array. *Synchronous remote mirroring* occurs when the copy of the data at two geographically different sites is identical. Remote synchronous mirroring can lead to a nearly instantaneous restart for storage. However, even if all the storage for an enterprise is mirrored remotely (which may very well not be the case), storage is only one aspect. The rest of the hardware infrastructure (servers and networks) and software infrastructure (applications, databases, and operating systems) also have to be in place. Additionally, people need to be in place.

An assessment process determines when to declare an emergency that results in a total transfer to a disaster recovery site, and that may take time. Note that this discussion applies only to a true disaster. In the case of a temporary local outage, automatic failover to a remote site (called an *active-active failover*) may occur with little or no apparent downtime. (By the way, synchronous remote mirroring may not be suitable for true disaster recovery, as the distance between the two sites for which synchronous remote mirroring is suitable may not be far enough apart for disaster recovery purposes. For example, the same earthquake or hurricane should not be able to take out both of two geographically separate sites because they were too close to each other.)

Interestingly, operational recovery can often take more time than disaster recovery. While the secondary site may benefit from synchronous mirroring, recovering a primary site either from the secondary site or from a tape backup can take hours—or days.

Most IT organizations have never experienced a true disaster and hopefully never will. That does not mean, however, that the second site is not necessary. In order to get the most out of the investment that needs to be made anyway, one objective might be to make the second site as useful as possible under normal business conditions. For example, failing over to a second site temporarily for planned maintenance or equipment upgrades at the first site and workload balancing are two reasons that the second site might be useful outside of disaster recovery. But, since all that could probably be done at a single site with better economies of scale, the real reason for the second site is "distance separation," to minimize the risk of both sites being affected at once. And even though disasters are relatively rare, that "insurance premium" is probably well worth the incremental cost.

2.6   Operational Recovery: Think Logically

The SNIA ILM definition of operational recovery (SNIA Dictionary at www.snia.org) is

> *Operational Recovery (OR):* Recovery of one or more applications and associated data to correct operational problems such as a corrupt database, user error or hardware failure.
>
> OR may use point-in-time copying or other techniques to create a consistent set of recoverable data.

Note that an operational recovery may be necessary as a result of either a logical problem (say, a virus or an accidental file deletion) or a physical problem (say, two drives failing in the same disk array, where there was protection against only one failure before the drive that initially failed was rebuilt). That said, operational recovery has a strong emphasis on logical data protection once the basic physical data protection technologies are in place. Since hardware is fairly reliable and operational issues occur frequently, logical problems play a prominent role in operational data protection.

There is one caveat: Many errors are user errors, such as an IT administrator configuring something improperly. User errors are classified as logical problems rather than physical problems even though no data may be changed from what it should be. For example, a configuration error that prevents a backup job from running so that the original data is not protected properly exposes that data to risk. Physically, the data could have been protected (because all the physical equipment was working properly); logically, it was not protected.

Operational recovery is within the control of the IT organization and is the responsibility of the IT organization. Operational recovery assumes that all (or nearly all) of the users are able and willing to use the applications—that is, normal working conditions prevail.

2.7   Disaster Recovery Requires Judgment; Operational Recovery Requires Automation

Disaster recovery responds to a systemic event that affects all applications either simultaneously or in a rolling manner. Disaster recovery requires a triage approach to recovery, by which the most time-sensitive and business-critical applications are restored first.

Operational recovery is a response to a non-systemic single event. A logical event typically affects a single application (although dependent applications may also be affected). In the case of a hardware failure, such as that of a disk array, all applications that use the affected disks will be involved, but other applications (unless there are dependencies) will not be. If disaster recovery is like responding to an epidemic, then operational recovery is like responding to events in an emergency room.

If *disaster recovery* is like responding to an epidemic, then *operational recovery* is like responding to events in an emergency room.

An operational recovery may involve people in the IT infrastructure other than storage personnel (such as a database administrator), but it should be able to be handled within the IT organization itself. The same is not true with disaster recovery.

Disaster recovery is really the responsibility of the entire enterprise, although the leadership role for the process may be assigned to the IT organization. (In many cases, IT may be in the unpalatable position of being charged with overall responsibility, but not given sufficient authority or resources to ensure the disaster recovery plan.)

Disaster recovery can be a people-intensive process. Although key aspects of the process can be automated (such as failover to a remote site), disaster recovery requires professional management. The range of possible disasters is so wide that human beings have to be able to adjust and compensate for the nature of the particular type of disaster. Although some degree of automation may be possible, adjustment to unplanned situations requires human judgment.

Disaster recovery is therefore always about a service-level-impacting event. A long-term active-active failover to a remote site for disaster recovery purposes with little or no downtime is unlikely. That is why it is a disaster. The goal is to minimize the effect on long-term business continuity.

In contrast, operational recovery may be able to respond to a service-level-threatening event before it becomes a service-level-impacting event. For example, a monitoring system may note that a backup job has failed to run to completion. Depending on circumstances, the backup job may be able to be rerun without having any impact whatsoever on service levels.

Speaking of service levels, IT needs to specify service-level agreements (SLAs) that spell out the level of service—for example, the availability of an application that IT promises its user community. Such agreements may be formal or informal. Some businesses (particularly larger ones or those that are very information-intensive) may require a formal agreement, in which expectations are spelled out in a written agreement between the IT organization and its various user communities. Other businesses may adopt an informal approach whereby IT specifies to itself what it feels it can achieve, but does not communicate those service levels to its user communities as an ironclad agreement.

Some IT organizations may deny that there is a need for SLAs. That is a mistake. SLAs can serve three purposes: management of user expectations, justification for acquiring resources, and better management focus. For example, a user community may want high availability for an application (and its associated information), but budgetary resources may not be available to provide that level of service. But whatever level is decided on it has to be measured. While it is probably not true that whatever cannot be measured cannot be managed, measuring SLAs for compliance is important not only for meeting user expectations but also for best deploying IT resources. This is also true for deploying IT resources for data protection. And that is where automation comes in.

Whenever it is feasible for operational recovery, IT professionals want to delegate continuity and recovery responsibility to processes with the highest degree of automation available. The reason is simple: Automation can sense potential SLA-impacting events before they happen (such as an out-of-space condition on a disk array) and may be able to take corrective action based on established policies (hence there is much discussion of policy-driven management).

IT administrators will welcome automation that can correct SLA-impacting or-threatening events (i.e., self-healing) whenever they occur. Software that helps by monitoring, alerting, and advising is available and very welcome.

This does not mean, however, that policy-based automation can solve all problems or that IT administrators need not be concerned about possible loss of control. IT operations always run into surprises that require judgment to resolve. The anticipation is, however, that concern over loss of control will probably give way to recognition of the benefits of automation in minimizing SLA commitment-breaking unavailability.

2.8   Logical Data Protection Gets Short Shift in Business Continuity

Operational continuity and disaster continuity need different mixes of logical and physical data protection technologies to achieve the planned levels of data protection that an enterprise requires. Yet enterprises may not have a clear understanding of the differences between physical and logical data protection—and that may result in a dangerous lack of attention to logical data protection.

The starting point is to examine both physical and logical data protection more closely. As already pointed out, data protection is divided into two classes: *physical* data protection and *logical* data protection. To provide full data protection, both are mandatory. Physical data protection focuses on *storage* devices, allowing a storage system to recover from dysfunction, failure, or destruction of one or more physical components. Logical data protection focuses on protecting the *data* itself: Bit patterns must retain their designated order and completeness. In other words, a user must get back exactly the data that was put in—reordered bits or missing bits will destroy the integrity of the data. That may render the data unusable: Even though the data—say, a database record or file—appears to be there, the data has for all practical purposes been lost (unless a true copy of the data is available). A danger is that the data may not be known to be bad (since it appears to be in place). That might lead to potentially serious consequences if an attempt is made to use the data. For example, a program may not be able to calculate the correct results of a financial calculation, or the calculation itself may fail to complete.

Physical data protection is built on redundancy (through expansion of storage requirements beyond actual usage, such as an additional full copy of data) and locality (separating an "original" copy from a second copy through geographical separation). Logical data protection may use redundancy, but it is built primarily on isolation (taking a set of data out of the input/output [I/O] path so nothing can be changed), locking (using software to prevent I/Os from changing a particular piece of data), and fixation (using hardware or software for "write once, read many" capability).

The first focus of *physical* data protection is on data *availability*, while the first focus of *logical* data protection is on data *preservation*. Physical data protection can do error correcting and consistency checks to determine that the data is the same as was written. However, that does not mean that the data is correct. The reason is that the infamous adage GIGO—garbage in, garbage out—applies.

Why does GIGO apply? Physical data protection cannot prevent I/O processes from changing data, because that is what those I/O processes are put in place to do. Yet those processes (say, a virus or data corruption) may change bit patterns so that the data is unusable. Therefore, making an exact copy of the data (say, local or synchronous remote mirroring) provides physical data protection. The exact copy does not provide any logical data protection because any change in the original—whether right or wrong—is reflected in the copy.

2.8.1   Logical Problems Feature Prominently in Data Loss or Downtime

Site disasters account for only a small fraction of data loss or downtime events. This low percentage, however, does not excuse under investing in disaster recovery implementations as part of the overall business continuity process, because the expected value of loss is high if the probability of a disaster is multiplied by the large magnitude of loss that could result from a disaster.

Of course, hardware and system problems are a significant concern for data loss or downtime, but logical problems are also important. Human error is likely to be a key part of logical problems (note that automation may pay large dividends by avoiding human error). Other logical problems, such as software program malfunctions, can include a wide range of problems, including database corruption. And even though computer viruses and other online attacks are probably only a small fraction of all logical problems, online attacks on data integrity are only likely to increase, and with them the possibility of a devastating impact.

Why is this important? Because much planning focuses on delivering disaster continuity, but the most likely threats to continuity are likely to come from the operational side. And on the operational continuity side, logical data protection problems shout for attention. But can logical data protection problems really have a significant impact on an enterprise? A further examination is in order.

2.8.2 Logical Data Protection Problems Manifest in a Number of Ways

Hardware, software, and people are all extremely complex, so together they represent a combustible mixture in a data center environment. In complex IT environments, what is perhaps surprising is not that problems

Table 2.1 Logical Data Protection Problems and Sources

Problem	Source
Data corruption through loss or alteration of data without the application's knowledge and consent	▪ Faulty hardware (bit loss or incorrect ordering) ▪ Software bugs (unexpected conditions reached and responded to incorrectly) ▪ User or IT administrator error (accidental file deletion)
Downtime and/or data corruption through application errors	▪ Faulty application version (introducing new software without sufficient testing) ▪ New system interfaces (semantic interpretation errors) ▪ Database errors (out-of-order transaction commits, accidental deletion of rows, dropped tables, etc.)
Data corruption through willful action	▪ Externally, from viruses and worms ▪ Internally, from deliberate tampering
Downtime through unintended human error	▪ Storage system configuration error ▪ Allowing out-of-space conditions to occur

arise, but that there are not more of them. Among the myriad of potential logical data protection problems, the ones listed in Table 2.1 represent just some of the possible sources that can result in data loss or downtime.

Problem diagnosis and assessment is not always easy, especially if the problem is intermittent, manifests itself in only small ways from which it has to be deduced that a larger problem is likely to develop, or is buried as a "time bomb" set to explode under certain conditions. Early detection to prevent a service-level threat from becoming a service-level-impacting reality requires eternal vigilance on the part of those people responsible for dealing with such issues.

A logical data protection problem can affect a key application, whether the application crashes or not. The inability to dispense cash from an automated teller machine or the inability to correctly deliver the right goods to a customer in a timely fashion, if systemic and not just isolated incidents, might affect an enterprise's credibility (and even market valuation).

Whether the logical data protection problem is pernicious and persistent or quickly diagnosed and corrected, logical data protection must get its full measure of attention.

2.9   Do Not Neglect Any Facet of Data Protection

No aspect of data protection can afford *not* to be protected. The target starts with four simple boxes (Table 2.2). Both operational continuity and disaster continuity have a physical *and* a logical component to them. Each box has to be considered individually, and all four boxes together have to be considered collectively to devise a data protection solution that meets an enterprise's needs.

Table 2.2   Data Protection Category Matrix

	Operational Continuity	Disaster Continuity
Physical		
Logical		

Although it seems simple, filling in the matrix is not that easy. The first challenge is in knowing when the levels of data protection are enough. The second challenge is in understanding that the target is moving and knowing how that will affect what needs to go into the matrix to get the right levels of data protection.

2.10   Key Takeaways

- Business continuity attempts to prevent the *risk* of major disruptions to business processes and hence is a key component of risk management.
- Business continuity is much more than data protection (people, processes, physical assets); data protection—protection of IT-managed, electronically stored information—is a vital aspect of business continuity.
- From an IT perspective, business continuity must deal with local operational recovery issues (operational continuity) and disaster recovery (disaster continuity) issues that result from a local IT site being rendered inoperable.

- Disaster recovery deals with the physical unavailability of a primary site, so the primary focus is on physical data protection (i.e., recovery from the physical loss of hardware).
- Operational recovery occurs at a primary site and, while physical data protection problems may occur, the basic focus is on logical data problems, when unauthorized changes to the data may have occurred.
- All facets of data protection—for both operational and disaster purposes as well as for physical and logical problems—have to be covered to prevent any gaps in data protection coverage.

Chapter 3

Data Protection—Where the Problems Lie

3.1   What to Look for in This Chapter

- What data protection really was and why that protection was severely limited
- How the introduction of RAID technology changed data protection
- Why RAID alone is not enough
- What needs to be done to provide better logical data protection
- Why disaster continuity faces issues related to cost, distance, and under protection

3.2   Data Protection as It Was in the Beginning

Understanding IT's heritage of data protection technologies is essential to understanding the thinking that still permeates the IT community regarding the nature of data protection. The genesis of that "thinking" was the limited choice for data protection technologies in the recent past, as well as cost considerations. Note that this focus has been on data protection technologies as related to risk management because, except for data security-related technologies, the role of governance and compliance in data protection was not generally recognized. In fact, even from a risk management perspective, not that many years ago, data protection and backup/ restore processes using tape were synonymous. All the other numerous data protection technologies in use today were not only unavailable; they were unthinkable.

The big change in data protection technology started with the introduction of what is now called RAID (Redundant Array of Independent Disks) in the 1990s. This was a major advance because before the introduction of RAID technology, all data on a particular disk drive was "lost" if the disk drive experienced a permanent failure that rendered access to the data permanently unavailable. That data loss was *temporary* if the data had been copied (i.e., backed up) to magnetic tape. Assuming no errors on the tape, the data could be restored to a working disk drive and the data would once again be available to an application for use. The data loss would be permanent if the data had not been backed up (or if the tape media failed). Backups typically were run once a day, at night, after most of the business applications had shut down at the end of a normal business day (the practice of applications running 24 hours a day, 7 days a week, was not common). The data that had been created during the course of the day since the previous night's backup could be permanently lost (unless special logging of transactions took place).

The introduction of RAID changed things dramatically, in that a group of disks could now have much higher availability as a whole than the same set of disks would have on average without RAID technology. A RAID group contains a set (an array or part of an array) of disks drives with at least one more disk than is necessary to house all the data (the redundancy part in the term). The "raw" capacity of a RAID group is the sum of the individual capacities of all the disk drives in the group. The "usable" capacity is how much data can actually be stored given that the equivalent of one or more disk drives has to be reserved for data protection purposes (using techniques that use "parity" or "mirroring" to protect the data). From a physical perspective, a RAID group can tolerate at least one disk failure before any data is "lost."

Prior to the introduction of RAID, the lack of such technology required forging a close relationship between magnetic disks, which provide the random access that most applications require, and magnetic tape, which provided a medium on which data could be written and preserved for data protection purposes.

So, just before the introduction of RAID technology, the primary storage media in use were, as today, Winchester disks and tapes (Figure 3.1). Winchester disk technology itself offered no extra measure of data protection. Winchester disks are disks on which the disk medium itself and the disk drive are sealed into a single unit. Prior to the introduction of Winchester technology, disk pack media could be removed. (The removability of disks is being reintroduced in limited cases with the removability of RAID groups—which include both drives and media—but this is typically not a general practice.) Each Winchester disk (hereafter referred to as simply a "disk") had to stand on its own, so that the mean time between failures (MTBF) for multiple disks was far less than for one disk. Although the technology for disk copies existed, the cost—except for extremely critical online

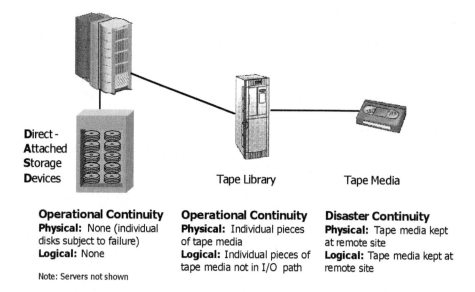

Direct-Attached Storage Devices	**Tape Library**	**Tape Media**
Operational Continuity	**Operational Continuity**	**Disaster Continuity**
Physical: None (individual disks subject to failure)	**Physical:** Individual pieces of tape media	**Physical:** Tape media kept at remote site
Logical: None	**Logical:** Individual pieces of tape media not in I/O path	**Logical:** Tape media kept at remote site
Note: Servers not shown		

Figure 3.1   Data Protection: The Way It Was

transaction processing systems—was prohibitive. Practically, neither physical nor logical data protection existed.

Magnetic tape solutions provided not only the first line of defense against data problems, but also the last (and any intermediate) line of defense as well. A tape solution consists of tape media, tape drives, and tape automation. Tape media have evolved from reels (almost like old movie reels) to more easily manipulatable cartridges. (Some 4-inch by 4-inch by less-than-1-inch cartridges can hold a terabyte or more of data.) Tape drives (into which a piece of tape media can be inserted) have shrunk dramatically as a consequence. Furthermore, tape automation (such as a tape library, which contains multiple tape drives, extra slots to store tape cartridges that are not in a tape drive, and a robotic arm to move the cartridges around) has improved the flexibility of management of a large number of pieces of tape media. In the old days (such as the 1980s), a tape operator had to physically change tape reels manually from a free-standing tape drive, whereas now the robotics in an autoloader (which has only one tape drive) or a tape library (which has multiple tape drives) move tape cartridges around automatically. However, under most circumstances, tape is intrinsically slower than disk, and the process of transfer of information from tape to disk or vice versa is a lengthy one.

Unlike disk, an individual piece of tape media is easily removed from a tape drive and can run in any compatible tape drive. This capability is important, because it allows tape media to be transported to and put into use at a remote site independent of the primary data center. Thus, movement of data is dependent on the availability of transportation, but not on the availability of a network. Tape drives can operate independently, but they are often embedded in tape automation solutions (such as an autoloader or tape library).

The copying of data from disks to tape media is done through the use of backup/restore software. This is the traditional backup/restore process, and it was for a long time essentially the only software available for data protection.

This process actually provides a great deal of both physical and logical data protection for both operational and disaster continuity. Since each tape copy is on a piece of physical media other than the primary disk, tape delivers physical data protection. Since any tape cartridge that is not in a tape drive is not in the I/O path, tape media also deliver logical data protection. Since a tape copy can be physically transported to a disaster recovery site, tape provides both physical and logical data protection for disaster continuity.

Multiple copies of the same data may be stored on tape. These are called *generations*. For example, suppose a full copy of a set of data is backed up on Saturday night. That is one generation. Now suppose that every night during the week, an incremental backup is made, which backs up new and changed data that particular day. On Saturday night another full backup is made. That is the second generation. And so on. In fact, many businesses used a generational scheme called *grandfather–father–son*. (At some point, the oldest pieces of tape media were rotated out of the generational scheme and put in what was called a *scratch pool*, to be used in creating a new generation of tapes.)

Since several generations of tape copy are available, no tape copy represents the only copy, and no single point of failure exists—thus, tape is both the "front line" and the "last line of defense" for data protection. However, this system does not address what tapes should be kept in-house for operational recovery purposes, and what should be sent off-site for disaster recovery purposes. Moreover, in many cases, not only would a full backup have to be used for recovery purposes, but also one or more (up to perhaps six) incremental backup tapes would have to be used in a recovery.

Apart from scalability, reliability, and manageability issues, the key concern with a tape-only solution therefore is lack of "high" availability, where high availability might be defined as minutes per year (and surely no more than hours per year).

A major recovery using tape may require hours at best, a day or more as a likely occurrence, and a week or more in extreme circumstances. This is because the recovery process, called a *restore process*, is actually a *rebuild process*. Tape, as a sequential medium, is too slow to handle random online processing. Therefore, before the data can be used for online processing, the contents of tape have to be copied to disk—and that can take a long time. If a mirrored disk copy were already available, the process would be a *restart* using the mirrored disk, and might take seconds to minutes.

The second reason that tapes are not always an optimal solution for recovery is that a number of tapes are likely to be needed to restore a disk system, and that can lead to problems if a part of the physical tape system (such as a piece of tape media) fails or requires significant resuscitation work (such as in the case of an intermittent error condition or constant read retries), or if there is a mistake in the sequencing of the tapes.

Considering the above, tape by itself is not sufficient to meet the demands of modern IT organizations. Note that the converse—disk is sufficient—also cannot be assumed to be true. Although disk plays a strong role in data protection, the proper role of tape in conjunction with disk has to be examined carefully.

3.3 Typical Data Protection Technology Today Still Leaves a Lot to Be Desired

A lot of change has taken place in data protection since the early days (Figure 3.2). As discussed, one of the primary improvements in data protection technology was the introduction of redundant array of independent disks (RAID), which provided physical data protection for the price of one or more additional disk drives. (RAID originally stood for redundant array of *inexpensive* disks, but the word *independent* was substituted for inexpensive as the price of disks fell dramatically and the relationship of disks to one another became more important than their cost.)

A number of RAID levels exist, but only a few are in common use. RAID 1 is a synonym for mirroring—for every disk that contains "original" data, a corresponding disk contains a "copy" of that data. This means that the usable disk space for RAID 1 is only 50% of the total available disk space. Parity RAID levels enable the recalculation of "lost" data in the event of a single failed disk through the use of parity check data. (*Parity data* is extra data that enables re-creation of all data from a failed drive from the other drives in the RAID group.) A RAID 5 group requires only one more disk than the number of disks required to hold the working data, although the parity check data and the working data are actually spread across all the disks.

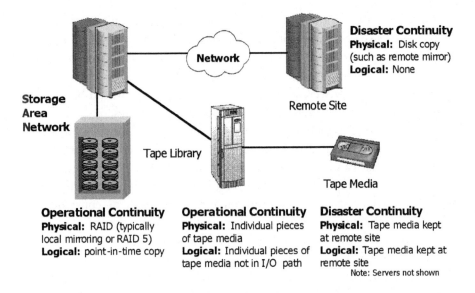

Figure 3.2   Typical Data Protection Until Recently

RAID technology delivers dramatically improved availability over an array of unprotected individual disks, and RAID technology typically now forms the first line of physical defense.

Remote mirroring, a variant of RAID 1, delivers fast-restart physical disk protection at remote sites, to aid in disaster continuity.

A second major advance is point-in-time copy capability, which is a fixed view of the data and therefore is not subject to change from I/O processes. This independence enables a point-in-time copy to deliver logical data protection as of the instant that a point-in-time copy (in some circumstances called a snapshot copy) was taken. Since that instant is unlikely to be the instant when a logical failure occurs, the aim of point-in-time copying is to be able to recover with a minimal loss of data. And even though point-in-time capability is available, some organizations do not use it for logical data protection on the disk array itself, but rather to provide a consistent point for invoking the standard backup process.

Although data protection has significantly improved from pre-RAID days, improvements over the typical data protection configuration are still necessary for a large percentage of enterprises in all four boxes in the data protection category matrix. This necessary improvement may not be a technology issue, but rather an education, adoption, and cost issue. In other words, the technology may be available, but understanding the affordability as well as the appropriateness of using the technology has to be carefully examined.

The myriad of new data protection products that have become available over the past few years, as well as the continued evolution of data protection products and services expected in the near future, indicates that the availability of the necessary technology is probably not the primary inhibitor to implementing effective data protection for business continuity. Understanding, finding, affording, and implementing the appropriate *mix* of data protection technologies is more likely to be the key issue.

The following sections address the state of the art in each of the four boxes in the data protection category matrix (review Table 2.2).

3.3.1   Operational Continuity/Physical: Generally Strong, but Some Improvement Needed

The addition of RAID technology has made physical operational continuity a strong area and, with concepts such as triple mirroring, an enterprise can buy its way to a desired level of physical availability. The operative word is "buy," as incremental changes in availability can become very expensive. The Achilles heel in RAID technology is that a typical RAID array can only allow one disk failure and still protect the data. During the period in which the RAID group is being rebuilt, the data in the array is exposed to the risk of data loss if a second failure should occur. And the chance for a bit error in rebuilding a large disk drive, as compared to a smaller drive, is by no means insignificant.

With that said, would not an advance in RAID technology to allow more than one failure in a RAID group be useful? The answer is yes; and that has already occurred. The general term for this technology is *multiple-parity RAID*, but the practical implementation of this is RAID 6, which can tolerate two disk failures before a rebuild process completes without loss of data. The cost for doing so could be low, as the "hot spare" that is typically found in RAID arrays could be put to active use for the extra drive in a RAID group. As a recommended strategy though, keeping at least one spare drive is still desirable, because the spare drive can be used for rebuilding the data from a failed drive. Although there is typically a slight performance penalty, such multiple-failure-tolerating RAID technology is be the closest thing to a higher-availability "free lunch" that is likely to come along soon.

3.3.2   Operational Continuity/Logical: More Attention Needs to Be Paid to Logical Data Protection

Point-in-time copy capabilities, including snapshot copy capability, have proven to be helpful for logical data protection. But point-in-time copies typically cannot be taken continuously, so some data can theoretically be lost. A powerful use of an *any*-point-in-time copy capability called *continuous data protection* (CDP) has now become generally available. A number of other technologies, including replication technologies, virtual tape libraries, and "write-once, read-many" (WORM) technologies, are also available to aid with logical data protection. In short, tape now has a number of allies, in addition to basic point-in-time copy capability, to help with logical data protection.

Many of the technologies, such as continuous data protection and virtual tape libraries, are still relatively new, so IT organizations may be either unfamiliar with the technologies or still in some stage of evaluating the technologies. However, point-in-time technology has been around for quite a while and has been used successfully by a large number of organizations. Nevertheless, point-in-time functionality not yet been adopted to the extent that it needs to be in order to provide the right level of logical operational continuity. The lack of adoption may be due to an IT tendency to focus on disaster recovery in general and the physical side of recovery for both operational continuity and disaster continuity, rather than the logical side; but logical operational continuity needs its fair share of attention as part of a comprehensive data protection strategy.

3.3.3   Disaster Continuity/Physical: Done Well, but Cost and Distance Are Issues

Remote mirroring has proven its worth, and has been justifiably successful in the data protection marketplace as a result. However, unless an enterprise already has a data center that can serve as a secondary disaster recovery site for the enterprise's primary site, the cost for establishing a disaster-specific site can be quite expensive.

For many organizations, cost—network equipment, software, and remote disk array cost—is a barrier to synchronous remote mirroring implementation. One reason is that many of the original synchronous remote mirroring products required that the disk array at the second site be the same model as the disk array at the first site. However, more cost-effective remote replication technologies are now available for organizations that are willing to make some concessions in exchange for cost savings. For example, if an organization can tolerate the performance loss penalty in case of a disaster, the ability to use less expensive disk arrays as targets for mirroring is an option that the organization might find attractive.

The second issue is that the distance between a primary site and a secondary site should be targeted at 300 miles (480 kilometers) or more. Although 300 miles (480 kilometers) is an arbitrary figure, it is a distance being mandated for certain compliance activities. Even if an organization is not subject to compliance restrictions, common sense says that if you are planning a long-distance data center, there is no sense in choosing one 250 miles (400 kilometers) away if there is any possibility of stricter compliance restrictions being imposed at a later date.

However, synchronous remote mirroring is typically used between two data centers that are no more than 100 miles (160 kilometers) apart. Once again, this is an arbitrary limit, but one that is based on experience with acceptable response-time latency for the valuable online transaction processing (OLTP) applications that can justify the expense of synchronous remote mirroring.

A sibling of synchronous remote mirroring is asynchronous remote mirroring. Asynchronous remote allows data between a primary site and a disaster recovery site to be kept *relatively* current. The operative word is "relative." The disaster recovery site may be behind by up to several minutes. Although the potential data loss of minutes for some applications may be unacceptable (e.g., an order-revenue-producing OLTP application), other applications may find that exposure acceptable.

Remote mirroring techniques create an undated replica (i.e., copy) of data. A dated (i.e., time-stamped) copy of the data, for example, a point-in-time copy for which the time and date of creation is known can also be used as a basis for a replica (i.e., copy) at a remote site. Dated replication is a more cost-effective way of protecting data at a disaster recovery site for data that does not demand up-to-the-second or up-to-the-minute protection. And that could be a good deal of a company's data.

In summary, asynchronous remote mirroring and other remote replication technologies are available to accommodate the needs of physical (and in some cases logical) data protection at a distant site. The challenge to IT organizations is how to meet the necessary data protection requirements while not having to use more remote sites than is absolutely necessary.

3.3.4 Disaster Continuity/Logical: The Danger of Being Under Protected May Be Very Real

If primary site processing has to move to a secondary site because of a disaster, the former secondary site has to assume the mantle of the primary site. One of the first questions that needs to be asked is "What is the length of time that the original primary site will be out of service?" If the answer is either permanently or for an extended period of time, the enterprise may want to implement a complete logical data protection solution if one is not already built in—and it may not be if only production disks were replicated at the disaster recovery site.

However, even if an outage may last a week or more, additional logical data protection may not be needed if the disaster recovery site replicates not only disk storage, but tape storage as well (a subset of the original tape solution may be enough in a pinch if the data center environment's configuration, e.g., its space and power, can accommodate expansion to the full solution). If the disaster site does not replicate tape storage, a third-party disaster accommodation arrangement might suffice. Note also that disk storage for data protection purposes (such as the target for disk-based backup) may serve as either a substitute for, or a complement to, tape storage.

A point-in-time copy (or equivalent) capability might serve as a stop-gap measure, but tape (or the disk equivalent) will provide secondary physical data protection as well as logical data protection as a target when restarting backup software processes.

In any event, a strategy for logical data protection needs to be put in place now, if the organization has not already done so. There is no point in making a large investment in a disaster recovery site if there is no protection from permanent loss of data due to database corruption, accidental file deletion, virus, or other logical data protection problems.

3.4 Summing Up Data Protection Challenges by Category

IT organizations need to examine the data protection technology challenges to determine how they affect the data protection planning process within their enterprise (Table 3.1). These should be kept in mind when setting the objectives for data protection for the enterprise.

The key is to blend newer technologies in with older technologies as either a substitute or complement ingredient in the data protection "stew." RAID 6 gives higher physical availability to a series of disk drives

Table 3.1   Data Protection Challenges by Category

	Operational Continuity	Disaster Continuity
Physical	**Key available technology:** RAID 1, RAID 5, and variants **Key challenge:** Relatively inexpensive and low-performance-impact RAID 6	**Key available technology:** Synchronous and asynchronous remote mirroring **Key challenge:** Getting potential data loss as close to zero as possible over long distances for time-sensitive information and adoption of data replication technology for less time-sensitive information
Logical	**Key available technologies:** Point-in-time copy capability and tape **Key challenge:** Acceptance of virtual tape library and continuous data protection technology	**Key available technologies:** Vaulting and electronic vaulting **Key challenge:** Acceptance of dated replication technology as a complement to existing technologies

for physical data protection for operational continuity. The increasing traction of virtual tape libraries and continuous data protection bodes well for improving logical data protection for operational continuity. (Incidentally, both technologies also improve physical data protection, as at least one additional physical copy is made.)

In terms of disaster continuity, combining synchronous and asynchronous remote mirroring can improve physical data protection. Perform synchronous remote mirroring to an intermediate site that has only limited disk capabilities, and use asynchronous remote mirroring for the true disaster recovery site. If a true disaster hits only the primary site, the intermediate site can deliver the last few minutes of data. (If the intermediate site is also affected by the disaster, the loss of a few minutes of data is likely to be the least of a company's concerns.)

For logical data protection, the disaster recovery (DR) site has to be able to manage the data that was not protected by remote mirroring techniques. That might mean backup copies on tapes that were vaulted manually to a third-party DR facility, or remote copies for a virtual tape library, or continuous data protection that were electronically vaulted to the DR site (or created remotely at the DR site originally).

3.5   Key Takeaways

- The first generation of risk-focused data protection relied on tape technology for both physical and logical data protection because there was no other way to protect against the failure of individual disk drives. The downside was that the time to restore data for access by applications from tape could be quite long (perhaps hours, or perhaps much longer).

- RAID dramatically improved the availability of disk drives in a physical sense. The always on (24/7) applications that are taken for granted today, while technically feasible, might have seen unacceptable levels of service in the absence of RAID.

- RAID by itself was not enough, because RAID deals only with physical data protection, not logical data protection. Other technologies, starting with point-in-time copy capabilities, have been and are being introduced to deal with logical data protection, where many day-to-day operational recovery issues occur.

- Doing disaster recovery right can be a challenge. A disaster recovery site has to be far enough away from the original production site that the same disaster cannot affect both sites, but that requires special technology. Moreover, the costs to replicate equipment at two sites (plus networking, people, and other costs) can be quite high. And, in the case of a real disaster, the costs at a disaster recovery site can go up with the need to provide enough logical as well as physical data protection.

Chapter 4

Data Protection—Setting the Right Objectives

4.1   What to Look for in This Chapter

- How organizations should think about high availability for data
- Why high value for data and high availability for data do not always go together
- Why availability objectives for operational recovery and disaster recovery are not necessarily the same
- What the other three key objectives of data protection are, other than availability

Recognizing *where* there may be problems in an organization's data protection strategy is not enough. Organizations need to understand *what* the right objectives for the risk management part of a data protection strategy should be. Setting the right objectives is critical, but not necessarily easy.

The objectives that an organization should consider are data availability, data preservation, data responsiveness (i.e., getting the data to the user within a reasonable time), and data confidentiality. These objectives must be kept in balance with one another, because changes in one area affect others, and therefore too much focus on one objective can lead to problems meeting another objective.

4.2   How High Is High Enough for Data Availability?

High availability, in which unplanned downtime is no more than seconds or only a relatively few minutes per year, is frequently a key objective in a data protection strategy, and one of the keystones of business continuity. However, an overemphasis on high availability can lead to problems with data preservation (all the money goes into keeping the systems up, and very little goes into preventing data loss when they do go down), data responsiveness (fault-resilient storage often does not restore as quickly),

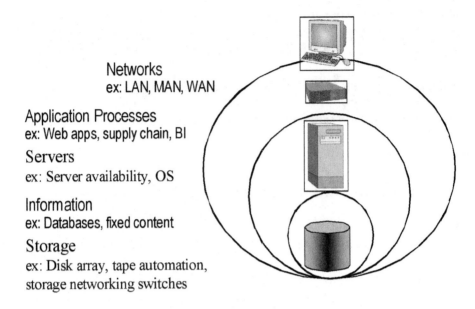

Networks
ex: LAN, MAN, WAN

Application Processes
ex: Web apps, supply chain, BI

Servers
ex: Server availability, OS

Information
ex: Databases, fixed content

Storage
ex: Disk array, tape automation,
storage networking switches

Figure 4.1   High Availability Depends on the Entire IT Infrastructure

and data confidentiality (all the money goes to keeping the systems up, and very little to protecting the data from unauthorized exposure). As a result, an organization may not meet its real data protection goals and probably will spend more than necessary for data protection.

High availability depends on the entire IT infrastructure (Figure 4.1) and not just on the storage part of that infrastructure. For example, if a network is unavailable for any reason, data on a disk array that an application accesses over that network is also unavailable, even if the disk array is working perfectly.

All applications do not have to have the same level of availability. However, for those applications that need high availability, all of the relevant components of the IT infrastructure have to be tuned to the same relative level of protection. Otherwise, a weakest-link-in-the-chain problem exists.

Under normal circumstances the overall IT infrastructure is unlikely to have been designed for high availability. High availability is a relative term. There are actually higher and higher levels of availability, where each additional level shaves off less and less improvement in overall uptime in terms of seconds or minutes. Unfortunately, as availability increases incrementally, costs tend to rise quickly. That is because moving from a single point of failure (where, if a component fails, there is no alternative component to fail over to with little or no downtime) to a situation where there is no single point of failure is expensive. That is because the second component is redundant and therefore results in more expense than was necessary to provide the original functionality without it. (Sometimes, the alternative component can share the workload with the original component, which improves performance. However, when one component fails, the remaining component has to do the work of both, which may degrade performance to an unacceptable level.)

However, if any part of the infrastructure can be significantly improved for a relatively small increase in cost, the investment is probably worthwhile.

All else being equal, incremental investment to increase the availability of storage is preferable to incremental investment to increase the availability of other parts of the IT infrastructure, such as servers or databases. The reason is that, if carefully done, investment in storage availability typically can improve data preservation as well. The data is more likely to be preserved from permanent data loss because there are one or more additional copies from which the data can be restored if necessary. That is an important side benefit that investing in another component, such as a network switch, cannot provide.

4.3   SNIA's Data Value Classification: A Point of Departure

The Storage Networking Industry Association (SNIA) has defined two key terms with respect to the availability of data through data protection (from the SNIA Dictionary at www.snia.org):

> *Recovery Point Objective (RPO):* The maximum acceptable time period prior to a failure or disaster during which changes to data may be lost as a consequence of recovery. Data changes preceding the failure or disaster by at least this time period are preserved by recovery. Zero is a valid value and is equivalent to a "zero data loss" requirement.

This is a definition of the amount of permanent data loss. *Permanent data loss* means that the data cannot be restored through use of IT. In some cases, manual reentry of data may be possible, but that ability may be infrequent.

Recovery Time Objective (RTO): The maximum acceptable time period required to bring one or more applications and associated data back from an outage to a correct operational state.

This is the maximum downtime that an application should suffer for a single failure event.

The Data Management Forum (DMF) within SNIA has further defined a third term (from the "SNIA Implementation Guide for Data Protection," March 2004).

Data Protection Window (DPW): Like the backup window, this is the available time during which a system can be quiesced and the data can be copied to a redundant repository without impacting business operations.

Table 4.1   DMF Data Value Classification

Data Value Class	Data Availability	RPO (Data Loss Risk)	RTO (Max. Recovery Time)	DPW (Copy Data Time)
1. Not Important to operations	90%	1 week	7 days	Days
2. Important for productivity	99%	1 day	1 day	12 hours
3. Business important information	99.9%	2 hours	2 hours	10 minutes
4. Business vital information	99.99%	10 minutes	15 minutes	None
5. Mission-critical information	99.999%	1 minute	1.5 minutes	None

Source: Derived from SNIA "Implementation Guide for Data Protection," March 2004.

This is critical, because data has to be protected. The question is how that protection can be provided without unnecessary "unavailability" of systems.

Building on these definitions, the DMF goes on to define five classes for data value classification and the resulting RPO, RTO, and DPW for each data value class (Table 4.1).

The DMF then defines a five-step implementation guide for data protection: (1) identify data value class, (2) define best solution, (3) select specific components, (4) check system cost, and (5) confirm decision or change. The five-step process seems reasonable, but then the implementation guide adds that "if cost is too high, change data value class or specific components." In other words, if you can't afford it, change your mind about how important it is!

That work was a valiant effort to tackle the very difficult issue of how to equate the value needed for risk-based data protection with an implementation strategy. And it serves as a good starting "straw man" point to thinking more deeply about the issue. The problem is that accepting the data value classification and implementation strategy at face value might not be the best strategy for IT management. An enterprise attempting to use that approach should think clearly about its applicability to the enterprise's circumstances. The reasons for looking closely at the pertinence of Table 4.1 are as follows:

- *Value is not the same as availability*—making the assumption that they are equivalent can lead to a misallocation of data protection investment dollars.
- *The RPO and RTO for operational recovery and disaster recovery are not necessarily the same*—making the assumption that they are the same can lead to a misapplication of resources when making a recovery.
- *Availability is only one data protection objective*—giving availability excessive weight versus the other objectives can lead to mistakes in protecting data.

The following sections elaborate on these findings.

4.4   Do Not Equate Availability with Value

No statistical correlation has been proven between the value of data and the need for the availability of that data, yet that is the fundamental assumption of the data value classification scheme. It is likely that if the information for an application *requires* (not just desires) high availability, the information is mission-critical (or at least has a high enough value to warrant the extra cost that high availability might entail). Everyone can point to applications that need (i.e., require) 99.999% availability—at least because of the severe financial penalties (such as lost revenues) for minimal downtime—and therefore can be considered mission-critical applications. Although there may be counter-examples (applications that require very high availability but that do not have high business value to the enterprise itself), the exceptions themselves might not be enough to override the assertion. Finding an application that requires high availability and is also mission-critical is easy. For example, a telephone billing system is an obvious example of a highly-available application that is mission-critical for a phone company. Note that with the increase of importance of Web applications for online ordering, the number of applications requiring extreme availability will only go up.

However, the converse—if the information for an application is mission-critical, it requires high availability—is not true. Mission-critical information is information whose permanent loss could severely impair an organization's ability to thrive—or even survive. The value for mission-critical information or other key information may come from several sources. The intellectual property value of digital assets, such as CAD/CAM designs or a film library, may actually have a quantifiable value. Accounts receivable actually collects customer revenue and is vital to sustaining the cash flow of a business. A data warehouse may serve as the basis for a business intelligence analysis that changes pricing strategy or decides where best to invest funds in a marketing campaign. An e-mail system used to facilitate customer service may be considered mission-critical (if customer service is deemed to be vital). Yet none of these applications is likely to require that downtime be limited only to seconds or minutes per year.

Equating mission-criticality and high availability can lead to "straight-jacketed" IT, which means that IT may think it has to provide higher availability than is really necessary for key information, because it follows a formalistic approach rather than thinking through what availability each set of application data really requires. The revenue-generation, operational, and decision-making processes of a business may run only during normal or extended business hours or at specified times that can be known in advance. Even if the applications that support those processes are scheduled to run 24 hours a day, 7 days a week, some reasonable amount of downtime, say even hours in a year if absolutely necessary, may be acceptable if it can be spread out over time (say, once a quarter) and if it is planned.

Why? Unavailability as described in the RTO and RPO definitions describes unplanned downtime. But, if an application can only tolerate minutes per year of unplanned downtime, does it make sense to assume that planned downtime can be any longer? The answer is no. Practically, then, there should be no distinction between planned and unplanned downtime. Yet planned downtime can be very beneficial to the enterprise and to its customers—an application upgrade that provides additional functionality, an operating system upgrade that enhances security and reliability, and a server upgrade that improves performance are all cases where downtime becomes beneficial. On the storage side, a migration to a new generation of storage may be necessary. IT needs flexibility to improve services—not a straitjacket that requires Houdini-like performance to make the simplest improvement.

IT needs flexibility to improve services—not a straitjacket that requires Houdini-like performance to make the simplest improvement.

IT applications that have critical business applications that require extreme availability typically have to live with them. However, IT should not go about creating the need for extreme availability unless absolutely necessary. An application for which a little downtime has significant serious consequences is something to be avoided if at all possible. Unless the reward is high, IT organizations should not take on both increased risk and expense.

By the way, a side benefit of a mission-critical application getting high availability for its data is that less critical but still important applications may also get the same availability. This "coat-tail" effect comes about because the less critical application shares a resource with the more critical application (such as sharing a storage area network switch). The more critical application, in effect, absorbs all the additional cost that is necessary to ensure higher availability than before, but the less critical application gets the benefit of the same higher availability. For example, an e-mail system may be able to tolerate hours of downtime per year (although not necessarily all at once), but, if downtime is only minutes per year, no one is likely to complain. However, the e-mail system may not be able to justify the additional expense all by itself.

4.5   Availability Objectives for Operational Recovery and Disaster Recovery Are Not Necessarily the Same

The response to an operational problem or a disaster situation is different (Table 4.2) because each has different characteristics. RPO and RTO may be conditional and contingent depending on circumstances.

Table 4.2   Differences Between Operational Recovery and Disaster

	Operational Recovery	Disaster Recovery
Problem Locus	Concentrated (typically one application)	General (typically all applications)
Mindset	Fire drill	Disaster relief
Management Control	"Emergency room"	"Control center"
Response Team	Ad-hoc as particular problem requires	Designated disaster recovery team
Resolution Strategy	Intensive care	Triage

An operational problem is typically isolated to an individual IT infrastructure component, such as an application, database, disk array, or tape library. There may be dependencies (say, among applications) that can cause the impact to magnify over time. Generally, however, there is a single triggering event and a single solution (however complex).

A disaster, by contrast, affects all applications. Applications have to be recovered and restarted based on a set of priorities, i.e., triage. In an actual disaster recovery situation, the people who are responsible for restarting the applications may not be the ones who had operational responsibility for them.

A mission-critical application that automatically fails over to a remote site may have the same RPO and RTO for both operational and disaster recovery. However, an enterprise typically has many important applications in its portfolio, and many of these do not require that same level of protection.

An accounts payable (A/P) application can serve as an illustration. If an operational problem occurs with the A/P system during normal business hours and there are no other major problems, the application recovery focus will be on the A/P problem, with an intention to restore as quickly as possible. An RPO and RTO serve as the upper bounds of reasonableness for the recovery process. Since the problem is an operational problem, zero data loss is a feasible goal, but a recovery from tape, if necessary, might take hours.

However, a major disaster changes the rules. Enterprises have to pay their bills, but the A/P application is likely to be pushed to the *bottom* of the priority stack and might take from a few days to a week or more to restore. The chief financial officer (CFO) has a reasonable defense for paying creditors late. (However, the accounts receivable [A/R] application is likely to have a higher priority for restoration in case of a disaster, as enterprises want to maximize cash inflow and minimize cash outflow!)

4.6   Availability Is Not the Only Data Protection Objective

The driving goal is to have *data always available securely, with optimal performance, to authorized users anywhere via any connection on any device.* Availability is certainly critical to obtaining that goal, but from a data protection perspective there are really four objectives that are part of that goal and that have to be met in working toward it:

- *Data preservation*—data must be consistent and accurate all the time, and also must be complete within acceptable limits.
- *Data availability*—the ability of I/O requests to reach a storage device and take the appropriate action.
- *Data responsiveness*—the ability of I/Os to deliver data to an authorized user according to measures of timeliness that are deemed appropriate for an application.
- *Data confidentiality*—data is available only to those authorized.

Note that data availability is not the same as data preservation. Not all preserved data needs to be immediately accessible. It may take a week or even longer to get some historical records back from the tape warehouse for discovery during a legal proceeding, but a week or more may be adequate time.

Moreover, all data that needs to be accessed quickly for business intelligence needs to be preserved—in some cases, financials can be quickly reconstituted from sales and other data if the financial spreadsheet is lost.

Job one in data protection is the preservation of digital assets. RPO states what the acceptable level of data loss is. RPO should be negotiated between the user and the IT group. Quite frankly, RPO will generally be zero for most applications, regardless of RTO requirements. To return to the A/P example, most CFOs would not rate the RTO of accounts payable as being very high at all, but (while they might like to!) the same CFOs would probably not agree to any permanent loss of data. (In a litigious society, creditors might object to accounts receivable having an RPO of zero [highly likely] and accounts payable having a nonzero RPO, which means that they might not get paid unless they complain.)

But RPO is only one measure of data preservation. RPO is what is planned, but intention and reality are two different things. If a RAID 5 or

Table 4.3   Consequences of Data Loss

	RPO Data (Acceptable Data Loss)	All of an Application's Data (Unacceptable Data Loss)
Temporary (within RTO)	Acceptable	Acceptable
Long-term (over RTO, but not permanent)	Acceptable	Pain level depends on many factors
Permanent	Acceptable	Devastation

mirrored array has two drive failures before the drives are rebuilt from the first failure, *all* the data is at least temporarily lost. The fallback is to the next layer of data protection, which hopefully can deliver the planned-for RPO (even if the planned RTO takes a hit).

What keeps IT management up at night is worrying about how much failure they can accept and still be able to recover all the data (Table 4.3). However painful an hour-long loss of availability might be, even more painful would be an extended (weeks to forever) loss of data, which is why tape still plays a major role in the data protection investments of organizations. Tape is IT's safety net. IT organizations cannot abandon their traditional backup/restore processes until they are sure that the alternatives are equally safe. Once again, low availability is better than no availability.

Note that the loss of data within the RPO window is an acceptable data loss. If the data is recovered within the RTO or even long-term, that is nice, but the loss is still acceptable. Note also that the severity of the loss of all of an application's data depends on the length of time that the data is unavailable. If the data can be recovered within the RTO, that loss is temporary and acceptable. If the loss extends beyond the RTO, the data loss has negative consequences. If the data can be recovered at some point in time (and therefore is considered a temporary loss), the suffering to the organization depends on many factors, including how long the data is out and what would have been done with the data during the time that the data was unavailable. Organizations had better think about the impact of a permanent loss of data. The consequences could be quite severe.

Data responsiveness is also a key objective. For example, data may be available, but access might be slow. If access is too slow, an application becomes virtually unusable. However, some degradation in performance for some period of time might be acceptable. For example, a remote mirrored array at a disaster recovery site may use lower-performance disks in order to be affordable. Degraded performance might be acceptable for the time required to swap in another high-performance disk array at the primary site.

Data confidentiality is also a key objective of data protection. In fact, the Data Protection Act in the United Kingdom equates data protection with confidentiality. The Health Insurance Portability and Accountability Act (HIPAA) in the United States mandates confidentiality for health records. Authorized access must be maintained under all circumstances.

4.7 All Primary Data Protection Objectives Have to Be Met

Although availability is critical, the other data protection objectives require an appropriate level of attention as well (Table 4.4). No objective is an absolute—even missing or inaccurate data may be tolerable in some situations, or, if some information got out to an unauthorized user, the consequences might not be severe. Intellectually, one could argue that should never happen, but realistically, costs, limitations of technology, and

Table 4.4   Summing Up Key Data Protection Objectives

Data Protection Objective	Observation
Data preservation	The consequences of not having all data complete and accurate have to be thought through very carefully.
Data availability	There is no utility in having data that cannot be accessed.
Data responsiveness	Slowness kills—if response is too slow, the usefulness of information can go to zero.
Data confidentiality	Confidentially has to be applied at all times.

limits on the ability of people to do everything properly get in the way of perfection. Still, exceptions have to be thought through very carefully.

4.8   Key Takeaways

- High availability for application data is often desirable—and sometimes mandatory. But high availability depends on the entire IT infrastructure, and obtaining incrementally higher levels of availability may not be worth the cost.
- For each set of application data, organizations have to determine the recovery point objective, which is a measure of what is acceptable in terms of time of how much data can be lost, and recovery time objective, which measures the acceptable time that application data can be unavailable. Balancing those two objectives is one of the major challenges in risk-based data protection.
- Although some high-value data requires high-availability access, not all high-value data requires high availability. To assume otherwise might mean an unnecessary high expense to provide high availability to a set of application data that does not really require it.
- Availability for operational recovery and for disaster recovery may not be the same. In a true disaster recovery scenario, an organization has much more to do than for an operational recovery (since all applications and their data are affected, compared to a subset in most operational recovery scenarios), and the organization is likely to be cut much more slack.
- Availability is an important data protection objective, but there are three other primary data protection objectives. Data preservation requires that data be preserved from unauthorized changes. Data confidentiality keeps the data private from unauthorized use. Data responsiveness is protection from unacceptable response time slowness that would, in effect, render the data unusable. Each objective has its own of acceptability for each different set of data within an organization. All four objectives have to be taken into account—none of them can be ignored.

Chapter 5

Data Protection—Getting the Right Degree

5.1 What to Look for in This Chapter

- What the key characteristics of a copy of production data versus a copy of data protection data are
- Why degrees (or layers) of data protection are necessary
- Why at least three degrees of data protection are necessary for any set of data
- How different degrees of data protection provide different levels of availability and why that is important

A nightmare that an IT manager does not want to live through in reality is a serious data protection problem that causes major disruption to the business. That means that no manager should be willing to rely on only one line of defense in data protection. A fallback strategy is necessary in case the first line of defense fails for whatever reason. Lines of defense can be seen as providing degrees or layers of protection. Successfully setting up degrees of protection starts with examining and understanding the general classes of data being used.

5.2 General Use Classes of Data

There are three general classes of data from a use perspective:

1. Production data
2. Data protection data
3. Test data

Test data is actually a special case for application development activities. Although test data is useful, it really does not require data protection (except for confidentiality of the data provided), as it can be regenerated from scratch if necessary and does not affect the basic data processing activities of an organization. This book focuses primarily on production data and data protection data.

The same copy of data can be both production and data protection data. For example, the same physical storage system may contain both production data and data protection data at the same time. With RAID 5, for example, a pool of production data will also have physical data protection. RAID 5 calls for an extra disk, which through extra parity checks on information striped across all disks delivers enough redundancy that all the data will be usable even if any one of the individual drives in the array fails. A snapshot point-in-time copy can provide a measure of logical data protection because I/Os cannot write to the snapshot copy to alter or destroy the data. In this case (and even in the case of local mirroring [RAID 1], where there are two separate and distinct physical copies of the data), the production and data protection data are commingled. The data is still production data, since that it is the purpose of the copy. Data protection is *added in* (i.e., internal or built-in) rather than *added on* (i.e., external or built-on).

In contrast, a disk array that is a remote mirror serves to provide physical data protection at a distance. In this case, data protection is added on (in the form of a distinct and separate copy of the data), so its purpose is the same as that of data-protection data.

If the primary array fails, the remote target disk array assumes the mantle of serving as the source of production data. However, the remote array reverts to a data protection role if another primary can be brought up, or continues to serve a production role if another array is designated as a target for data protection purposes. Still, data protection was the reason for acquiring and implementing the remote array.

5.2.1   Tape Is a Special Case

If a piece of tape media is a copy of random-access disk data, then that copy is pure data-protection data (both physical because of the physical media and logical if no I/Os can write to it). That tape is always data protection data; unlike a remotely mirrored disk array, the sequential nature of the tape does not permit it to serve a random-access data purpose.

That is not to say that tape cannot serve production purposes. In fact, tape has a long track record of production use. Tape can serve a production role where sequential processing of a whole database is necessary (such as a data mining analysis or batch update of a data warehouse when it is offline). Tape can also be used to retrieve selected files that, in effect, use disk as a cache. The original Hierarchical Storage Management (HSM) system used tape. Very large files and large numbers of infrequently accessed smaller files may very well find a production home on tape.

5.2.2 Understanding Degrees of Data Protection

Data protection comes in degrees (which also can be thought of as layers). The first degree where data protection can be provided is for the primary copy. The primary copy may or may not have data protection. If it does, that is the first line of defense for operational continuity. Built-in data protection of the primary data copy can help prevent service-level-threatening events (such as a single disk failure) from becoming service-level-negative-impacting events.

However, built-in data protection cannot provide disaster continuity protection and the risk-protection diversification that is necessary for operational continuity protection. At least one add-on copy—a full copy of the data that is physically separate and distinct from the original—is necessary.

Some Crossover Protection from Disaster Continuity to Operational Continuity

Each of the four boxes in the data protection category matrix (see Table 2.2) is separate and distinct, but physical disaster continuity protection may also serve to benefit operational continuity. For example, suppose that two disks in a local RAID array fail and a failover to a remote site happens. Failure of individual disk drives is a normal outcome at times when using disk drives, not a situation that requires disaster recovery. For all practical purposes, in this case the array could have been located in the primary data center. The distance separation does not matter, but the presence of the other array does matter. Thus, counting the remote array layer in both physical disaster continuity and operational disaster continuity is legitimate as long as it is recognized to be only one layer.

The Limits of Data Protection Continuum Charts

In looking at a data protection continuum chart, it is important to understand layering. The different versions of data protection continuity spectrum charts that are available tend to show a range of data protection solutions on the basis of availability. On one end of the spectrum, tape solutions are often shown in hours/days to recover and triple mirroring at the other end in seconds. The charts are very useful for viewing a broad spectrum of options at a glance, but they do not typically distinguish physical from logical data protection, and they imply that availability is the only objective.

Not too many—if any—companies are giving up their tape automation systems, despite the fact that these are low-availability solutions. The message seems to be that low availability is better than no availability.

5.3 The Third Degree—Levels of Exposure

Call one layer of added-in or added-on data protection one degree of protection. One degree of data protection means that one failure is tolerable; data is recoverable. If a failure should occur, data protection is at zero degrees. Zero degrees of data protection means no more failures can be accommodated without total and permanent data loss. This is a level of exposure that IT organizations find unacceptable.

That is why additional degrees of data protection are necessary. The question is how many. The minimum number of layers is two. If one failure occurs, the degrees of protection are down to one. Given that technology is not perfect; having only one extra degree of freedom to fall back on is not advisable. So most users should consider a minimum of three degrees of data protection. Each additional layer beyond three adds expense, but one or more additional layers may still justify the expense.

5.3.1 Mapping Degrees of Protection

IT administrators should map out the degrees of data protection for each application (Table 5.1). The degrees of protection have to be split between higher-availability and lower-availability degrees. Once the higher-availability degrees are exhausted, availability depends on the lower-availability degree options. Note that the term *lower availability* should not be considered pejorative, but rather reflects the relative differences in the time-based ability of different technologies to restore information.

Table 5.1 does not exhaust all the possible combinations and choices of technologies, but should rather be considered as simply an example. IT administration has to determine if the levels of protection are adequate.

On the operational side, physical data protection may be adequately covered for many applications. Note that the remote mirroring form of remote replication is double-counted—once on the operational side and once on the disaster side. Remote mirroring may be synchronous or asynchronous, which can protect against physical, but not logical, failures. However, remote replication may also be remote dated replication, where the replica is made as of a certain time (rather than the non-dated replication

Table 5.1   Sample Degrees of Data Protection for Application n

	Operational Continuity	**Disaster Continuity**
Physical	Higher availability Degree 1: RAID/local mirroring Degree 2: Remote mirroring Lower availability Degrees 3+: Tape/disk-based backup	Higher availability Degree 1: Remote mirroring Degree 2: Remote dated replication Lower availability Degree 3+: Vaulted tapes
Logical	Higher availability Degree 1: Continuous data protection Degree 2: Point-in-time copy Lower availability Degree 3: Disk-based: backup Degree 4+: Tape-based backup	Higher availability Degree 1: Continuous data protection Degree 2: Remote dated replication Lower availability Degree 3+: Vaulted tapes

that mirroring provides). For example, a snapshot point-in-time copy can be made locally and then replicated (also called copying or duplication) to the remote location.

Note that once again tape plays a big role. Tape typically offers at least three degrees of failure (assuming that at least three generations of tape are used). The problem is that it is all lower availability. Moreover, having to use older generations of tape is likely to result in even greater time loss.

The advantage of tape, however, is that the addition of each degree of protection is mainly the cost of a piece of media for each additional generation or copy. While there may be a requirement to add more tape drives or to expand the overall tape library infrastructure, this is often administratively easier and may be more cost-effective than adding disk arrays.

The use of a disk-based backup solution (such as a virtual tape library) may improve availability somewhat, but there is still likely to be a gap between such a solution and higher-availability solutions.

On the operational side, logical data protection—if the newer continuous data protection approach is not used—does not have the same level of high availability that is available on the physical side. That could create exposure unless point-in-time copy capability is used and is managed very well for logical operational data protection.

As has been mentioned, Table 5.1 should not be used as a guideline, but rather as an example. The disaster continuity side of the house illustrates why this is so. For example, a large enterprise may have a triad of fully stocked data centers for disaster recovery (DR). The first DR site serves as the first line of defense, and the other DR site is in place should the first data center become the production site.

Other companies cannot economically justify the risk/reward for three sites and find that having two sites—one production and one DR—is fine. (Incidentally, all sites in a multiple-data-center environment may play both a production and a DR role.) Still others cannot justify even the cost of a second data center or prefer to outsource at least some DR requirements.

However, the number of sites is not the only issue. What is in a DR site is another issue. IT may have a full replica of its primary site at the remote site, it may have a partial replica with the ability to bring in additional equipment when necessary (such as tape automation), or it may turn to a third-party service provider for recovery. All involve time and cost trade-offs.

There are also logistical issues. Even if the remote site has a recent tape copy available, it may have only one.

Filling in the degrees of data protection for each application helps identify where the levels of data protection are satisfactory and where improvement might be necessary. But IT organizations first need to understand the impact of information lifecycle management on the requirements mix before they start filling in the boxes.

5.4   Key Takeaways

- Not counting test data, a copy of data can be either a production copy or a data protection copy. Sometimes a copy can serve a dual role, being both a production copy and a data protection copy. The distinction between the two is important in understanding how they work in conjunction with each other.
- Data protection comes in degrees (or layers), where each additional data protection copy provides another degree of data protection.
- A minimum of three degrees (i.e., three copies) of data protection is necessary to provide against multiple failures that could lead to permanent loss of data.

- Different levels of data protection are likely to have different levels of availability. The last-line-of-defense layer is likely to have much lower availability than the front line of data defense. If the last layer of defense has to be called on, the situation is an emergency, and failing to adhere to the service-level agreement for availability is not the key concern; preventing permanent data loss has the highest priority in those circumstances.

Chapter 6

Information Lifecycle Management Changes the Data Protection Technology Mix

6.1 What to Look for in This Chapter

- What information lifecycle management is really all about
- Why data lifecycle management is not a replacement for information lifecycle management
- What the role or tiering and pooling plays in information lifecycle management
- What archiving is really all about
- Why archiving requires a different software management approach
- Why information lifecycle management and archiving change the data protection category mix

Information lifecycle management (ILM) is a much misunderstood term in the IT community. Although ILM actually has deep implications for the management of IT and for data protection, understanding ILM starts with an apparently simple definition: Information lifecycle management is the *policy-driven management* of information as it *changes value* throughout the *full range of its lifecycle* from conception to disposition.

Understanding that information lifecycle management is much more than a shopworn term in the IT vocabulary is important to IT management. Along with being a process and a strategy, ILM is a new way of looking at the storage infrastructure and managing data throughout its lifecycle. That has profound implications for data protection. For example, ILM focuses attention on the management of fixed-content (i.e., unchanging) information as being different from that of dynamic, changing information, ("Information is all the same" was storage's traditional view of the world). Fixed-content information must be replicated as required for data protection. That replication is a one-time process, so the traditional day-in, day-out backup process can be skipped for fixed-content data!

Information lifecycle management is the *policy-driven management* of information as it *changes value* throughout the *full range of its lifecycle* from conception to disposition.

What is not included in the definition of ILM, but is critical to understanding ILM, is that every piece of data becomes fixed (i.e., read-only) at some time during its lifecycle—and that time is typically short compared to the full length of its lifecycle. Active changeable data reflects a creation and change process, where viewing the data at different times would reveal that the data had not stayed the same. At some point in time, however, this change ends. Even online transaction processing systems updating customer records create data that must be "frozen" after a certain period of time—say, at the end of the month or year, or after a certain event occurs. For example, when a hotel stay event has ended (and been paid for), the hotel reservation transaction has been completed and now is not subject to any further change (except perhaps error correction). That means that the information is fixed-content.

The same thing happens to non-transaction-processing applications, such as an e-mail system. An incoming e-mail is information that is fixed upon capture (because replies do not change the original e-mail). If an IT organization looks carefully at the data managed under its custodial care, a large percentage of the data will probably be fixed.

Of course, value—in the sense of worth and importance for business purposes rather than in a monetary sense—is likely to change even for information that is fixed. For example, the completed hotel stay is no longer a source of revenue, but it is now information that, when combined with other information, such as all completed hotel reservations, can be used in a variety of ways, such as hotel stay trends for hotel planning and marketing campaigns to get repeat business at the hotel. Changing value indicates a change in the information's lifecycle and leads to the ability to apply policy-driven software management—and that is where ILM steps in.

6.2   Why Data Lifecycle Management Is Not Enough—The Need for Metadata and Management

Some critics have said that ILM is overkill—that a concept called *data life-cycle management* (DLM) is enough. Storage at the device level is about the management of blocks of data, so the migration of data at the block level from one tier of storage to another is often referred to as *data lifecycle management.* (*Tiering* means that different classes of storage have different physical characteristics, such as employing faster but lower-capacity disks rather than slower, larger-capacity disks.) Claims have been made that data lifecycle management is enough; information lifecycle management is a pretentious marketing ploy. That is not true.

Examine what data lifecycle management does. Actions on blocks of data have to be taken on the basis of metadata (i.e., data about data). Block-level metadata has to be simplistic because there is very little of it, such as the age of the block. If actions are taken simply on the basis of age (when a block was created or captured) or if the date of last access exceeds a threshold, that migration is data lifecycle management, since there is no knowledge of the underlying content of the data (which is where the data becomes useful as information).

Migrating data in this manner might result in the use of more cost-effective storage for the migrated data and ease the burden of managing the nonmigrated data. However, data migration simply on the basis of last access or age does not mean that the migrated data is fixed-content data. The data lifecycle metadata does not tell us whether a long period without change is an aberration or an indication that the data has become fixed.

And the knowledge that a pool of data is fixed is critical, because policies for managing and allocating resources—applying policy-driven data retention and data protection rules—are different from those for non-fixed-content data. And to support these policies, metadata has to be at the record or file level, not a block level, and it must contain information about the data's use, not merely its physical block storage characteristics. Moreover, the contents of the record or non-bit-mapped files can be examined and an index created that is also metadata. Policies for data retention and data protection can now be applied using ILM, since there is a rich set of metadata with which to work. Policy rules can be applied using the metadata. For example, if a file is of a particular type (such as word processing) and contains one or more keywords, then the file should not be deleted for a specified length of time based on the date of last update. Policies can be made

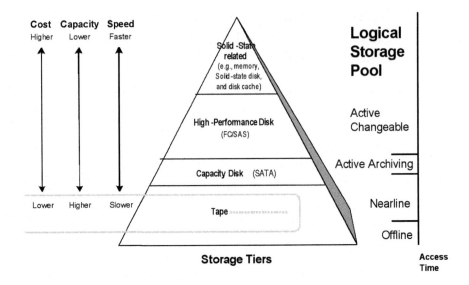

Figure 6.1   The Storage Pyramid—Tiering and Pooling

flexible enough to ensure that users get their *exact* needs met. This is a powerful endorsement for ILM, because getting the users' exact needs met may be critical for governance, risk management, or compliance reasons.

On the other hand, data lifecycle management simply does not cut it because it does not have the necessary metadata to enable the flexible range of policy choices that is essential for proper policy management. And that is why—paraphrasing Voltaire—if information lifecycle management had not been invented, there would have been a need to invent it.

6.3   ILM Is Deep into Logical Pools of Storage

Tiering and pooling are two of the key ideas in information lifecycle management. Figure 6.1 is a simplified storage pyramid that shows the interrelationship between tiering and pooling.

- *Tiering* is the separation of storage into classes by the characteristics of the storage itself: performance (speed and availability), functional capabilities, and cost. As such, tiering is a storage device-related concept.
- *Pooling* refers to a collection of information that is managed as a homogenous whole for quality of service (QoS) purposes, such as response time and availability. As such, pooling is an information-

related process. The objective is to map a pool of information to a choice of storage tier, and the net result is a storage pool.

By knowing the QoS that the information pool requires, a storage administrator can map the pool to the tier that can deliver the appropriate quality of service. The mapping has to take into consideration not only cost, capacity, and speed, but also data protection requirements, such as availability.

6.3.1   Logical Storage Pools at a High Level

In the past, whether data was fixed or not, there were generally only two choices for persistent storage: high-performance disk or tape (flash memory was not yet available). The distinction between active changeable and fixed data did not matter. Despite lower performance requirements, fixed data that still had to be available for reading on occasion might not be able to be moved to tape, even though tape was more cost-effective.

The introduction of capacity disks has changed all that. The largest-capacity disk drives have much more storage capacity than disk drives for which performance is important. Capacity disks are primarily Serial Advanced Technology Attachment (SATA) disks. Capacity disks are suitable for data that does not require the performance (both speed and reliability) of Fibre Channel (FC), Small Computer System Interface (SCSI), or Serial SCSI (SAS) disks. That typically includes fixed-content and very slowly changing data. By the way, solid-state drives are very-high-performance drives and affect the choice of performance drives for storage-performance-challenged applications.

The nearline and offline pools focus on data protection (where the sole purpose of the storage pool is on protecting data), whereas the active changeable and active archiving pools focus on using data for production purposes (that is, any business use except data protection). The distinction between production data and data protection data—how they can be separate and how they can be joined—is important for understanding what mix of data protection technologies can give the intended level of protection.

Note that active changeable pools and active archiving pools of storage are online pools of storage. An online pool of storage is one that can be accessed by a business-application user. An active changeable pool theoretically is composed only of production data that is likely to change, but practically speaking, a lot of data that is never going to change—and is hence fixed-content data—is still commingled in. An active archiving pool is more likely to be closer to being pure, because all, or at least most, of the data should be fixed-content data. The key is to remember that both pools are production data that can be accessed online.

Understanding the nearline pool is a bit trickier. The original meaning of "nearline" has been co-opted in at least one case. The use of the term here refers to the fact that a nearline pool of data is data that can be accessed "online," but only by an authorized IT administrator, not by an end user. The offline pool is easier to describe. That describes data—typically magnetic tape, but possibly a removable disk—that requires a manual effort to bring it back to a network-accessible online state. For example, a tape cartridge would have to be put into an import slot in a tape library to get it back to a state where it could be accessed online by an IT administrator.

6.3.2   Moving Information Across Pools—A Distillation Process

The mapping of a pool of information to a tier of storage is an assignment process, so the process may be static and manual. The tiering and pooling assignment process has nothing to do with the movement and migration of data per se (as the process simply describes what is and not what should be as in terms of where data is located). Yet pools of information are not static; inflows to a pool of information and outflows to another pool of storage have to be taken into account. Inflows and outflows are at the information-object level. An *information object* is the smallest information unit—perhaps a file or a record—that can be differentiated by access only to authorized users, by ownership, by compliance requirements, by identification, and/or by process control.

Migration can be viewed as a distillation process. One key distillation process is to separate information-object "molecules" that are currently active changeable (i.e., information that is likely to change in a foreseeable future) from those that are fixed-content (i.e., information that is unlikely to change in the near term). The fixed-content information-object "molecules" are distilled from their original storage pool into another storage pool "flask." And that new "flask" can be called "archiving."

6.4   Archiving Through a New Lens

Understanding the concept of the bifurcation of production data into two separate and distinct classes—active changeable data and fixed-content data—has achieved some measure of mindshare in IT organizations. A lot of words are being thrown about, such as content addressable storage (CAS), to refer to data with fixed content. These terms all have their place, but the most general term, and the one that is on its way to achieving the

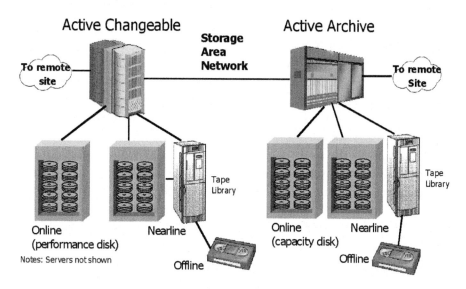

Figure 6.2   ILM Changes the Logical Topology Storage Look

greatest popularity and acceptance, is *archiving*. In dealing with archiving, ILM fundamentally divides the storage infrastructure into two separate halves: an active changeable side and an active archive side (Figure 6.2).

Note that this is a *logical* arrangement, even though the icons can be misinterpreted as indicating a *physical* arrangement. Mentally separating storage into logical pools is useful whether or not the different pools reside physically on one disk frame (sometimes called a storage system, a storage subsystem, or a disk array) and one tape frame (such as a tape library) or whether or not they are on multiple general-purpose and single-purpose appliance-oriented frames.

All the logical storage pools are contained in the topology shown in Figure 6.2. The online pools of storage for both active changeable and active archive data are for production data (with data protection added in). Nearline retains its data protection origins from tape automation solutions, but also adds in nearline disk. Offline remains data protection data that is removable and may or may not be taken offsite.

Note that for data protection purposes on the active changeable side, backup can go straight to disk (and then to tape as necessary) or directly to a tape library. Backup does not have to be used for an active archive (although backup software can still be used). A data protection copy can be made at the time of ingestion of data into the online active archive pool to either disk or tape or both. That is simply a replication process and only affects newly ingested data.

The fundamental changes from the typical data protection configuration today (see Figure 3-2) are really on the archive side. The importance of capacity disks is not only lower cost and a higher capacity with a performance trade-off, but also that the management of fixed data through an archive is fundamentally different from the management of active changeable data, even though the two have to work together and exchange information with each other.

For example, the focus on data retention in archiving is much greater than on the active changeable side. On the active changeable side, intermediate changes may (but not always) be discarded because work-in-process does not represent the committed transaction or a usable version of a document. On the archive side, data (no matter whether it is database or file data) may reach end-of-life and go through a destruction process, but that process should be managed and not ad-hoc.

6.4.1   Archiving: The Makeover

Much confusion exists about what archiving really is and what it means to IT organizations. One reason is that the definition of archiving is undergoing a transformation (and really was not well understood anyway!). A starting point for examining archiving is the original Storage Network Industry Association (SNIA) definition of archive:

> *Archive:* A consistent copy of a collection of data, usually taken for the purpose of a business or application state. Archives are normally used for auditing or analysis rather than for application recovery. After files are archived, online copies of them are typically deleted and must be restored by explicit action.

This definition, from the SNIA "Network Storage Terms and Acronyms" (2003 edition, page 10), is the "classic" definition of archive. A subset of production data has reached the end of its "production" life, but the enterprise has a need to preserve the data for an additional period of time (up to posterity). One or more tape copies are made and the production copy deleted. The tape(s) are taken to an archive in an underground salt mine (or the equivalent) somewhere, with the fervent hope that the data never needs to see the light of day again. This is equivalent to data death through suspended animation. The data is not really dead, but it is not really alive either.

That original definition corresponds to the dictionary definition of an archive as a place where documents of public or historical interest are preserved.

The SNIA later (circa 2004) redefined archive as follows:

Archive (noun): 1. (noun) a collection of data that is maintained as a long-term record of a business, application, or information state. Archives are typically kept for auditing, regulatory, analysis or reference purposes rather than for application or data recovery. 2. (verb) to copy or move data for purposes of retention; to create an archive.

That updated definition reflected the changing times. The reason for the new definition was that archives may have some real "production" purpose rather than serving no active purpose in a data mausoleum. There is a lot of read-only data that still can serve real business purposes, such as analysis, reference, and governance.

The makeover is significant. No longer is data, for all realistic purposes, "dead." Instead, most archived data serves a real business purpose. If archived, "not dead yet" data were small in size, there might not be an impact on data protection; but these days, fixed-content data may be the majority of the data in most enterprises, and the impact on data-protection architecture design is substantial.

However, the SNIA had not reached the end as far as defining archive is concerned. The current definition of archive from the SNIA online dictionary (www.snia.org/education/dictionary) is as follows:

Archive: 1. (Data Management) A collection of data objects perhaps with associated metadata, in a storage system whose primary purpose is the long-term preservation and retention of that data. 2. (Data Management) The process of ingesting data into an Archive.

This definition is a laudable attempt in that the long-term preservation and retention of selected data is a critical issue. However, the definition does not describe what the collection of data objects is really about. An archive is simply a long-term collection of data that is typically fixed-content data— i.e., no I/O writes are allowed to change the data. Understanding archiving is essential because archiving has a transformational role in data protection not only from a risk management perspective, but also from a governance and compliance perspective.

6.4.2   Protecting Archived Data

To reinforce the basic archiving mantra once more (since it may be a new worldview to many people), archived data is fixed data (i.e., the data does not change). Archived data must be protected data; the proper numbers of copies in the proper number of locations have to be prepared. However, archived data does not have to undergo a regular process of backup. Backup is a recurrent cyclical process; if full backups are run weekly, a file that had not changed in a year would be backed up 52 times even although only a limited number of copies of the file are available at any one time (since only a certain number of copies are retained at any point in time).

The new process involved in archiving fixed data is replication. All the necessary copies of a new piece of archived data can be produced through a replication process at the time of capture in the archive.

Although an individual file or record does not change, a fixed-data archive storage pool is not static in its contents. An archive has both inflows and outflows. Inflows are simply additive—a new piece of fixed data has been added to the archive. Outflows are subtractive; data is removed from the archive. If the outflow process results in data being migrated to another piece of storage media, the data is preserved on the target piece of storage media (and theoretically deleted from the original archive). If no data migration is involved in the outflow process, the archive copy of the data is simply deleted (i.e., destroyed) (Actually, for the data to be truly destroyed, all other copies of the same data would also have to be destroyed as well.)

The actual archive storage pool is a production pool of storage, and authorized users can access information in the pool for production purposes. The production pool can use data protection technologies for both physical and logical protection, but one or more data protection copies need to be made as well.

6.5   Active Archiving and Deep Archiving

The consensus term for the new type of archive is *active archive*. The term for the original archive is now *deep archive*. The distinction is very important. Fixed-content information that is deep-archived is stored on removable media, removed from online files, and may or may not be transported to an offsite spot for safekeeping. An active archive contains production data, no matter how old or infrequently accessed, that can still be retrieved online.

A deep archive is an electronic landfill, in that the data is likely never to be retrieved. That does not relieve an enterprise from doing the proper media management to ensure that it knows where the data is and how to get it back. However, the first question is why any enterprise would want to deep-archive data. If the data has reached the end of its useful life, destruction of the data—rather than deep archiving—should be the choice. If the data still retains some value—such as for regulatory compliance—keeping it in an active archive and sending a replica offline might be a better option. Deep archiving should be utilized only if the data must be preserved against significant future risks (e.g., changes in regulations), the volume of data is large, the chances of a need to recall the data are remote, and a long restoration time is acceptable.

6.5.1   Active Archiving Requires Active Archive Management

Active archiving requires archive management—the umbrella term for the overarching software that is necessary for managing data retention and other data protection policies on the archive. Active changeable data does not require a manager. Active changeable data is application-controlled; the creation, updating, reading, and deletion functions are all under the aegis of the controlling application, such as an e-mail application. An archive is controlled by a special archive manager application. That application may grant privileges to the originating application, but it does not have to.

The archive manager is key to the effective management of an active archive because it controls who, what, where, how, and why I/Os are allowed to take place. For example, policy management that works through the archive manager control who is allowed to delete a piece of data and when that deletion can take place. The production application is no longer always king of the I/O; in an active changeable pool of storage, an auxiliary application has to kowtow to Microsoft Exchange or Oracle, but an archive manager does not have to.

The reason is simple. Data protection (which includes data retention) is paramount in an archive; the I/O functions are tightly controlled, which was not the case in the production application with active changeable data, where, for example, I/Os that allowed the deletion of data without policy oversight might be permitted.

Metadata management is critical for the archive manager. The metadata (other than the basic information of name, size, and date) includes the following categories:

- *Ownership*—creator, owner, last update, organization, application
- *Access control*—security clearance; access control list (ACL); browse, read, and write privileges
- *Compliance/governance*—retention policy, earliest deletion date, who has authorization to delete, etc.
- *Identification*—version, identification codes, relationship to other objects
- *Process control*—workflow information, including approval process

Many IT and security managers might be concerned about taking on the additional management responsibilities that an active archive requires, so reviewing the benefits may be useful.

Moving data from active changeable disks to the archive side of the IT infrastructure house obviously reduces the amount of data that has to be managed on the active changeable side. This has several benefits for managing the storage on the active changeable side:

- Less data to be backed up on a regular basis minimizes the time needed for backup (and thereby improves either data availability or data access performance), reduces the need for storage assets to back up the data, and reduces the likelihood of problems (such as the failure of a backup job to complete, or tape media failures).
- Reduces the time required to restore the data from disk or tape should that become necessary.
- Shortens the time that it takes to run a query that spans the entire database.
- Cuts the investment required for high-performance disks.

The trade-off is between these benefits and the additional management burden. If managing fixed content today as inseparable from active changeable data is not a major burden, IT managers may want to delay moving to an active archive and therefore delay taking on the extra burden. However, an honest examination of the whole information infrastructure may reveal that the benefits of moving to an active archive in an evolutionary manner (say, by starting with a selected application) will far outweigh the additional responsibilities.

6.5.2 Long-Term Archiving as Part of an Active Archive

The adjective "active" in active archive implies some reasonable frequency of access; however, much of the data in a large active archive may never (or very infrequently) be accessed. Active also means that the data is online, which implies a "reasonable" response time; however, a reasonable response time to a governance or compliance request may be a day (or more) and not the subsecond or a few-seconds response time that might be more typical when working "online."

Those two parameters—expected frequency of access and acceptable response time—can lead to the placement of data in different storage pools, e.g., information pools on different storage tiers.

The age of the data and how long it is expected to be kept is not an issue for that placement. For example, one United States county keeps well over 100 years of property deeds online with a response time in seconds. That information is likely to be kept as long as the county continues to function.

Long-term archiving raises the specter of technological obsolescence. That obsolescence is not only storage obsolescence, when the piece of storage media on which data resides exceeds its physical life span, but also software obsolescence, when the software that is used to access the data is no longer available or no longer works with an operating system.

Deep archiving is likely to be most affected, as there is little incentive to migrate data or to ensure that applications can really work with the data. Active archives may be less subject to technological obsolescence for the simple reason that they have to be online and IT administrators pay attention to online applications. Therefore administrators usually know when the time has come for a technology churn, either from a storage or an application perspective. They might get some nasty surprises, however, such as that migration takes too long or there is no easy way to move to a newer application that can manage the data. The long-term obsolescence problem is being worked on at present (and that work is very welcome). However, it should not be a major issue of concern today when setting up an active archive.

6.6   ILM Changes the Data Protection Technology Mix

The addition of an active archive for fixed content information changes the data protection category matrix (Table 6.1). The reason is that some of the data protection strategies for active archiving are different for active archived information than for active changeable information, such as not necessarily requiring the use of backup/restore software, but rather making dated replicas of the data.

Table 6.1 Adding Archiving to the Data Protection Category Matrix

	Operational Continuity		Disaster Continuity	
	Active Changeable	Active Archive	Active Changeable	Active Archive
Physical				
Logical				

As another example, an application may have data on both the active changeable and the active archive sides of the house. That might mean that the RPO and RTO for each side will be different. For example, active transactions in online transaction processing (OLTP) may require a different (and probably more stringent) recovery point objective (RPO) and recovery time objective (RTO) than closed transactions that are retained for business intelligence purposes.

The finer granularity that is expressed in the doubling of the cells in the matrix requires more work on the part of an IT administrator to fill out, but also permits the design of more effective data protection strategies.

6.7 Key Takeaways

- Information lifecycle management is essential for the proper management of information as it changes value over its lifecycle.
- Data lifecycle management manages only blocks; blocks do not have the rich metadata that is necessary to ensure the proper granularity to which policies can be applied for data retention, in specific, and data protection, in general. ILM does not suffer from those limitations.
- Information can be classified into pools in which a homogenous set of information has the same quality-of-service characteristics, such as response time and availability. A pool of information can be assigned to a tier of storage, where the characteristics of the storage meet the necessary quality-of-service requirements of the pool.
- Archiving is all about managing the special needs of fixed-content data. Archiving comes in two forms; active archiving is about managing fixed-content production data which has to be kept online for possible retrieval, versus deep archiving, which can be stored offline because there is little chance that the data will ever need to be accessed again.

- An active archive needs to be policy-managed for data protection purposes, especially for data retention purposes. That requires an overarching active archive software management application through which all I/Os must flow.
- The data protection technology category mix has to be expanded to include active changeable and active archive pools of storage that ILM dictates must exist. That is important because the quality of service and the technologies that support that quality of service may be different for each pool for each cell in the matrix.

Chapter 7

Compliance: A Key Piece of the GRC Puzzle

7.1 What to Look for in This Chapter

- What compliance is all about
- What the relationship is between compliance and risk management
- How a financial reporting compliance requirement illustrates the need for data quality and data auditing
- What implications data privacy laws hold for data protection
- What are the different roles of people, processes, and technology in compliance

7.2 What Compliance Is All About

Compliance is typically defined as the necessary mandatory response to an authorized third party, such as a government regulator. However, it can also be

- A voluntary response to a trade association or vertical industry body, to adopt common practices that make it easier for customers to work with the industry as opposed to a substitute industry
- A response to a mandated industry standard, such as PCI DSS (Payment Card Industry Data Security Standard) for the handling of information such as that related to credit card transactions
- An intentional response to protect an enterprise against lawsuits
- A voluntary response to follow good practices to protect intellectual assets (e.g., patents or trade secrets)

Note that compliance and governance are not the same. *Governance* deals with the processes and systems designed to ensure the proper accountability for the conduct of a company's business. In that sense, governance is broader than compliance. Governance, risk management, and compliance

(GRC)—although they can be described separately, individually, and distinctly—are interrelated and overlap, so integration of a GRC framework in which all three are considered simultaneously is important. This is important so that the focus can be on what needs to be done rather than on how to divide responsibilities among each of the three GRC pillars. Note that organizations may want to consider compliance before governance, such as complying with a specific regulation without having a formal governance structure in place. However, the inverse should be the case. Governance is concerned with the overall conduct of an organization, whereas compliance only results in constraints on that governance.

7.3   The Relationship Between Compliance and Risk Management

If compliance to regulations is not followed in an acceptable fashion, a business faces the threat of a financial penalty (or other sanctions) that could range from minor to very severe. That threat represents a risk to the business, hence the importance of risk management to compliance.

However, the reason that risk receives such prominence in any discussion of compliance is that without the risk associated with noncompliance, businesses would have no incentive to comply with regulations. As with data protection, compliance is something that businesses *have* to do, not something they *want* to do. The reason is very simple: Regulatory compliance is perceived as a pure cost burden. Now, that may not be strictly true, because compliance may lead to other benefits, including improved data quality and the overall ability to use better-organized data, such as targeted marketing campaigns for up-selling. Additionally, voluntary vertical industry compliance may lead to greater overall demand for all participants in the industry in a rising-tide-raises-all-boats scenario.

In general, however, regulatory compliance is a hard sell, because it comes with a more or less certain (and quite possibly expensive) cost to avoid the uncertain cost of the risk of noncompliance. The tangle of regulations is already complex for many businesses and is not likely to get any simpler, as devising new regulations seems to be a growth business. This can create a number of problems for even the most conscientious of businesses attempting to meet regulatory compliance requirements. Add to this that different jurisdictions sometimes have conflicting requirements. One may require the deletion of certain information after a certain period of time, whereas another requires that the information be kept for a longer period. A regulation may be ambiguous, which means that a business has a hard time figuring out how to comply.

In theory, businesses should comply with all regulations to the best of their ability, but practically that may not be economically (or technically) feasible. Businesses therefore may put together a portfolio to balance the risks of noncompliance against the costs to comply with regulations. Although the use of the words *minimum* and *maximum* in an uncertain risk environment is probably a stretch, the goal is to minimize the risk of non-compliance while maximizing the use of the dollars that a business allocates to the management of compliance processes. (The danger is that a large, unexpected risk event, popularly called a "black swan," may devastate even the best of plans.)

7.4   Compliance and Data Protection

From a legal perspective, the number of local, national, and international regulations is overwhelming. They may be confusing, complex, and conflicting. They may apply as a general rule to all organizations and individuals, or they may apply to more targeted audiences—say, a vertical industry such as health care. Meeting compliance regulations requires laborious work and attention to a myriad of details. Still, the need exists to try to simplify thinking about compliance—especially as it applies to data protection.

Simplifying compliance from a data protection perspective generally takes two forms: *what must be done* and *what must not be done.* Compliance is really about controlling organization behavior. Those rules, laws, and regulations that predominantly prescribe doing *something new,* such as having more controls on financial reporting, are really about what must be done. Those that predominately prohibit or limit certain behaviors on the part of organizations, such as the ways that organizations manage data privacy, are really about what must not be done. Of course, elements of both what must be done and what must not be done are carried in each law, but the overall intent of the law or regulation is what is important.

7.4.1   What Must Be Done—Financial Reporting

As an example, consider the U.S. law called the Public Company Accounting Reform and Investor Protection Act of 2002—more commonly referred to as the Sarbanes-Oxley Act (SOX). SOX establishes standards for financial reporting requirements (including the need to preserve financial records) by publicly held companies and public accounting firms.

According to SOX, among other things, management has responsibility "for establishing and maintaining an adequate internal control structure and procedures for financial reporting" (Sarbanes-Oxley, Section 404). In addition, a set of internal procedures must be in place to ensure accurate financial disclosure (Sarbanes-Oxley, Section 302). Moreover, financial information has to be certified at certain processing points.

Planning and design, development, deployment, and ongoing management of the necessary financial manual and automated controls have required a lot of work on the part of companies. SOX is a watershed act not only from a financial reporting perspective, but also because of the significant requirements that compliance to the act imposes on data protection.

One focus of this type of regulation is the accurate and timely reporting of information. This requires, first, that an enterprise have the information: An enterprise has to know *what* information it has and *where* that information is located. The enterprise also has to follow the data preservation and data availability objectives of data protection. Data availability is essential so that reporting requirements can be met in a timely manner.

Data Quality Must Go Hand in Glove with Data Preservation

Data preservation is essential in order to ensure that the information is accurate and complete, but another essential element has to be included: *data quality*. Data preservation alone is information-blind: whatever preserves data (i.e., bits) has no knowledge of the correctness of the information (i.e., data that is usable for business purposes). (Recall GIGO: "garbage in, garbage out.")

From a compliance perspective, data preservation alone is not acceptable. Not only does the data have to be preserved properly, the information that makes up the data has to be accurate, complete, and consistent. And that is what data quality is all about—the accuracy, completeness, and consistency of the underlying information.

Accuracy is the condition or quality of being true and correct for an intended business purpose. *Completeness* is the state that nothing (i.e., no part or element) is lacking that is essential for a business purpose. *Consistency* is the state of constantly adhering to the same form. All three conditions must be met as necessary.

Note that accuracy tends to apply to each and every database record and file. If the individual parts are not accurate, then the whole (i.e., an entire application database or set of files grouped for a business purpose) cannot be accurate. Completeness applies to the individual parts to ensure that nothing essential is lacking, but also to the whole because if any individual record or file is missing, the whole is not complete.

Consistency has both a technical and a business perspective. From a technical perspective, a database for one application on one storage system may provide input to another database on another storage system (e.g., information on shipped orders from one database may be shipped to another database for accounts receivable so that invoices can be generated). Those applications compose a consistency group in which I/O writes must be maintained in time-stamp order. The reason is that backup processes must ensure that the data from the different databases comes back consistent to the same point in time (otherwise, two or more applications may not be synchronized, which could create an inconsistent-reporting nightmare). The technical issue of consistency is for the technologists to deal with.

From a business perspective, consistency means that different reports (by time or by business view) should give the same total/summary results. A couple of examples can illustrate the point. The sales from all regions for March should be the same as the sales of all products/services for March and should also equal total sales. The sales for March should remain the same if they are reported as part of future reports (say, last month's sales in the April report).

How can data be inconsistent if each item is accurate and complete, and all items are accounted for? One answer is that business rules for how individual sales are aggregated into total sales in different views of the data may be inconsistent. For example, Manufacturing may record a "sale" upon shipment of an order (because that is where its responsibility—except for returns—probably ends), whereas Sales may record a "sale" only when a customer has paid an invoice (because that may be the event that triggers a sales commission). Moreover, proper changes over time, such as adjustments due to returns after the fact, have to be taken into account. Since many businesses have a hard time agreeing on the definition of basic data entities, such as customers and products, dealing with consistency issues related to business rules may be a real challenge.

However, businesses should not make the subject of data quality any more complex than it has to be (and that is likely to be complex enough by itself). No absolute standard exists for data quality. The level of data quality should be fit for the purpose. That is, if financial reporting is involved, the data quality should be fit to serve that purpose. This does not mean that the data can serve a marketing purpose, such as customer relationship management. Improving the data quality even further to meet such a need may be valuable for the business as a whole, but it may not be necessary for strictly compliance purposes. However, if the improved quality of data, such as for financial reporting, can be used for a non-compliance-related business benefit, such as a business intelligence analysis to identify performing/nonperforming product and sales combinations, go for it!

Data Auditability Is a New Data Protection Objective

Data quality improvement is not the only challenge that a company faces in meeting compliance requirements. A company also has to be able to trace the history of actions that have affected the data. This requires being able to provide an audit trail of the information at all points in time during its lifecycle. So not only does the data have to be collected, it also has to be tracked. And that introduces a new objective for data protection: data auditability.

Data auditability is the ability to verify that data is always correct. Note that before compliance mandated the verifiability of information, companies tried to have accurate, complete, and consistent information (i.e., data quality), but did not suffer legally (as long as generally accepted accounting practices were followed) if the information was not "up to snuff" from the perspective of an audit. Today, however, data quality alone is not enough. Now data auditability is a requirement.

A question to consider is when the auditing process starts for any particular piece of data. The answer is "when there is a triggering event for which the particular piece of data has to be tracked." For an e-mail, that might be when an attempt is made to send the message (by a sender) or received (by a recipient). For a transaction processing system, that might be when the transaction is in its first actionable state, such as when an order has been booked, which for an online Web store would mean that the order can be shipped or for a manufacturer that the order can now be scheduled for manufacture and a parts inventory reserved for the fulfillment of the order.

This implies that not only information in an active archive (say, a closed order that has been shipped, delivered, and paid for), but also information in an active changeable database (such as an order released to manufacturing that may have change orders applied to it before the order actually ships) are subject to data auditing. This increases the complexity of auditing (because legal changes are possible in active changeable data) over making sure that no changes take place with fixed data in an active archive.

Even though data auditing is a necessity for compliance, it is a secondary and not a primary objective of data protection as a whole.

7.4.2   What Must Not Be Done—Data Privacy Illustration

Another focus of regulation is *what must not be done*. Data privacy is an important illustration. Three types of legislative initiative can illustrate the basic concerns about data privacy and what it means for data protection:

- European data privacy initiatives, especially that of the European Union (EU)
- The U.S. Health Insurance Portability and Accountability Act (HIPAA) for health providers
- U.S. state data breach laws

The European Union Data Protection Directive

Recall that the term *data protection* has been used instead of *data privacy* in some legislation, especially within the EU.

The broadest initiative is the European Union Data Protection Directive (DPD), which sets significant restrictions on what personal information can be collected, stored, transmitted, and retained. Although the DPD was originally passed in 1995, work on "data protection" is ongoing in order to apply the basic principles to new and emerging IT requirements (such as those on the Web). The four general provisions are broad and sweeping:

- Personal data can only be collected for "specified, explicit, and legitimate purposes," such as being necessary for contractual or compliance requirement.
- The person who processes personal information (who is called the data controller) has to inform the person about whom data is kept about who is processing that information and the specific purposes for which the data is being gathered.
- Access to as well as the ability to change or delete incorrect information is the right of any person about whom data is being kept.
- The right to pursue remedies through the court system for the misuse of personal information is the right of any person.

Note that while the DPD specifies guidelines, each member country of the European Union can determine how to implement them. For example, the United Kingdom's Data Protection Act of 1998 focuses on the processing of information about individuals, such as the obtaining, holding, use, or disclosure of that information.

Note that personal data can be transferred to non-EU countries only if those states have a satisfactory level of protection as defined by the EU.

The Health Insurance Portability and Accountability Act

A U.S. law that focuses on data privacy is the Heath Insurance Portability and Accountability Act (better know as HIPAA). Basically, HIPAA deals with the availability and breadth of group health plans as well as certain individual health insurance policies. From a data protection perspective, HIPAA requires that health providers adopt privacy and security policies to protect the health record information of individual patients.

The Privacy Rule regulates the use and disclosure of Protected Health Information (PHI) by any covered entity, which is basically any organization that touches PHI. PHI includes any part of an individual's medical record or payment history. Individuals have a right to access their PHI and to request that errors be corrected. PHI typically is disclosed to facilitate treatment, payment, or health care operations.

The Security Rule complements the Privacy Rule and deals specifically with Electronic Protected Health Information (EPHI) (whereas PHI can be either manual or electronic). The Security Rule specifies administrative safeguards (which specifies the policies and procedures on how a covered entity will comply with the act, such as access authorization), physical safeguards (which specifies controlling physical access to protect against inappropriate access to protected data, such as workplace monitors not being in public view), and technical safeguards (which means access to computer systems and preventing interception of PHI over an open network by unauthorized individuals).

U.S. State Data Breach Laws

California's landmark SB1386 was the first data breach law enacted. A data breach law covers the requirements companies have to notify consumers whose personal information has been compromised (such as a copy being stolen or lost, and presumably in the hands of someone not entitled to have that information). A significant majority of U.S. states have followed suit, although each has its own requirements. The four basic tenets are as follows:

- *Notification guidelines:* when a company is required to inform people whose data privacy has been breached
- *Penalty for failure to disclose:* whether or not there are criminal or civil penalties for a failure to disclose

- *Private right of action:* if/when individuals have the right to file a lawsuit
- *Exemptions:* what kind of breaches are exempt from reporting, such as those for encrypted data

Data breach laws typically have a "safe harbor" provision, under which notification is not necessary if the stolen/lost data has been encrypted. The presumption is that encrypted data cannot be read, so the data will not be usable by any unauthorized party.

Implications for Data Protection from Data Privacy Laws

None of the three illustrations is universal, but, not only does each have broad applicability in its specific domain, each also reflects a trend that is likely to become more prevalent.

The European Union Data Protection Directive takes a totally different perspective on data privacy than in the United States. In the EU, personal data exists for the benefit of the individual, and the possessor of the data is simply a caretaker who can use the data only for limited purposes and a limited time. In a sense, anything not specifically allowed to the caretaker is prohibited. The opposite is true in the United States. Businesses collect personal data for their use first and typically have no responsibility to tell an individual that the data even exists (e.g., credit card ratings). In the United States, everything not specifically prohibited is allowed with personal data. Data breach laws say only that personal information cannot be exposed to unauthorized individuals; they have nothing to say about the use of the data otherwise. HIPAA specifies a number of prohibitions and regulates use and disclosure of EPHI, but are for the health-care domain only.

Although data privacy regulations in the United States are likely to evolve somewhat, moving all the way to adopt the EU approach to data privacy seems unlikely (although anything is possible).

HIPAA illustrates, however, that specifying *what* needs to be done (processes and procedures), as well as *how* (a specific type of technology), is a feasible approach. HIPAA gets to a level of detail (such as the use of checksum, double-key, message authentication, and digital signatures to ensure digital integrity) that forces covered entities into a level of data security that they probably should have done on their own, but now have to do (a mother-made-me-do-it scenario), which provides cover when asking for budget dollars.

Data breach laws are a retroactive attempt to remedy the loss of confidentiality, in this case the data privacy of personal information. They serve a very useful purpose in letting individuals whose data privacy has been lost know that they may have a problem, such as an identity theft, but it is a closing-the-barn-door-after-the-horse-is-out solution. A better approach would be to prevent the problem before it occurred. One way of performing this is through encryption, but the technical solutions should be thought out by businesses, because technical solutions are evolving, and all solutions require careful consideration of all the trade-offs. Laws are point-in-time solutions and may be hard to modify to meet changing conditions. So although they are not perfect, data breach laws bring attention to the problem.

Overall, the primary data protection objectives have a role in data privacy:

- *Data availability/data responsiveness:* Individuals are more and more likely to have the right to access personal information and to access it in a specified period of time.
- *Data preservation:* The right to make sure that the data is accurate and the ability to rectify mistakes will become more and more critical, and issues of data retention are likely to become more prominent.
- *Data confidentiality:* Data privacy is a subset of data confidentiality—a loss of data confidentiality is at the heart of the loss of data privacy.

Finally, businesses must take action to comply with data privacy regulations. Except for data breach laws, compliance is not something that they can do after the fact, but rather are actions that must be taken to ensure that they are in compliance.

7.5   The Role of People in Compliance

People, processes, and technology are all critical to compliance, but people are the starting point. Compliance is a knowledge-intensive business because the ability to understand numerous regulations and interpret what their implications are is essential. Judgmental and decision-making skills are equally critical to determining the necessary business rules that can be part of policy-driven processes to carry out the actual business of compliance. Defining the processes themselves is also a challenge.

First, however, all the right players have to be involved. The first essential is internal knowledge workers who have the skills to deal with laws and regulations. These include people from the offices of compliance, privacy, the general counsel, risk management, and internal auditing.

These functions are actually roles, so in smaller businesses, one person may wear more than one role hat.

The second necessity is knowledge workers from functional business organizations such as, but definitely not limited to, human resources, finance, sales, and executive offices. These are the stakeholders who may be responsible for actually complying with regulations and so have to know and understand what their responsibilities are with respect to specific regulations. Although the focus here is on compliance related to data in electronic systems, many of these people have to deal with non-IT-related compliance requirements. For example, human resources personnel understand the rules relating to the hiring process, including questions that are prohibited in the interview part of the hiring process.

The third important type of knowledge workers comes from the organizations of the chief information security officer (CISO) and the chief information officer (CIO). These are the technologists who are responsible for making sure that the electronic systems and the data associated with them that instantiate the compliance processes do the tasks that are required of them—not only in terms of functionality but also in terms of monitoring and control.

These three types of knowledge workers are all internal to the organization. Two types of external knowledge workers also have a significant role. One is the regulator, who has the right to examine what is going on and verify that compliance is taking place on an ongoing basis. The second type is the external auditor, who acts as an independent safety valve to ensure that the internal processes and systems are actually performing as desired, so that the regulator will find everything as it is supposed to be.

Identifying the *dramatis personae* in the compliance play is one thing. Getting them to learn their lines and repeat them on a regular basis is the real challenge. Even though a lot of work for compliance with specific laws and regulations is project-specific, overall compliance should be part of an overall corporate governance strategy within the overall GRC framework.

7.6   The Role of Process in Compliance

Process is essential to compliance. Recall the 4Ps—policy, processes, procedures, and practices. Nowhere are they more important than in compliance. The problem is that compliance typically not only has to develop new processes, it also has to mesh with existing processes. Retrofitting new processes with old ones can be quite challenging. Moreover, the level of process maturity of businesses varies considerably. What may be perfectly fine for normal business operations may be unacceptable to meet compliance regulations.

Recall the data quality and auditing requirements that are necessary for Sarbanes-Oxley compliance (in addition to all the other requirements). Successful processes require good policies, which are what business rules are all about. If existing business rules are incomplete, inaccurate, and/or inconsistent, businesses will have a difficult time getting off to a good start. Then processes that have to implement those policies with the necessary procedures have to be specified. Finally, practices (such as data auditing) may have to be put in place to ensure that proper procedures are carried out. And that can be difficult.

7.7 The Role of Technology in Compliance

Non-compliance-specific processes in the data security arena (i.e., information security) take on increased prominence because compliance heightens the awareness of their importance, such as in access control and authentication procedures. Even more stringent requirements may have to be put in place for compliance, but non-compliance applications may well benefit from more stringent applications of sound security principles.

Nowadays, processes are typically instantiated in information systems, which is also true of compliance-specific processes. This instantiation includes software that carries out the compliance behaviors based on policies that have been set by authorized individuals. One type of software enforces compliance directly. For example, active archiving management software might enforce data retention policies to dispose of information on a legally set schedule. Another type of software might enforce data privacy laws by preventing an e-mail being sent to a person who is not entitled to see specific sensitive information. That is an implementation of data security technology, but it requires a careful development of necessary policies that the technology can execute automatically.

The other type of software actually helps to manage the compliance process itself. This software is more than a set of policies that are executed by an automated software policy engine. Imposing IT controls—such as monitoring, reporting, and auditing—is essential. The software may be available as a package rather than requiring internal software development, but implementing the package may still be time-consuming (as businesses that have implemented enterprise resource planning systems can well attest).

Technology plays a key enabling role in compliance, but technology can only reflect the quality of the work that went into the 4Ps.

7.8 Key Takeaways

- Compliance is generally a response to governmental regulation, but it can also be a response to industry or internal requirements.

- Noncompliance carries a business risk, so compliance and risk management are interrelated (which is one of the reasons for the GRC framework).

- A financial reporting compliance requirement, the federal Sarbanes-Oxley Act, illustrates the need for two data protection requirements—data quality and data auditing. Data quality imposes the constraint that compliant data *must* be accurate, complete, and consistent. Data auditing imposes a new data protection objective,e that compliant data must be able to be tracked and verified at every step of its lifecycle. These are both significant requirements.

- Three approaches—the European Union Data Protection Directive, HIPAA, and state data breach laws—illustrate different requirements for data privacy. All basic data protection objectives have a role in data privacy, even though data confidentiality is the most applicable.

- Not surprisingly, complying with a multitude of compliance regulations can be very complex. People, processes, and technology all play a role. Many people from many business disciplines play key roles in compliance, so coordination is a challenge that has to be met. Process can raise a number of issues, but one is making sure that the right business rules are in place in order to develop the appropriate policies. Though many forms of technology are necessary to enable good compliance, technology only reflects the outcome of the process management work—it does not guarantee it.

Chapter 8

Governance: The Last Piece in the GRC Puzzle

8.1 What to Look for in This Chapter

- Where data governance fits in the governance hierarchy within a business
- Why the changes to the Federal Rules of Civil Procedure have an important impact on data governance within businesses
- Why data knowledge and data auditability are two additional data protection objectives of data governance
- What the issues are that businesses face in managing litigation holds
- How the principles of data protection apply to the GRC business responsibilities
- How different pools of data map to the GRC business responsibilities

The term *governance* is in vogue in corporate executive circles these days. Governance is typically seen as a broader term than *management,* referring to the planning, influencing, and conducting of the decision-making affairs of an enterprise. Governance also concerns itself with the processes and systems that ensure the proper accountability for the conduct of the enterprise's business. Beneath the umbrella of corporate governance are IT governance and data governance (Figure 8.1).

IT governance is the structure of relationships and processes that govern IT decision-making in investment decisions, infrastructure management, client relationships, and all other aspects of the IT business function

As a subset of IT governance, data governance includes the people, policies, processes, practices, and procedures required to ensure the preservation, availability, confidentiality, and usability of an enterprise's data. Note that data governance can exist independently of a formal IT governance (or even corporate governance) structure, although having a formal corporate and IT governance structure would be best practice.

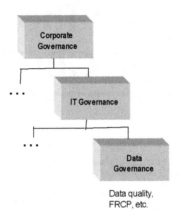

Figure 8.1   The Governance Hierarchy

8.2   Data Governance Must Respond to Changes in the Federal Rules of Civil Procedure

Why should data governance receive so much attention? The changes to the Federal Rules of Civil Procedure (FRCP) that became effective on December 1, 2006, are the tipping point in making a formal data governance strategy, policy, and process mandatory, because they apply to any enterprise that can be sued in the U.S. federal court system. The rules themselves seem fair and impartial (as well as being open to some interpretation, as is typically true with any rules). However, the rules also have profound implications because of ripple effects that will take enterprises a good deal of time to assimilate fully—if ever.

In essence, the FRCP rules govern the discovery process for civil litigation, which decrees how an enterprise must provide legitimately requested information to requesting parties in a civil litigation case. FRCP Rule 26(a) clearly defines electronically stored information (ESI), i.e., information stored in electronic systems, as discoverable. Electronic discovery (eDiscovery) is the process used for making available electronic records (eRecords).

This matters because if a company fails to comply with the new eDiscovery rules, it can be subject to substantial fines and sanctions. Moreover, unfavorable publicity (including the public disclosure of fines and sanctions) could lead to a loss of corporate net worth. Even if a company can comply with the requests, the burden of doing so can be arduous in terms of money as well as a productivity drain that keeps people from more important, mission-fulfilling tasks.

8.2.1   Data Knowledge Is a Data Protection Objective of Data Governance

Data governance includes the secondary objective of data auditability (which is also present in compliance), but it introduces a new data protection objective as well—data knowledge. For example, an enterprise needs to know what eRecords (i.e., data) it has. However, that requires more than knowing that all the application data for an application is in a particular array. Knowledge also has to extend to the content itself, and not just the file or record metadata associated with it.

An enterprise not only needs to know what data it has, it also has to know how to access it. That includes knowing what formats that data is stored in as well as the associated metadata. In addition, IT has to know what formats the data can reasonably be converted into.

One key implication of these requirements is that IT needs to perform an inventory to establish whether eRecords are available and where they are located. That inventory starts with the IT-managed servers and storage as well as the applications that use them. However, the process does not stop there: It must also include remote locations, such as distributed offices and branches, as well as distributed equipment, including desktops and hard-to-control mobile devices, such as laptops and even personal digital assistants (PDAs).

8.2.2   Litigation Holds

Some of the key impacts of the changes to the FRCP have to do with litigation holds, good faith as a safe harbor, inaccessibility of data, and distribution of responsibilities for data protection

A litigation hold means that an enterprise is required to preserve data that may be subject to civil litigation in the U.S. court system. Relevant data in the form of eRecords must be made available to a legitimate requesting third party. The primary goal of a litigation hold is therefore data preservation, from the perspective of both data survival (no destruction) and data integrity (no modification is authorized). Legal circles talk about preventing *spoliation,* which is the "the destruction, alternation, or mutilation" of the data.

The obligation to put a litigation hold on selected electronically stored information is triggered not only when a company learns of pending litigation or is put on notice that litigation is imminent, but also when a company "reasonably anticipates" litigation. In certain industries and markets, that anticipation is virtually universal.

8.2.3   Data Auditability Is a Data Protection Objective of Data Governance

When data serves as evidence, a *chain of custody* has to be invoked. This means that a record must be kept of how the data is used and protected from the time that attorneys request a litigation hold, which makes system audit logs and access controls essential. A chain of custody is necessary to authenticate a piece of data, which in turn is necessary to ensure that ESI and its associated metadata is accurate, complete, and not been altered. In turn, authentication leads to data auditability, the ability of all records to be authenticated by an outside third party.

Governance shares the data auditability objective with compliance. However, there is one difference between governance and compliance with respect to data auditability: timing. Compliance applies to ESI from the time the data is created, and so the chain-of-custody process starts at the time of data creation. By contrast, litigation holds are established only at some time after the data has been created, and the chain of custody requirement refers only to the time after a litigation hold is approved. This means that an eRecord may have been improperly modified (or even destroyed) prior to the placing of a litigation hold. But nothing in a litigation hold can speak to the prior condition of ESI. Otherwise, all data would have be placed under chain-of-custody control from the time of creation, and although that is certainly possible, it could represent an unnecessary burden to businesses. That burden would be due to the cost of and administrative effort to manage the software to provide the required data retention controls. That burden would be unnecessary if the data was not needed for compliance and unlikely to be needed for civil litigation reasons.

Please note that data auditability means that a sound system of audit logs and access controls has to be implemented, which implies that automatic tools have to be in place on systems—tools that no one can tamper with. High data security rises from a very desirable objective to mandatory status. Moreover, someone (probably an external auditor) is going to be looking over IT's shoulder—and not just metaphorically. IT is going to have to get used to it. While the *quis custodiet custodes ipsos* (who watches the watchers) issue certainly exists in the scenario, the watcher issue will not be addressed. There has to be a line somewhere.

8.2.4   ESI in Litigation Hold Should Be Placed in an Active Archive

By definition, eRecords placed on litigation hold as part of a possible eDiscovery process should to be fixed-content. This requires that they be separated and placed into an active archive where they can be managed by data-retention management software that is not the original software that created the eRecord in the first place. This is not to say that the original production software cannot use the data for ongoing business purposes, such as business intelligence, but no software can alter or destroy the eRecord. Note that the archive may be a separate and distinct copy simply for litigation purposes rather than a general-purpose working archive.

Note that fixing content does not mean that business stops. If a copy of the data is placed in an active archive for litigation purposes, another copy that can be changed can be kept in an active changeable pool of production data. However, any changes that affect the eDiscovery process will also have to be reflected appropriately in the active archive.

Note that even though having data on litigation hold in an archive is the preferred approach, active transaction data in an active pool of data can also be managed for litigation holds (as well as for chain-of-custody considerations). How is this possible? Keeping logs of all transaction changes (as well as who made the changes) is possible so that all versions of a transaction (or a document) are kept. The key is to ensure that the logs cannot be tampered with. Overall, software and a management process have to be put in place to ensure that everything works properly. As mentioned earlier, doing this could represent a burden to the business. It may not be necessary today, but some businesses may want to select it as an alternative to setting up a formal archive. Going forward, businesses may find it necessary to install the necessary processes, for example, to ensure that orders are not tampered with over time to change revenue claims or to ensure that stock options are not backdated or changed in value inappropriately.

8.2.5   Deciding What Data to Put on Litigation Hold May Be a Challenge

Typically, parties to a lawsuit have an early meet-and-confer meeting to discuss eDiscovery issues and to resolve concerns about what data needs to be protected. Such discussions may also help limit the amount and types of information to be subject to litigation hold.

However, businesses should not rely on a friendly outcome, because a meet-and-confer meeting occurs only after a lawsuit is either pending or very likely. For that reason, all that an enterprise may be able to do is reasonably anticipate the need to respond adequately to a litigation hold.

As a result, enterprises need to carefully preserve all *relevant* data (i.e., data that needs to be preserved as possible evidence in potential litigation). Unless a clear separation can be made between irrelevant and relevant data, one trade-off is between preserving all data—which may or may not be burdensome but is likely to be costly—or preserving data selectively and thereby risking the spoliation of data that might be relevant in future litigation.

8.2.6   When Is Good Faith a Safe Harbor?

Rule 37(f) of the FRCP, which contains what is known as the Safe Harbor provision, states in part that "absent exceptional circumstance a court may not impose sanctions as the result of the routine, good faith operation of an electronic information system." This applies to the deletion of potentially discoverable eRecords.

A company that is sued has to show that the data destruction occurred as the result of the "routine" operation of an electronic information system. In addition, the company must also show that such "operation" occurred in "good faith," that is, without intent to circumvent the legal process. Without demonstrating "good faith," it is impossible to take advantage of the Safe Harbor provision. This should not be construed as a "get-out-of-jail-free" card even with "routine" operations and definitively not with potential litigation holds.

Note that this rule does not apply whenever litigation is "reasonably foreseeable"—even before a lawsuit is actually filed. A company has to cease and desist even normal destruction of what might be considered relevant ESI under a litigation hold.

8.2.7   The Burden of Inaccessible Data

Determining what data should be put on litigation hold and what data can be safely destroyed are not the only challenges facing IT organizations trying to meet the changes to the FRCP. So is what might be called the burden of inaccessible data. Part of FRCP Rule 26(b) states that: "A party need not provide discovery of electronically stored information from sources that the party identifies as not reasonability accessible because of undue burden or cost." While flexible on its surface, this is not a Monopoly-like get-out-of-jail-free card, since the IT organization from which discovery is sought (i.e., the responding party) must prove the data's inaccessibility.

And the operative word is *prove,* not simply assert that the data is inaccessible. To succeed, a company has to understand its data—not only where it is located, but also how it is mapped within data sources. Though a costly and burdensome planning process is likely necessary to determine what data can be declared inaccessible, that still may not be enough. Rule 26(b) goes on to state: "If that showing [burden] is made, the court may nonetheless order discovery from such sources if the requesting party shows good cause. . . . The court may specify conditions of the discovery."

The reason for this apparently contradictory stance is that the overall goal of the changes to FRCP is to facilitate the use of ESI in civil litigation. Proof of inaccessibility may be tolerated by courts today, but will likely decline over time as companies put in place the necessary policies, processes, practices, and procedures (the four Ps) to make the data more accessible.

8.2.8   Sharing Responsibility

Responsibility is all about accountability in a particular situation and who has the obligation to do what. In most organizations, IT has a custodial role in controlling the infrastructure for electronically stored information. Within budgetary and other constraints, IT makes the decisions on what IT resources to provide and what access to allow.

On the other hand, the business (as an asset-owning entity) has the ownership rights to ESI and sets the business rules that govern information. Business controls the creation, reading, updating, and deleting of ESI within the constraints imposed by the business rules. The key differentiator is that the business has knowledge of (and makes its governance decisions according to) the content of information, whereas IT (except in limited circumstances) does not. As a result, IT is considered a service-oriented function, and IT and the business come together through the use of formal or informal service-level agreements (SLAs).

However, despite the fact that that senior management has little to do with day-to-day data management, it cannot abrogate—i.e., put aside or end—its data preservation obligations. The question is to when and to whom senior management can delegate—that is, commit powers or functions to others as its agent. A compliance example might help to clarify the distinction. Clearly a company's CEO and CFO cannot abrogate their fiduciary responsibility for Sarbanes-Oxley as discussed previously. That does not exonerate IT from its delegated management responsibility in the case of a technical meltdown, such as the inability to restore financial records properly from backup files. However, senior management cannot use IT mistakes or missteps as an excuse and remains on the hook.

Compliance fulfillment rests on the traditional chain-of-command, according to which each level of responsibility subsumes the responsibilities of the one below it and assumes additional responsibilities of its own.

In comparison, governance is more of a shared responsibility among the Office of the General Counsel, IT, and targeted data-owning business functions than as a straightforward chain of command (even though executives still bear the ultimate responsibility). For example, a corporate legal department has to take responsibility for *when* and *what* data needs to be put on hold, while IT has the functional responsibility of actually putting the data on litigation hold.

Note that part of the task may require knowledge of the content itself (which means looking inside a file or record). IT should not view the content itself, as it is neither the subject-matter expert nor the decision maker in terms of what should be done about information derived from the data. Moreover, IT should not breach the confidentiality of the data, because it is not authorized to do so. Thus there is a need for shared responsibility.

8.3   The Impact on Global Civil Litigation

The discussion so far has focused only on the U.S. federal court system because the changes to the FRCP are the leading driver of change that affects the governance of data for civil litigation reasons. What about other jurisdictions?

Within the United States, a number of states have already adopted rules that are similar to the FRCP, and other states are considering such rules. However, international jurisdictions differ in whether or not something similar to the FRCP will be adopted.

Those countries with a common-law heritage (which includes the United Kingdom, Canada, and Australia, in addition to the United States) already have the concept of mandatory pretrial disclosure. For example, England and Wales, as part of the United Kingdom, require in-house counsel to preserve relevant documents as soon as litigation is reasonably expected. Businesses must disclose documents or face possible sanctions, such as cost awards and contempt of court.

By contrast, much of the European Union (EU) comes from what is called a civil-law heritage, and no pretrial disclosure is required. This does not mean that no disclosure is ever required, but there is a different focus. For example, in Italy, each party is only required to disclose materials on which it intends to rely. Neither party is required to assist the opposing party in proving the opposing party's case. The obligation of each party is only to prove the facts that it alleges. Consequently, the principles of the changes to the FRCP are not likely to be followed except in countries that have an English legal heritage. However, global businesses that are based in countries outside the English legal heritage cannot dismiss the FRCP requirements out of hand if they are likely to face civil litigation in a jurisdiction that applies FRCP-like rules.

8.4 The Big Three—Governance, Risk Management, and Compliance—and Data Protection Objectives

Each of the three responsibilities of governance, risk management, and compliance (GRC) has a different purpose. Consequently, the rationale for each responsibility differs (Table 8.1).

Some of the similarities among the three GRC objectives as well as some dissimilarities start to become apparent. For example, all three aim to preserve data in its entirety if that is possible, but the rationale for doing so is different for each. In governance the objective of preservation is to demonstrate that the data has not been spoiled, whereas in risk management the objective is to ensure the continued functioning of the IT applications of the business, and in compliance the data has to be certifiable as being complete and accurate.

Confidentiality is more or less the same for all three responsibilities, although the emphasis may differ slightly. Availability is definitely not the same. The concept of recovery time objective (RTO) has meaning for risk management in terms of application uptime, but really has no meaning in terms of either governance or compliance. For compliance, proving that the required data is available accurately and completely is the key, but this does not have to be done within seconds or minutes of a request. For governance, delivering the required information on time is important, but the time frame may be months.

In terms of availability, the need for responsiveness also differs. Responsiveness for governance has to do with providing the data in a format that is useful to the requesting party. For both risk management and compliance, providing the data in a timely manner is important (though "timely" means different things for each).

Formal data auditability is mandatory for governance and compliance processes, but it is simply a good thing to have management oversight for risk management.

Table 8.1   Applying the Principles of Data Protection to GRC Business Responsibilities

	Governance	**Risk Management**	**Compliance**
Purpose	Find and make available legitimate electronic records	Prevent or minimize business process impacts	Conform and acquiesce to appropriate third-party demands
Example	**FCRP** eDiscovery	**Business continuity** Operational and Disaster Recovery	**Regulatory compliance** Sarbanes-Oxley, HIPAA, etc.
Data protected	IT systems and beyond	Standard IT systems	Subset of IT systems
Data Protection Objectives			
Data preservation	Prevent spoliation of data	Accuracy and completeness for business continuity	Authentication through chain of custody to ensure auditability
Data confidentiality	Limit access to legitimate requestors	Prevent misuse by unauthorized parties	Prevent breech of confidentiality
Data availability	Delivery on promised date	Online access path available	Demonstrated availability as mandated
Data responsiveness	Delivered in a proper usable format	Data provided in a timely manner for user	Data provided for auditing in a timely manner
Data auditability	Verify nonspoliation of data	Management oversight only	Verify that data is correct
Data knowledge	Content awareness is mandatory	File/database metadata only, typically	File/database metadata primarily, with possibility some content awareness and user metadata

Data knowledge in the sense of content-awareness is mandatory for the governance responsibility, but is important only at the file/database metadata level for risk management and compliance.

By the way, a useful mnemonic for remembering the six objectives is: PRACtiKAl, where P stands for Preservation, R for Responsiveness, A for Availability, C for Confidentiality, K for Knowledge, and the second A stands for Auditability.

8.4.1   Data Protected Differs by Management Responsibility

It is important to note that the data that requires protection is different for each of the three responsibilities (Figure 8.2).

A complex set of Venn diagrams would more correctly reflect the overlaps of the different sets of data. However, those Venn diagrams would be industry (and possibly company)-specific and add nothing to the basic conclusions.

Risk management data tends to be the same data used for business continuity, referring to the preservation of the basic business processes and standard IT systems. This does not mean that there is not important data for the enterprise outside those systems, merely that these are the systems and applications that IT formally protects as part of its business continuity responsibility within overall risk management.

Compliance data is typically a subset of the data already protected within IT. Compliance regulations tend to focus on particular types or classes of data, such as financial records for Sarbanes-Oxley and medical information for HIPAA. Since compliance data is likely to be critical in some way, IT (as either a corporate or functional entity) is very likely to already have formal procedures in place to protect the data from a business continuity perspective. Compliance simply implies (and inspires) tighter constraints.

An argument might be made that much sensitive data that is required for compliance to data privacy laws is not found in IT systems—consider, for example, the large number of data breaches involving lost or stolen laptops that contained information relevant to data privacy laws. Although there are examples of sensitive information that originates on laptops (such as a strategic presentation), most of the data privacy-related information—which is probably in bulk, as it would cover a lot of individuals—probably originated in selected IT systems, and that is where control should radiate from.

Data that is subject to governance is likely to incorporate a much broader area than the data that IT formally protects currently. For example, IT may not have in place a formal policy for protecting mobile devices, yet a word processing document located on an executive laptop may be relevant in the eDiscovery process. Although governance data is unlikely to encompass all the data in an enterprise, the boundary of what data is subject to

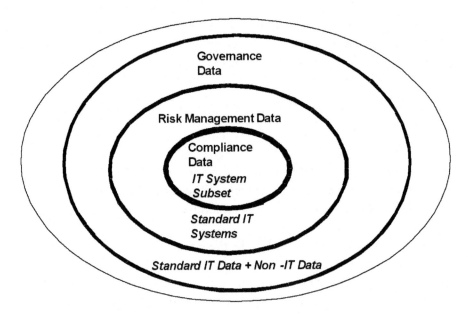

Figure 8.2   Mapping Data Requirements to the GRC Business Responsibilities

governance and what is not is not clear. Moreover, when a lawsuit is filed (or a litigation hold put on in anticipation of one), the data that requires actual protection may be only a tiny slice of all a company's data; however, if there are multiple lawsuits, there may be many slices. Overall, the potential for data to also qualify as governance data is much broader than what is traditionally protected. IT must take this issue into account.

8.5   Key Takeaways

- Data governance is about the structure of relationships and processes necessary to meet business objectives for use of its data. Although data governance can exist independently, data governance should be a subset of IT governance, which, in turn, should be a subset of overall corporate governance.
- The 2006 changes to the U.S. Federal Rules of Civil Procedure describe how electronically stored information can be used in the discovery phase of civil litigation. Failure to comply can result in significant sanctions, including the possibility of heavy fines.
- The implications of the FRCP rule changes are important to businesses. An enterprise now has to know what data it has and how to access it. That leads to a data knowledge objective for

data governance. An enterprise now has to be able to prove the authenticity of data so that the data (as information) can be submitted as evidence. That leads to a data auditability objective for data governance.

- Enterprises have an obligation to put data that might reasonably be expected to be used in civil litigation on litigation hold. A litigation hold means that the data must be preserved and authenticated. Businesses must deal with a number of issues around litigation holds, such as deciding what data should be placed on litigation hold and whether the data should be placed in an active archive.

- Each of the GRC responsibilities has different requirements for data protection along the four basic data protection objectives—preservation, confidentiality, availability, and responsiveness—and the two new objectives—auditability and knowledge.

- Each of the GRC responsibilities revolves around certain pools of data. Compliance tends to be limited to a targeted subset of all IT-managed data. Risk management includes not only compliance data, but all the other standard IT-managed pools of data as well. Governance data includes all the data managed for risk management and compliance, but may also contain data that is not easily (or at all) managed by IT, such as on mobile laptops.

Chapter 9

The Critical Role of Data Retention

9.1 What to Look for in This Chapter

- Why data retention policies are required
- What the three roles in data protection are and what the limits are on each role
- What a data governance team can do to get the three data protection roles to work together
- How an active archive can help in data retention management
- How to create data archive storage pools by data retention attributes

Data retention is about the policies, processes, procedures, and practices related to when data should be kept and when it should be disposed of.

9.2 The Need for Data Retention Management

Why should data be kept beyond the first use for which it was primarily intended? For example, why retain a revenue-producing transaction that has been closed because payment has been received? The first reason is that the information has an ongoing business use, such as being able to help verify revenues if financial systems are audited or serving as part of a customer history for sales and marketing efforts. The second reason is that the information might be needed to satisfy legal requirements including compliance or simply to have on hand in case of a lawsuit.

Retaining data longer than necessary for business and legal reasons imposes actual and potential costs on a business. The actual costs that the business bears are the IT costs of unnecessary storage as well as the administrative costs to manage that storage. The potential cost is that of eDiscovery on the extra data, and that can be very expensive. (Of course, the legal department has to weigh the fact that the undeleted data might expose the business to unnecessary risk against the chance that the extra data might have been able to prove its case.)

The proposed extremes for data retention are ether to delete everything as soon as possible after its initial use or to retain everything forever. Neither of these is sensible. Deleting everything exposes a business to unnecessary legal and business risk. Retaining everything is the pack-rat mentality gone wild. Not only does it directly increase business costs for storage and data management, it also increases the burden of being able to find needed data as it accumulates in electronic landfills.

Setting retention policies and enforcing them can be trying, but businesses can do two things to simplify the problem. The first is that they need to understand who has the responsibilities for data retention and how a data governance team can help. The second is to understand why the move to active archiving with overarching archive management is essential.

9.3 Where the Responsibility for Data Retention Policy Management Lies

A key issue in data retention is policy management. Who sets and maintains the policies? Who is responsible for enforcing policies? The facile answer is the legal department or the data "owner," but the answer is a bit more complex than that.

There are three general roles for data protection (Table 9.1). These roles are appropriate wherever policy-driven management is required—for example, in determining the sensitivity of data. So data retention is not the only area where these three roles influence policy management. In fact, misunderstanding the three roles often leads to a conflict between the IT organization and business units.

9.3.1 The Limits of Ownership

Unless a business is a sole proprietorship (or perhaps a partnership), information is owned by the enterprise itself. That is because the enterprise has the ultimate responsibility for what happens to its information. However, such ownership (including ownership by governmental or nonprofit organizations as well as by for-profit businesses) creates a problem. An enterprise is a legal entity, but it is also an abstraction. Responsibility lies with the enterprise, but individuals are the ones who take action. Note that these actions might be taken by computers on behalf of individuals without their knowledge, as long as the actions conform to policies established

Table 9.1   The Three General Roles in Data Protection

Role	Definition	Who
Ownership	Legal right of possession, which means the full body of rights to use a property	The business as a whole and a functional organization for specific types of data
Stewardship	Manages another's property	Role-based individuals
Custodianship	Guardianship or care of property	Whoever has custody—from general IT and security organizations to particular individuals

by approved individuals (although the reasons for the approval may have been lost in the mists of history).

In order for a business to take actions on information, it can delegate day-to-day management to role-assigned individuals, who may incur serious responsibility as a result, such as fiduciary responsibility. This is what the role of stewardship is all about. Still, the ultimate responsibility for the information rests with the business.

Note that the word *ownership* implies that the owner has full use of the data, including processes such as creating, deleting, and sharing. However, legal jurisdictions may impose rules, such as those for data privacy, compliance, or civil litigation reasons, that impose restrictions on what the "owner" can do. Those restrictions (i.e., boundary conditions) have to be accounted for in any policy that is established, such as for data retention.

9.3.2   The Limits of Custodianship

Before considering stewardship (which is likely to be a new concept for some readers), consider custodianship first. Custodians provide guardianship or care of property. For example, IT provides storage on which data resides, and security professionals manage the access control process. But that custodianship is not limited to physical equipment, such as servers and storage, but also includes processes that protect the data, such as backup/restore software and authentication.

However, custodians do not perform information management tasks, such as managing the content and decision-making relationships of information as it moves through the lifecycle of a business process. This means that the custodian does not create the data, nor should he or she determine the sensitivity of the data or the data retention policies. Why not?

The reason is separation of duties, which is a means of keeping a set of checks and balances within an organization to avoid possible damage. For example, should IT have the right to determine how long historical accounts receivable (AR) transaction records are kept before being destroyed? The answer is no. IT should simply carry out policy directives that have been formally communicated to it by the AR department. The AR department (in consultation with the general counsel's office and the tax department) should know the governmental rules and regulations regarding how long the data must be kept (such as for tax records compliance) as well as any internal policies that might extend the legal minima. Custodians should be held accountable for failure to carry out specified policies; they should not be allowed to set the policies.

As a side note, a severe problem that many businesses face is that all data custodians are not professional custodians. Users, who are generally not IT or security professionals, may have physical custody of mobile devices such as laptops, which may contain sensitive information that should not be revealed or copied without authorization. Dealing with that is an issue for security and IT personnel.

9.3.3   The Limits of Stewardship

By comparison, stewards are individuals who are actively involved in some aspect of the management of the information resources of a business. Depending on their role, they may have responsibility for creating, reading, updating, or deleting data.

A common problem is that there is unlikely to be a single steward who is responsible for all stages of the lifecycle of information. Consider e-mail for example. If e-mails contain no sensitive data, do not need to be held for any legal reasons, and do not serve any ongoing business purpose, the creator or receiver of an e-mail may be allowed to delete those messages. However, if any one of the reasons to retain the data is in place, the original steward may not be allowed to set policy. That responsibility falls to another steward.

And that new individual may be a reluctant steward—for example, a member of the legal department. Reluctance can stem from many reasons, including a lack of intimate understanding of the information and what it is used for, the amount of work it may take to determine what governmental rules and regulations apply now (and what might apply in the future), and the need to make a managerial decision (say, to set a policy for when certain

Table 9.2   Assigning Focus to Stewards and Custodians

	Mission-Enabling	Mission-Defending
Stewards	Business user	Legal
Custodians	Information technology	Information security

data can be deleted) that may expose the business (and consequently the decision maker) to risk.

So the hard part of stewardship is setting policy. Fortunately for the new steward, the responsibility of enforcing the policy may belong to others.

However, identifying a steward may be difficult. In fact, multiple stewards may be acting simultaneously. For example, an AR professional, who understands the requirements for AR data, and a legal professional and a tax professional, who know (or can find out) the rules and regulations relating to AR, may have to work together.

9.3.4   The Focus of Different Stewards and Custodians

Some stewards and custodians share an overall common focus; other stewards and custodians have a different focus (Table 9.2). On one side are the stewards and custodians whose *primary* (not sole!) focus is on *mission-enabling* activities. That is, their tasks are organized so they can do what is necessary to fulfill a mission, whether that is to provide a product or service, pay a bill, or whatever else is required to perform the necessary mission. Business users and members of the IT organization fall into this category.

On the other side are stewards and custodians, whose primary focus is on *mission-defending* tasks. That is, their tasks are organized to ensure that the mission does not fail because of the lack of the necessary security controls and policy constraints. Legal personnel and members of the information security function fall into this category.

Note the use of the term *primary focus*. For example, IT performs many mission-defending tasks, such as the backup/restore process. But typically, if the backup process fails, a business software application will continue to run. Only if there is a problem will the failure to run a backup properly be noticed. So exceptions do not disprove the rule.

And the rule is important in order to understand where each set of stewards and custodians is coming from. Business users set business rules (in the form of policies) to enable business applications to perform mission-enabling functions. IT puts in place an infrastructure (including applications) to ensure that the business user can carry out mission-enabling tasks using IT infrastructure capabilities.

Legal sets business rules as policies to protect against violating laws, minimizing the threat of lawsuits, and defending the intellectual property assets of a business from misuse. Information security acts to prevent the inappropriate use of information technology assets, notably information.

Note also that even though a general term is used, such as business users, there are actually many different functional roles that are played, and multiple individuals may have the same role.

Understanding the difference in focus and understanding the fragmentation within each category of stewardship and custodianship makes it even more imperative to make sure that the different sets of domain knowledge and focus are taken into account in managing the data retention process (or any other process, such as compliance) with which data governance must deal.

9.3.5 The Data Governance Team

One of the responsibilities of the data governance process is to understand the need for data governance policies and what it takes to bring them about and enforce them. Data governance is a responsibility not only of IT and security, but also of business units and functional organizations within business units, including legal, compliance, and IT auditing representatives probably as permanent members. The roles and responsibilities of individuals have to be defined. There may be permanent members and ad-hoc members, and the data governance team has to coordinate with other activities that are going on that directly affect data governance, notably data security. In other words, the data governance team has to sort out who has stewardship and custodianship responsibilities and how they all fit together in setting data retention policies.

Although a core cross-functional team should exist permanently for overall coordination and oversight at the executive and managerial levels, project teams may come into and go out of existence dynamically to deal with particular issues. These teams are also likely to be involved in the get-the-fingers-dirty detail of what has to be done. Coordination with other work efforts, such as a compliance team that is working on compliance to a particular regulation, is also essential.

The data governance team then has to face the data retention management challenges. Among them are

- What data is available that needs to be retention managed, and where is it?
- What are the legal implications of keeping or not keeping the data?
- How can policies for retaining specific sets of data be established?
- How can data retention policies be enforced, and what is necessary to prove that they have been enforced?

9.4   Making the Case for Archiving for Data Retention

When production data was held in only one pool, data retention was the responsibility (from an operational perspective, not from the perspective of setting or enforcing policy) of storage administrators and storage administration tools for that pool. With the separation of data into two production pools—an active changeable pool and an archive pool—the responsibility shifts to the archive pool, since the active changeable pool does not have to worry about data retention. The active changeable pool saves data, but it typically does not have a formal process for deleting old data. The reason is the implicit assumption that active data may change and therefore should not be deleted. When data moves into the next stage of the lifecycle as fixed data and migrates to an archive pool, data retention becomes an issue.

Data retention now attracts more attention because data retention plays a key role in both compliance and governance. However, data retention is also about data destruction. An archive is a place of long-term storage, but long-term does not mean that data lives forever.

9.4.1   Disposition of Data

One of the basic rules of thumb of information lifecycle management (ILM) is the principle of accumulation: Enterprises tend to add data to their storage pools faster than they dispose of data. This can lead to problems ranging from increasing the burden on the data protection processes to overspending on physical storage to overworking storage administrators. A key focus of the data retention process therefore should be data disposal.

Data disposal may be complex in two ways; the first involves defining policies, and the second involves actually making sure that all copies of data that is to be disposed of are actually destroyed.

Disposal policy can no longer be implemented "laissez faire," where the original creator (or recipient) of the data may have been entitled to destroy or alter the data (such as certain classes of e-mails) without interference by administrators. Approval of a disposal policy must take into consideration the inputs from the chief legal counsel, senior management, and business unit management. IT organizations are custodians of data, but IT must act on direction from the owners of the data—and in this case the owners are those who speak officially for the enterprise as stewards of the data.

However, IT management is not just an order taker; it is also a partner in this effort. IT management has the knowledge and experience to put together recommendations that form the context of the discussions. For example, the disposal policy probably should not be benign neglect, where nothing is destroyed—ever. This raises manageability, cost, and, perhaps service-related issues. The recommendations of IT management should include an impact analysis of the advantages and disadvantages, both quantitatively and qualitatively, of different choices.

Policy-setting is at the front end of the disposal process; the actual data destruction is at the back end of the disposal process. This presents a dilemma because if all copies of the data are to be destroyed, including data-protection-only copies, the IT organization may lack the knowledge or ability to find and destroy copies outside its control. IT administration can set policies for deletion of the production copies as well as the data protection copies that are within the IT "walls" of the enterprise, but cannot control those copies that go to either internal non-IT users or external-to-the-enterprise users. This dilemma is especially acute when discussing the management of compliance data.

9.4.2 Data Retention Required for Both Compliance and Governance

Much of the data that is subject to compliance regulations is compliant data, while data that is subject to, for example, litigation holds, in data governance might be called governable data. Both compliant data and governable data are subsets of data retention-managed data, and their management must adhere to special conditions. In effect, working with and preserving this information is data retention on steroids.

For example, a compliant/governable set of data has at least logical data protection built in, but the data may still serve a business use (other than compliance or governance). Data protection in this case is not optional; the data protection has several special conditions built into it, including a chain-of-custody process, serious controls on authorization of access, and inalterability of the data, in order to fulfill the objective of data auditability.

Both compliance and governance, from a data protection perspective, require putting into place the policies, processes, procedures, and practices that are necessary to preserve it in an unalterable state and to safeguard the confidentiality of data that fall into designated classes for a prescribed (sometimes indefinite) period of time.

On a more positive note, following compliance and governance rules may help enterprises manage their data resources for competitive advantage via approaches such as those called master data management and customer data integration. Consequently, businesses should not regard compliance and governance as reactive strategies used only to meet mandatory regulations or rules of civil procedure, but rather as elements of a proactive approach that enables overall data retention.

Of course, enterprises that are struggling to figure out how to comply with multiple evolving, complex, and sometimes apparently conflicting compliance and governance requirements face a challenge to which there are no easy answers, but certain basics apply even to them. For example, chain of custody is both a process and a technology issue in that it is a legal concept that relates to the handling of evidence—in this case, data. From a compliance perspective, every transaction between the time of creation or capture of the data and the time it becomes fixed must be completely documented so as to avoid later allegations of tampering or misconduct. From a governance perspective, the clock starts when data is put on litigation hold. Since only authenticated data can qualify as worthy evidence, authentication is a primary part of overall data auditability objectives.

As far as possible, an IT organization needs to put in place an automated process for controlling all transactions (e.g., all data I/O requests) to ensure compliance with the chain-of-custody requirement.

9.5 Creating Data Archive Storage Pools by Data Retention Attributes

Logically, an archive can be broken into different storage pools by many characteristics; one of the most notable is by data retention characteristics (Figure 9.1). At first glance, Figure 9.1 may seem shocking—fixed content, by definition, should mean that the information is unchangeable, i.e., immutable (and many discussions of archiving affirm the immutability requirement). Unfortunately, that is not quite the case. By itself, data is not immutable as long as there is an application change process that is allowed to update the data. An archive management process may close down the ability of an application to change an information object once it is in an archive, but that constraint might not need to be a universal criterion for all information objects.

Compliance Not Necessary		Compliance Necessary	
Slowly Changing	**Practically Immutable**	**Guaranteed Immutable**	**Guaranteed Immutable, but can be Appended**
Any change may result in the replacement of (or appending to) the original information object	Any change results in an additional and new unique information object.	Any change results in risk contamination with a new unique information object.	Need to be able to handle new information.

Figure 9.1   Data Retention Archive Pools

The four basic I/O processes are create, read, update, and delete (a very old acronym for this was CRUD). In an archive, the create I/O process becomes a capture process in which information is brought into the archive through a migration process. Read I/Os are allowed to authorized users, and often what can be read can be modified to create another version of the information even if no update processes are allowed on information objects already in an archive. Delete I/Os, that is, destruction of an information object, should be permitted to an authorized user only under the control of an archive management process.

Data in the form of information objects is placed in an archive because there are voluntary reasons for doing so (and therefore compliance is not necessary) or there are mandates for doing so (and therefore compliance is necessary). Voluntary migration of data to an archive may be useful for data retention, data protection, and storage asset utilization reasons. However, some voluntarily migrated data may be slowly changing. For example, a 30-year mortgage may be paid off early, or a life insurance policy may be paid off. These changes are relatively infrequent and straightforward, but they need to be accounted for. An archiving process that can handle this may be important. The creation of a new, unique information object that reflects changes while keeping the original information object may be a satisfactory solution if additional storage requirements are minimal and if the user application points to the correct version of the information object. Alternatively, the original object might be deleted, since the information object is not subject to compliance requirements.

In the "practically immutable" case, any unanticipated revisions to the original information object should result in both the original and revised versions being stored in the archive.

Information objects that are subject to compliance requirements have greater constraints placed on them. In the "guaranteed immutable" pool, information objects cannot be changed at all, but they also cannot be deleted without the permission of the archive manager. A potential problem does exist, however: If a read copy of the information object is changed without the consent of the archive manager, it might be put into a separate archive as if it were a data protection copy. Then, if the original copy were physically destroyed, the compromised copy could be misconstrued for the original. Although the risk of such contamination is small, the archive manager must have policies in place to deal with this type of potential problem.

"Guaranteed immutable, but can be appended" data is an important class. Consider medical records, for example. They are subject to privacy and confidentiality requirements, but also to inalterability requirements. As such, they have to be considered fixed content, but, by their nature, they may not only be slowly changing, in some cases they may be rapidly changing. Events that happen are fixed, but there is a need to accommodate new and continuing events. That can be done by appending new information to the old information. However, appending to existing information and retaining the original may lead to a lot of wasted disk space. Managing this process using space management techniques so that not a lot of extra disk space will be used will be a requirement for a solution where adding new information over time is a necessity.

The reason to sort into these categories is to facilitate the ability to manage each pool with a different set of retention policies. Of course, other strategies for dividing the active archive pool logically by different attributes of the data may also be necessary.

9.6   Key Takeaways

- Retaining data longer than necessary increases the cost and management of storage.
- There are three general roles in data protection: ownership, stewardship, and custodianship. The problems in setting policies for data retention relate to who has the right responsibilities. Custodians guard and care for data but do not manage data. The management of data is the responsibility of stewards who act on behalf of ownership, which is the business itself. Stewards "own"

responsibility for managing data, but they cannot absolve the business of actual ownership of the data.

■ A data governance team has to sort out who has stewardship and custodianship responsibilities so that tasks and responsibilities can be established for setting and executing data retention management policies.

■ An active archive facilitates the ability to apply data retention management policies using active archiving management software.

■ Although a data archive may be in one physical storage array, businesses can use data retention attributes to logically separate the archive into logical pools. For example, data that resides where compliance is necessary can be logically separated from data residing where compliance is not necessary. That allows different retention policies to be effectively applied to different data.

Chapter 10

Data Security—An Ongoing Challenge

10.1 What to Look for in This Chapter

- How data protection and data security relate to each other
- What the role of data security is in data preservation
- What the role, process, and focus of information assurance are
- What the role of information risk management is
- When confidentiality is a public concern and when it is a private concern
- What role data security plays in data availability and data responsiveness
- How confidentiality through limiting access to data is achieved
- How confidentiality through limiting use of information is achieved with data loss prevention, and what implications this has for information management
- How confidentiality can be preserved through the use of encryption

10.2 How Data Protection and Data Security Are Interrelated

With today's heightened focus on data security, the question arises as to how data security relates to data protection. In some sense, data protection can be considered synonymous with data security. *Protection* means "making safe from harm and defending or guarding from loss." *Security* means "protecting or making safe." However, in common parlance, data protection is an umbrella term that covers all aspects of protecting data. Traditionally, data security focused primarily on unauthorized access to or use of data. This is still a major focus of data security, but with the new focus on compliance and governance, as previously discussed, the definition of data security has to be expanded.

Data security implementations traditionally focused on defenses to man-made threats; that is, threats of human origin, whether intentional or not. For example, data security was concerned with stopping viruses that could corrupt data, but not with the corruption of a database table by an application. Yes, the result would be the same—corrupted data—but a security professional would deal with the virus, while a database professional would deal with the database corruption. However, that was then and not now. With today's increased compliance and governance requirements, there is a need to ensure that data is preserved safely and is available for use. A security professional may not be able to perform a database administrator's job of fixing database corruption but might well monitor and audit to ensure that the end result is an accurate and unspoiled database. So the definition of data security must be expanded to include all unacceptable threats to data and not just willful ones.

Note that this task is complicated by the fact that many approaches to fixing database corruption (typically called "inaccurate" data) allow initial storage of inaccuracies, then "cleanse" the data as it is replicated to, say, a data warehouse. There is good reason for this—in many cases, data inaccuracy can only be detected when data from multiple sources is combined—but the result is that data security must deal with a world in which both corrupt and accurate versions of the same data are permitted to coexist.

In fact, all four basic objectives of data protection—data preservation, confidentiality, data availability, and data responsiveness—can benefit from improved data security. Although data security requirements were implicit in previous discussions—such as on compliance and governance—this chapter has more emphasis on data security and reexamines some basic concepts in that light.

Keep in mind that the discussion of data protection has built on first principles in order to foster a better understanding of all of its aspects. Data security is a well-known and ongoing function that delivers a lot of data protection naturally. Data security fits like a glove into the overall discussion of data protection.

10.3   Information Security Versus Data Security

For most purposes, the terms *information security* and *data security* can be used interchangeably. However, there is a distinction between data and information that is important from a security perspective. Much security can be done at the data level, where no knowledge of the contents of an information object, such as a file or a database, is necessary. For example, access to a company's human resources database or personnel files can be restricted to certain individuals without any knowledge of what that database or those files specifically contain. At times, however, the contents of a database or a particular file has to be known. For example, transmission of files that contain Social Security numbers or credit card numbers may be severely restricted. Therefore, when knowledge of a data object (such as a file) is required, the focus is on information and the term *information security* is a more accurate description of what is necessary.

In recent years, the task of information security has been complicated by the recognition that in the real world, multiple disparate versions of information about the same thing (customer, partner, supplier, product) typically exist. Merged or acquired companies have their own data formats; so, sometimes, do lines of business. Master data management, on the database administrator side, seeks to create master records of key information to ensure that all of these disparate data-item versions are kept synchronized. In turn, information security must now ensure that "what is sauce for the goose is sauce for the gander"—i.e., that all versions have the same security—else an invader may be able to access the most vulnerable version.

10.4   Information Assurance

Information assurance is another essential term. *Information assurance* is sometimes used interchangeably with *information security*, but it is a formal, well-recognized approach in itself that commands attention.

Information assurance has a long and distinguished history and is a well-established discipline in the U.S. government (especially within the U.S. Department of Defense), although information assurance is also well represented elsewhere around the world, including in private businesses and academic institutions. For example, a multidisciplinary degree program called the Master of Science in Information Assurance (MSIA) is offered by a number of academic institutions. Note that information assurance as a discipline deals with electronic information, but it also deals with security issues that do not involve computers.

A key definition of information assurance from the U.S. government's National Information Assurance Glossary is this: "Measures that protect and defend information and information systems by ensuring their availability, integrity, authentication, confidentiality, and non-repudiation. These measures include providing for restoration of information systems by incorporating protection, detection, and reaction capabilities."

Five key words in the definition are *availability, integrity, authentication, confidentiality,* and *non-repudiation.* If, for purposes of this discussion, integrity is the same as preservation, then availability, integrity, and confidentiality are the same as three of the basic objectives of data protection. In fact, *c*onfidentiality, *i*ntegrity, and *a*vailability make up what is known as the CIA triad and have for decades.

Here, authentication is not about requirements to ensure the legal admissibility of evidence, but rather the process that ensures that users or objects (which could include documents) are genuine (in the sense that the credentials have not been forged or fabricated).

Non-repudiation is the concept that the receiving party in a transaction cannot deny (i.e., repudiate or refute) having received a transaction, nor can the sending party deny having sent a transaction. However, from a digital security perspective, non-repudiation can take on a couple of other meanings as well. First, it can mean a service that provides proof of the integrity and origin of data. Methods that establish that undetectable changes to data are highly unlikely to have happened are valuable for ensuring integrity. Methods such as digital certificates can help to establish origin. Second, non-repudiation may imply reasonable assurance that the data is genuine. Non-repudiation techniques are important to electronic commerce, or eCommerce (for example, there is a convention that any electronic funds transfer sent from one bank must be honored by the receiving bank, hence establishment of transfer authenticity is vital to the financial system), but could also be applied to authentication from a legal evidentiary perspective.

10.4.1   Defining the Information Assurance Process

As applied in practice, information assurance is not only about technology, but also about people (including the management of teams) and process. Process management planning is a key strength of applied information assurance. Key steps in an information assurance process might be the following:

- Enumerate and classify the information assets that need to be protected.
- Conduct a risk assessment that examines both the probability and impact of unwanted events.
- Develop a risk management plan.
- Implement the risk management plan and then test and evaluate as necessary.

The whole process is iterative, and changes to the risk assessment and risk management plan should be made as necessary.

In the risk assessment step, the probability of both threats and vulnerabilities may be identified. In a sense, this approach is similar to the strengths, weaknesses, opportunities, and threats (SWOT) analysis approach that many businesses use in strategic planning. Then the impact might be measured in terms of cost. Multiplying the probability times the impact cost gives the expected value (EV) (in the negative cost sense) of any event.

Carrying out such a process is useful for thinking about what might happen and for risk management planning, but organizations should not put too much faith in the actual numbers. Assessing probabilities is itself a difficult task, and trying to identify rare but severely impacting "black swans" is an exercise in futility. Risk assessment should be made, but users should explicitly recognize the limits of its applicability.

A risk management plan details actions that can help to mitigate, eliminate, accept, or transfer the risks and examines prevention, detection, and response measures. The cost and benefit of each possible action is carefully examined (using well-developed frameworks); the goal is not to eliminate all risks, but rather to try and manage them with the most cost-effective use of resources.

10.4.2   The Focus of Information Assurance

Information assurance has a network-centric and governmental heritage (e.g., the beginnings of the Internet). A network focus is a natural one for a government agency. While the permanent loss of data could have severe negative consequences for a government agency, typically the survival of the agency itself would not be affected by the loss of information.

Today, information assurance continues to emphasize network-based threats and vulnerabilities. This is not a bad focus, as the increased dependence on a public network infrastructure, notably the Internet, exposes all organizations to greater and greater risk. However, the priorities of private business are different from those of a government agency. For example, data protection from a business continuity perspective is an issue for private businesses because the permanent loss of most if not all of their most important information could have serious financial consequences and might even lead to shutting down the business.

So businesses may waffle between integrity and availability as their number-one data protection priority, but confidentiality will almost certainly be in third place. Governments may hesitate between considering availability or confidentiality their first priority, but integrity will be in third place. This is not to say that businesses do or should ignore confidentiality (they definitely should not), nor that governments do or should ignore integrity (they do not), but data-at-rest is the primary focus for businesses, data-in-motion is priority one for governments. Although all businesses and governments face a number of common threats and vulnerabilities, the emphasis they place on different threats and vulnerabilities is understandably different.

In any case, today's information assurance models can still be applied to businesses as a solid foundation for data security and for business continuity and regulatory compliance. Information assurance can bring a lot to the table in the data governance work that is necessary for ensuring proper data protection for an organization.

An Aside on Nation-State Attacks

Note that while individual private businesses worry primarily about themselves, governments are concerned with protecting not only their own constituent parts, but also with protecting individual businesses in a general sense from certain types of threats.

A key example is what is called a nation-state attack. A nation-state attack might be a highly sophisticated electronic attack as part of a cyber war or other attempt to wreak havoc, such as creating an economic crisis by significantly disrupting eCommerce. Such an attack might be launched by a foreign country (hence the name nation-state attack), a terrorist group, organized crime, or political activists.

Such an attack could be a devastating black swan; but governments, not businesses, have the responsibility for trying to prevent it. And that is where the principles of information assurance come into play. By following government's lead in establishing information assurance, businesses become part of a more integrated system for defense against nation-state attacks.

Note that all businesses can do is keep their individual cyber defenses up to date, not anticipate the nature of the attack. Since even up-to-date defenses may not be enough should such an attack occur, businesses should have at least one data protection copy of their critical information that is offline—for example, on magnetic tape cartridges that are not in a tape library or on removable disks. Businesses can do little about the availability issues that would be brought on by such an attack (isolating parts of the network may sometimes be possible), but data preservation should be achievable.

10.5   Information Risk Management

Another term that can be added to the mix is *information risk management* (also called information system risk management). Information risk management (IRM) is a proactive approach that promises to help businesses think about and deal with the data knowledge and data quality challenges that were discussed earlier with reference to compliance and governance and apply it to a formal approach to risk management. Until recently, businesses really did not have to know what data they had and where it was in detail (although that might have been nice), and they may not have had a sound risk management plan in hand. Now, not handling those challenges may expose businesses to an unacceptable level of risk.

Information risk management introduces a formal approach to dealing with data-knowledge and data quality challenges. As such, IRM supposedly represents an additional cost burden to an enterprise. However, doing a risk/reward analysis across an information portfolio may actually save money, when the rewards of risk reduction exceed the costs. Moreover, the work done may lead to new and innovative business uses for the information.

The focus of IRM has to be on the management of risk. Risk can be seen as the likelihood that an event will occur and the consequences if the event does occur. The four basic strategies for managing risk are the following:

- *Mitigation* reduces the potential severity of an identified risk; this is done by fixing a flaw that creates an exposure to risk or by putting compensatory controls in place that either reduce the likelihood of the weakness actually causing damage or reduce the impact if the risk that is associated with the flaw actually materializes
- *Transference* transfers the risk to another party that is willing and able to accept the risk; this can be done through insurance, where the premium pays for the other party to assume the risk. Recall, however, that businesses are self-insured for data protection—for example, delegating tasks to a third-party service supplier does not relieve the business of its responsibility if the exposure event associated with a risk occurs.
- *Acceptance* means to go on doing business as usual with the knowledge that a risk exists, but without taking any action with regard to the risk; this can occur when the cost of mitigation exceeds the negative expected value (the likelihood of the event occurring times the cost of impact should it occur) or when the cost of mitigation is simply so high that a business cannot afford to undertake it.

- *Avoidance* removes that which creates a vulnerability; in IT, that may mean removing a device, application, or database that is vulnerable and perhaps substituting an alternative solution that is not vulnerable to that particular threat.

One way of looking at IRM is as three phases:

1. *Discovery and classification*—Where does data exist, what is its lifecycle (i.e., what events impact it, and how do those events change its value, usability, and mobility), and to what threats and vulnerabilities is the data exposed at each stage of its lifecycle?

2. *Investment prioritization*—Investments to manage risk can be prioritized on a risk/reward basis, i.e., relating the amount of risk that an event entails to the potential business reward for not spending to reduce the risk. Thus, when the cost of risk reduction is greater than the negative expected value of the risk event, risk management investment has a low priority; naturally, a risk assessment has to be prepared before prioritization.

3. *Control implementation*—Controls have be defined to measure risk, and mechanisms for enforcing, measuring, monitoring, and reporting on those controls have to be put into place.

Note that a business can find a lot of help in putting together a risk management framework. For example, the U.S. government uses the National Institute of Standards & Technology (NIST) methodology that is covered in *Risk Management Guide for Information Technology Systems* (NIST Special Publication [SP] 800-30). Businesses may find the ISO 27002 framework available from the International Standards Organization useful.

Isn't much of what IRM does already covered under the rubric of information assurance? The answer is probably yes and, if it isn't, the concept of information assurance could be extended to include it.

However, remember that whether it is called data security, information security, information assurance, or information risk management, all those functions exist to serve the business; so they should fit into the overall governance, risk management, and compliance (GRC) framework. In fact, they should fit into data governance and into IT governance, as they relate to overall corporate governance. The name is not as important as getting the required functions performed properly within the organization.

10.6   Data Preservation Is Data That Is Good to the Last Bit

When seeking data security, the business user's first focus has to be on data preservation (because none of the other data protection objectives can be met otherwise). Data preservation can be divided into two parts, data integrity and data survival. *Data integrity* means that the data that is retrieved from storage is the same data that was put in; the bit patterns are the same and all the bits are there (i.e., completeness). Data integrity also means that the data has not been subject to unauthorized modification since creation or the last authorized change. If an unauthorized modification has taken place, the result is either corruption—the data is unusable—or potentially inaccurate, misleading, or false alteration of the data that deceives the user or an application. (Note that this definition is about the validity and accuracy of the information; in the database world, data integrity is that a change is fully carried out so that the data continues to be in the proper format or it is not carried out at all.)

Data survival means that the data is there and can be found—that is, the data has not been subject to unauthorized destruction, and linkages that enable the data to be retrieved have not been disabled or deleted. "Death" of data may lead to malfunctioning business processes (such as the inability to invoice a customer) or the inability to furnish evidence (which could lead to serious economic consequences in a legal case). Data survival and hence data preservation are therefore essential components of data security (and of data protection).

Data preservation is essential for achieving data compliance. Data preservation practices for noncompliant data are at the discretion of the organization that owns the data. That is not true for compliant data: Compliant data is subject to data retention requirements that may be set by regulators. The organization that owns the compliant data has a choice of policies, practices, procedures, and technologies to enforce the data preservation requirements, but it does not have the choice to do nothing.

10.7   Confidentiality as a Private and Public Concern

Confidentiality is also an essential goal of data security. Confidentiality is the prevention of unauthorized disclosure of sensitive information. However, whereas data *preservation* focuses on the *intrinsic* value of information to those authorized to use it; *confidentiality* focuses on the *extrinsic* value of that information to unauthorized parties.

Confidentiality concerns can be divided into *private* and *public* concerns. Private *concerns* are those that only affect a business itself. The unauthorized disclosure of proprietary information, such as trade secrets or nonconsumer customer lists, is a private matter in the sense that it is not subject to public regulation. If the owners of proprietary information fail to protect the confidentiality of that information adequately, then that business alone (along with its stockholders) suffers the consequences.

That loss of private confidentiality may be important to a business, but the loss of public confidentiality has attracted the greatest publicity. From a public (i.e., governmental) perspective, the issue with confidentiality has been the unauthorized disclosure of private information about individuals—such as Social Security numbers and credit card numbers—either intentionally or unintentionally, by organizations that have possession of that information for legitimate purposes, such as authorization of a credit card transaction.

Unless there are externally imposed consequences on those organizations (such as losing a lawsuit), possessors of other individuals' private information do not suffer from the exposure of that information to unauthorized third parties. However, individuals whose information has been exposed can suffer a loss ranging from a loss of legally defined privacy (exposure of medical records) to economic loss (identity theft).

Governments continue to create legislation that attempts to correct the risk imbalance between the possessor of an individual's private information and the individual. Possessors of private individual information now have to contend with laws and with threats of litigation. One of the consequences is public exposure of the failure to protect the confidentiality of private individual information. That can result not only in public embarrassment, but also in a possible negative impact on the brand or market value of a firm. Consequently, organizations are giving much more consideration to confidentiality policies and practices.

10.8   The Role of Data Availability in Data Security

Depending on the organization and its requirements, availability may or may not be as important—if not more so—than either preservation or confidentiality. However, from a traditional data security perspective, the same defenses that work well for data preservation should work well for data availability. (That is not true for overall data protection, as traditional data security was not concerned with issues such as I/O bottlenecks on a disk array or a storage-area networking switch, which had to be addressed to solve a data availability or data responsiveness problem.)

These defenses are global, logical, and data-focused. A business looks at the data security problem from a global infrastructure perspective—server security (e.g., operating system and application), network security, and storage security. These security defenses focus on the logical value of the data—if a magnetic tape is lost or stolen, no one is concerned about the cost of the tape, only the value of the information. And the defenses focus on the data: how servers process data, how networks move data, and how storage stores data.

All of these defenses tie together in layers, i.e., fallback positions. (Security discussions often revolve about such defense-related terms as threat vectors, attack surfaces, and perimeter defenses.)

How well the data should be protected depends on its value—and different data has different values to the organization—as well as the cost of protecting that data. Security costs money; what can an organization afford—the safe that is rated for 15 minutes of protection, the one that is rated for 30 minutes, or the bank vault?

Infrastructure-Centric Versus Information-Centric Security

Traditional security has been infrastructure-centric, such as the security of networks. Firewalls, anti-malware, and endpoint protection as well as capabilities such as a virtual private network (VPN), which protects the network connection over which sensitive data can be transmitted, are among the many vital components of this type of perimeter-centric security. Undoubtedly, this type of security is an absolute necessity for conducting business in the global, interorganizational, networked world of information technology. However, infrastructure-centric security is a blunt instrument: It does not consider the relative value of data items to the organization, and therefore it cannot adequately balance the organization's need to communicate data against its need to protect against misuse of that data. To infrastructure-centric security has to be added the constantly evolving functionality and capabilities of information-centric security.

Information-centric security protects information independently of the infrastructure components that transmit data (networks for data-in-motion), process data (servers for data-in-use), and store data (storage for data-at-rest). Information-centric security protects data throughout its lifecycle (which reinforces the concept of the information lifecycle) and while that information is in use, in motion, or at rest.

While infrastructure-centric security is vital and does play a role in data protection (such as preventing a denial-of-service attack that may threaten data responsiveness), the focus will be on information-centric security.

10.9   Three Strategies for Protecting Confidentiality of Information

A key focus of information-centric security is on maintaining the confidentiality of information. There are a number of reasons for keeping information confidential, such as not allowing a competitor to gain advantage from knowledge and use of confidential intellectual property that was obtained improperly. However, the one overriding reason that encompasses all organizations is compliance. Ensuring data privacy compliance is the number-one goal of information-centric security.

There are three basic strategies for protecting the confidentiality of sensitive information for compliance, such as data privacy, and other reasons. Confidentiality can be provided:

- By limiting access to sensitive information only to authorized users or "roles"
- By limiting the uses of sensitive information to only authorized uses
- By rendering sensitive information unusable to those who are unauthorized, even if they somehow obtain a copy of the information.

All three approaches should be used in conjunction with each other as appropriate. Even if all three strategies are employed to the fullest extent using well-thought-out processes and state-of-the-art technologies, there is no guarantee that a data breach of sensitive information will not occur. However, that should not excuse any organization from making its best efforts to prevent data leaks.

These approaches or strategies also differentiate between data-in-use (say, on a user PC), data-in-motion (or transit) (say, over a network), and data-at-rest (on a piece of storage media).

The strategy of *limiting access to sensitive information only to authorized users* has long been a staple of data security. The focus has been on access control and identity management. That strategy traditionally has had an infrastructure-centric focus: Networks, servers, and storage, as well as applications and databases, are infrastructure components where access has to be controlled, and integrated with information security. However, as information access has become more granular, access limitation has become more information-centric.

The strategy of *limiting the use of sensitive information to only authorized uses* takes an information-centric—rather than an infrastructure-centric—tack in providing confidentiality. Sensitive information is discovered and identified according to predefined policies. The uses of that data are also described by policy. Those policies may be negative in the sense of identifying actions that are proscribed, for example, not allowing users to send e-mail containing sensitive information outside a particular business. The most common name for the "limiting of use" strategy is data loss prevention (DLP).

The strategy of *rendering information unusable to those who are unauthorized* is a long way of saying encryption. Encryption renders information unusable to those who do not have the proper encryption key. As such, it is an information-centric rather than infrastructure-centric strategy.

10.10   Confidentiality Through Limiting Access to Data

Data breaches have attracted a lot of attention, and deservedly so. Identity management and access management are staples of data security that focus on preventing data breaches. The familiar username, password combination is a simplistic way of providing that type of control, but more sophisticated techniques exist that extend beyond just what an individual knows to what an individual possesses (such as a key or access card) and to what an individual is (biometrics such as fingerprints or retinal scans). These are only part of access control, which is standard operating procedure in all businesses today.

10.10.1   Access Control Basics

Access control permits or denies the use of a particular operations on a particular system resource by a particular entity. An *entity* is something that is a self-contained unit, such as a user, a software program, a process, or a system. Key capabilities in the access control process include authentication, authorization, and auditing.

Authentication is the process that verifies the claims of an individual, application, or device to be the entity that it purports to be. Note that this is sometimes called *identification and authentication* (I&A), where, for example, a username is the identifier and unique within a particular security domain, and a password is the authenticator. In fact, the password challenge-and-response process is the most familiar approach, but advanced authentication should be used for critical data. This may include the use of digital certificates or biometric readers, such as a fingerprint scanner.

Four different types of factors can be used as authenticators. *Something that is known* includes a passwords or a personal identification number (PIN). *Something that is possessed* can include a "smart card" or security token. *Something that a person is* gets back to biometrics. *Location* determines physically or logically from where an access attempt is made, such as inside or outside a company firewall.

Authorization determines what can be done to a system, a resource, or groupings of data. Among other things, authorization defines the rules and responsibilities of individuals, applications, and devices for creating, reading, updating, and deleting data.

Auditing is a key function of any data security system. Auditing requires capturing and retaining logs that detail attempts (successful and unsuccessful) to obtain access, as well as attempts to make unauthorized modifications, to data of any type. After the fact, auditing can be used to assist in determining what caused a breach of security, so that it can be corrected, as well as in assessing the damage, to help determine the requirements for reconstructive actions. During an attack, alerting can trigger a response to limit further damage (if any have already occurred) and to end the attack. Non-repudiation also plays an important role in auditing. Note that databases often store logs for the purpose of backup and recovery, and these logs can also be used for auditing purposes.

10.10.2   Access Control Techniques

Subjects are entities that are allowed to perform actions in a system. *Objects* are entities that represent resources to which access control may need to be applied, such as a file or a database. Although making a subject equivalent to a human user may be convenient, it is also wrong. For access control purposes, a subject is a software entity. In an electronic system, a software process actually accesses a system; a human user only accesses a system through a software entity. Technically, to have a human user as a subject violates the principle of least privilege, a well-known and well-accepted principle in information security, which states that a user should run at all times with as few privileges as possible. However, for convenience of understanding, subject and user will be used interchangeably.

Because an application is typically an intermediary between a user and the data, access control often combines access control for the application (i.e., what operations the user can perform at the application level) and access control for the data (i.e., what data-level operations the application can perform). This splitting of access control responsibilities typically means that data-level access control is the "security mechanism of last resort," as attacks can seek out the application with the loosest access controls. However, the data-level access control must also ensure full access to the data by some users, such as administrators. Therefore, successful data-level access control requires sophisticated understanding of sources of access.

An access control list (ACL) contains a list of permissions that apply to an object. The list identifies what transactions (i.e., operations) are permitted to be performed on an object as well as identifying who or what is permitted to access the object. An ACL-based security model typically uses one of three techniques: discretionary access control, mandatory access control, or role-based access control.

Discretionary Access Control

In discretionary access control (DAC), an owner of an object determines who is permitted access to the object. The owner also determines what privileges these other subjects will have when they access the object. DAC therefore introduces the concept of ownership of an object by a subject. An object's initial owner is typically the subject that created the object. The word *discretionary* is used to indicate that the owner, at its discretion, can give out access and action-permitting privileges. This is the least restrictive access control technique.

From a data protection perspective, this technique cannot be used when the guaranteed preservation of the information object is a requirement, such as for data retention purposes for compliance or governance (litigation hold) reasons.

Mandatory Access Control

In mandatory access control (MAC), the access control system—not the owner (if any)—determines the access policy. MAC uses a multilevel approach that allows a computer system to manage multiple classification levels between subjects and objects. MAC is used in an environment where there is sensitive data. The classification scheme requires that all subjects and objects be given a sensitivity label that has a level of sensitivity assigned to it. For a subject, the sensitivity level represents the level of trust that is required for access. For an object, the sensitivity label represents the level of trust that is required for access. Naturally, a subject's sensitivity level must be equivalent to or higher than that of the object in order to be granted access.

From a data protection perspective, this technique is good for granting access to sensitive information only to those authorized. However, using the technique requires a classification process on the part of businesses that might be more work than it is worth. Moreover, the security-level approach can be inflexible when subjects vary in security level on a case-by-case basis.

Role-Based Access Control

Role-based access control (RBAC) is sometimes called nondiscretionary access control, because the access control system, rather than the subject that owns the object, determines which subjects are allowed access to an object. RBAC assigns permissions on the basis of roles. For practical purposes, roles are assigned to individuals, so the term *user* is appropriate (although technically, roles are assigned to subjects). In the real world, roles are the job functions within an organization. All users who are assigned to the same role have the same access privileges to the resources permitted for that role. No way exists to give an individual user additional permissions over and above those available for other users who have been assigned the same role.

Three fundamental rules of RBAC—role assignment, role authorization, and transaction authorization—work in conjunction to give RBAC its power for access control. In role assignment, a subject has to be assigned to a role before the subject can execute a transaction, i.e., an operational task. In role authorization, the subject must be authorized for an active role. In transaction authorization, a transaction must be authorized as appropriate for a role. Therefore the subject has to have an active role assigned to it before it is allowed to execute a transaction that has been authorized for the role.

From a data protection perspective, the granular authorization capability of RBAC allows it to construct roles that divide responsibilities in such a way that the principle of separation of duties, where no one individual can subvert a function, is followed. That makes RBAC useful in compliance situations, such as those governed by the Sarbanes-Oxley Act, where no one person—either deliberately or unintentionally—should be able to alter information inappropriately.

10.11   Confidentiality Through Limiting Use of Information

Limiting access to data is one way of preventing data breaches, but insiders may inadvertently contribute to the problem by using sensitive information in a way that was not intended, such as copying personal information containing Social Security numbers and credit card numbers to a laptop that later gets stolen. Another example is violating data privacy of an individual by simply e-mailing a health record to an unauthorized person. Data loss prevention (DLP, sometimes known as data leak prevention) attempts to prevent unauthorized use of information.

Data loss prevention enables businesses to detect sensitive data in their organization and then be able to identify, implement, and enforce policies for protecting the data without forcing any modifications to the data to be made. DLP can work in conjunction with digital rights management.

Data loss prevention is a useful term, but it has to be used in the right context or it will cause confusion. Data loss has typically meant that data is temporarily or permanently unavailable due to the corruption or destruction of data, either because of a change in the logical order of bits on a piece of storage media or because the user is unable to read a piece of the physical media itself, because of a physical failure ranging from minor (such as bad blocks on a disk) to major (complete physical destruction of a disk). If the data is recoverable, either on the piece of media itself (such as through the use of a snapshot) or through reconstruction on a new piece of media (through the use of a data protection copy), the loss is said to be temporary; otherwise, the loss is permanent.

Data loss prevention, however, is about the loss of confidentiality of sensitive information. This, too, is a kind of data loss. Data protection is about the protection against "loss" measured against any of the objectives of data protection, say, data availability, as well. As long as everyone understands that, from a data security perspective, data loss prevention is only about the loss of confidentiality, then all will be well.

Data loss prevention, as well as digital rights management, is built around the concept of limiting the use of information to which an authorized user has access. This means that the user may not be able to perform actions on the information to which the user had previously been entitled, such as printing, copying, or transmitting via e-mail. That is so significant that it bears repeating. Previously, the purpose was to limit access to information to authorized users, but once the user had accessed the information, the user was able to perform any action (creation, read, update, delete, print, copy, transmit) permitted by the application used to access the data. Now another application somewhere in the I/O stack imposes rules based on policy to impose restrictions on the actions that the user was originally able to perform. This is a significant new constraint, and the organization has to understand the implications of this new constraint.

The challenge of DLP is to classify sensitive information at a granularity that is able to prevent critical data leaks but, at the same time, not impinge unnecessarily on users by denying them the ability to perform necessary tasks because the filters are so tight that operations that should have been permitted on information are disallowed. That may cause frustration and a lack of productivity.

10.11.1 Policy Stewards Play a Key Role in DLP

Data loss prevention means that someone other than the authorized-access user now has some control over what can be done with the information. The user is a "steward" of the information (as previously discussed), because the user can perform any accessing-application-allowed actions with the information as long as no proscribed actions are attempted. However, this means that someone has to set the policies that define the forbidden actions. That person is also is a steward of the information. By definition, a steward manages something; in this case, the policy steward manages the list of restrictions on the use of the information.

The difference between the two stewards is this: The mission-enabling user steward understands the business uses of the information, and the mission-defending policy steward understands the reasons for restricting the use of the information. The user steward is probably a knowledge worker, who may be part of a functional organization, such as sales, marketing, or human resources, whereas the policy steward is more likely to be part of an organization that deals with regulatory matters, such as a compliance officer or a member of the general counsel's office.

The policy stewards should not arbitrarily set policy restrictions without consulting with the business user stewards. Otherwise, a general policy rule may restrict the ability of a business user steward to perform a necessary and legal function. For example, upon. hiring a new employee, the human resources department may need to send the new hire's Social Security number to the payroll department. A general rule proscribing the use of Social Security numbers in all e-mails would be too restrictive. The burden on the policy steward is to define policies correctly, but the DLP software has to be able to handle the level of granularity of policies that may be needed. Not only must the policy stewards define policies correctly to start, they then have to keep the policies up to date. Policies must be dynamic, because regulations are changing all the time, so policies have to be managed on an ongoing basis.

10.11.2   DLP Software Now Has the Final Say

A fundamental concept in DLP is that some software other than the application the user steward uses to access and manage data has some overriding control. This is not a new concept, of course; digital rights management software performs the same function. Moreover, recalling the discussion of active archiving, overarching active archiving software had the last say (based on policy) on what could or could not be done, e.g., during data retention processes, as to whether or not data would be deleted. DLP now has the same control from an information security perspective, but it extends its control to all data that is accessed, even in an active changeable production pool of information, and not just to an active archive.

The DLP software has to be content-aware, because it may acquire the knowledge of whether to permit or deny an action only by examining content. At issue here is when the software acquires that knowledge. For an e-mail, the knowledge has to be acquired at the time an action is attempted—for example, trying to transmit an e-mail from one business to another business. The reason is that the e-mail was just created, so prior indexing is not possible. The key is that policy rules have to be applied quickly and without noticeable performance degradation. However, the e-mail may contain an attachment. The content may be examined at the time of the attempted action, but if the file is large, the performance of the e-mail system may degrade.

An alternative is to preclassify all documents as to their degree of sensitivity. However, the approach must be able to scale if the number of documents is large. Another risk is that the index may also be very large. However, this approach may be the one chosen, so it behooves an organization to apply data retention policies that reduce the amount of data to a more manageable amount.

10.11.3   Data Governance for Data Loss Prevention

The *dramatis personae* in the DLP play may include business users, compliance officers, members of the legal staff as stewards, and security and IT staff as custodians. Also included may be records management representatives, because of their extensive experience in being able to deal with this type of issue. Given the number of interested parties, one way of dealing with the DLP issue is to set up an ad-hoc committee to deal with a particular subject. This is, in effect, dealing with the pain of each stone in your shoe while jogging. A better way is to deal with it in a more formal, proactive manner.

The formal manner is to have a formal approach to data governance. A data governance team should focus on . confidentiality and retention, how to find data when necessary, data quality, and information management in general. The key is to bring all the necessary players, with a wide range of skills, to bear on each issue, such as confidentiality. Actually, a number of teams may be needed to focus on a number of issues, but each smaller team cannot work in isolation. There is no sense having a smaller team come up with a local optimum (i.e., a solution that works best to solve a specific problem) without trying to come up with a global optimum (i.e., a series to solutions that work together to provide a better solution than all the individual solutions together).

Note that both stewards (those who manage data on behalf of its owner, which is the business) and custodians (who perform a guardianship role such as applying access controls and running DLP software) must participate. The stewards specify what should be done, and the custodians specify what can be done.

10.12   Confidentiality by Rendering Information Unusable to Unauthorized Users

Much-publicized incidents involving the exposure of sensitive private information (such as credit card numbers), especially information stored on magnetic tape cartridges as well as on stolen/lost laptops, has led to a new interest in encryption. Encryption is the reordering the bits of data to make it unintelligible (and therefore useless) to an unauthorized third party, while still enabling authorized users to use the data after decryption.

10.12.1   Data-in-Flight Encryption

Encryption can be used for data-in-flight (a.k.a. data-in-motion, which is data being transmitted from one location to another) and for data-at-rest. Data-in-flight is currently the most popular use of encryption. In this case, sensitive and/or regulated data is protected from loss of confidentiality while being transmitted over a network. Since the data can be immediately returned to clear text at the receiving site if so desired, no issues of key management that could possibly involve the permanent loss of data are involved. The trade-off is the cost of equipment to perform the encryption/decryption as well as any perceived performance and manageability issues. Often the scales weigh in favor of encryption for data-in-flight.

10.12.2   Data-at-Rest Encryption

Encryption of data-at-rest is an entirely different matter, since careful key management is critical to the implementation of a successful—and safe— encryption strategy. The ability to be able to use the "safe harbor" clause in data breach laws, so as not to have to carry out a notification procedure in the case of lost or stolen data, is a primary motivating factor for data-at-rest encryption on disks. Another reason is to prevent internal misuse, such as inappropriate internal use of data. For example, having "superuser" privileges on a system means that the superuser can read (and copy) all the data. Encryption eliminates that problem.

Data-at-Rest Encryption on Disks

More than one approach is available to perform data-at-rest encryption on disks. One method is software, another is an encryption appliance, and a third is at the disk device level itself, which is called full disk encryption (FDE). Software may create a performance issue, and an encryption appliance raises a cost issue. Even though either may be appropriate in certain scenarios, FDE seems to be an alternative.

Data-at-rest encryption will take some time to be adopted; although FDE disk drives are now available. It appears likely that FDE disks will be used primarily on a replacement basis, for cost reasons (because an existing investment is too expensive to replace economically).

There are two scenarios where the process of converting to data-at-rest encryption might be accelerated. One is when storing sensitive/regulated data at a third-party site. A second is when highly sensitive data is stored locally—data for which exposure, even within an organization, might have serious consequences. But data-at-rest encryption will likely prevail over time even for data that really does not need to be encrypted. The reason is that it will simply be easier to manage all disks on an encrypted basis rather than having some that are encrypted and some that are not encrypted.

Data-at-Rest Encryption on Tapes

What about data-at-rest encryption on offsite backup tapes? The technology is now generally available for data-at-rest encryption on magnetic tapes (such as through software, an encryption appliance, on a router, or on a tape drive). Should an enterprise encrypt its tapes?

The question is whether the tapes contain information that should be private to the company, and whether, if the tapes are lost or stolen, that information might become public. One of the factors to be considered is the ease with which unauthorized individuals could use the data on the tapes. Note that in many cases, not only is unauthorized use not necessarily easy for a third party. (even if it is so inclined), it also exposes them to severe personal risk, such as to their future liberty.

Next, organizations have to weigh the risk of public exposure of a failure to protect the confidentiality of private information versus the difference in total cost of ownership with or without an encryption solution.

If an encryption solution is chosen, there may be two options. The first is to use electronic vaulting from disk at a local site to disk (or tape) at a remote site. This uses data-in-flight encryption to ensure the confidentiality of the data while it is being transmitted. The important point here is that the remote site is also the final-resting-place offsite location for the data.

A second option is to encrypt tapes locally and make sure that rigorous key management policies are in place so that the necessary key(s) are available remotely if necessary, even in the case of a disaster. These tapes can remain onsite or can be transported physically offsite using traditional manual vaulting (i.e., they are loaded on a truck).

As time goes on, organizations are more and more likely to encrypt their tapes as a matter of course. One reason is that they do have to worry about the content of the tapes remaining confidential; the second reason is that all tapes in the scratch pool (those returned for reuse as part of a tape rotation strategy) will automatically be encryption-ready, so the organization does not have to worry about which ones (and which data) go on each.

Key Management—The Key to Encryption

Good key management is essential to the success of an encryption deployment. Encryption scrambles data using an algorithm to make it unusable. An encryption key is used to encrypt the data, and a decryption key is used to decrypt the data to make it once more readable (readable data is often called clear text).

If the decryption keys are lost (say, in a disaster), all data that is encrypted is permanently lost. Key management is an issue that can be solved technically, but it may sometimes be difficult to reassure users psychologically. Advanced encryption management—not just simple key management—is essential to overcome this psychological resistance when encryption is necessary. Advanced encryption management is sophisticated management of the encryption process—for example, the ability to restore at any location, key sharing among more than one individual, and a secure key repository. The inadvertent permanent loss of keys, or the malicious destruction of keys by an insider, could be devastating, as it might lead to permanent data loss. The sharing of keys with unauthorized users might entail all the associated costs of the loss of confidentiality of sensitive information. Making sure that the key management strategy will work effectively within an organization is therefore essential to adopting data-at-rest encryption.

Keys must be managed throughout their lifecycle, which starts with generation and ends with deletion. The keys must be *generated* randomly, with enough strength that the keys can be considered unbreakable for all practical purposes. The keys must be *stored* in a fashion that allows quick and easy retrieval, but the storage system must meet essential security standards both locally and at a safe remote site. The keys must be securely *distributed* to those entities that must use them, using the necessary authentication and authorization processes. Keys must be *rotated* on a regular basis as a security best practice—this means they have to expire at a planned time. Keys must be able to be *recovered* whenever necessary, such as in the case of a disaster. Keys should also be able to be *deleted* (such as when suspicion arises that a key has been compromised); this means that all copies of the key have to be found and deleted in a secure manner.

Ease of use and use of the proper security processes are among the important characteristics of a successful key management solution. And except for very simple environments, a hardware appliance may be required to ensure the security of the keys and a central administrative process to manage all the stages of the key management lifecycle correctly.

10.13   The Special Case of Storage Security

When all disk storage was attached directly to the server, and all the I/Os flowed between the two, storage security was not an issue. When Fibre Channel storage area networks came into existence, the presumption was that the SAN was secure; after all, it was a physically-secure network within a data center that required specialized knowledge to access.

10.13.1   Remote Access to Storage as a Security Risk

Now administrators access SAN storage not only within a data center, but also through a switched long-latency network called the Internet. Storage administrators can now make changes to their SAN from a Web browser in the convenience of their own home if necessary. As a result, storage is no longer secure without a focus on making it secure. Traditional data security techniques can be used to limit access, but then some form of DLP may need to be applied. The reason is that access credentials of a storage administrator might be compromised and an unauthorized user gain access to storage. That unauthorized user may not know or care about storage, but his or her actions, deliberate or unintentional, could have serious consequences.

In this case, because it is unlike the usual situations handled by DLP, the storage administrator may have to set usage policies that cannot be changed remotely. The actions to be forbidden are things that an administrator does not want an unauthorized user to do that would be totally devastating. Since, after the new policies are in place, the storage administrator has to be able to take some actions, the unauthorized user could still create some problems that would have to be unraveled, but the potential damage has to be limited.

10.13.2   The Need to Secure SAN and NAS Storage

Then there is storage security itself that has nothing to do with remote access. Today, there is rising awareness that FC SANs themselves are not as secure as they originally were thought to be. That includes the storage switch, the storage controller, and the storage devices themselves. SANs have had only "security through obscurity." This means that SANs have generally been safe only because the security holes have not been highly publicized. While those potential holes are not likely to make the front pages, they are well documented in publicly purchasable materials.

FC SANs were not designed with security features that are common for IP networks. FC lacks certain access control features that security professionals consider necessary for a proper level of authentication. Among the problems that a FC SAN might face is World Wide Name spoofing, which is the process of bypassing authorization methods in a SAN, and session hijacking, which is the act of intercepting Fibre Channel sessions between two trusted entities. NAS and iSCSI cannot criticize FC SANs for lack of security, as they have their own structural security defects.

That is the bad news. The good news is that the situation has caught the attention of some storage vendors, including those who have the incentives and resources to address the situation. Some storage vendors are already trying to differentiate themselves on the basis of their storage security solutions. Hopefully, all the key vulnerabilities have or shortly will have been corrected.

However, any enterprise should check to make sure that its storage is secure, for compliance reasons if nothing else. For example, if a SAN or

NAS does not have standard capabilities for the basic access functions of authentication, authorization, and auditing, then the internal controls that are necessary for Sarbanes-Oxley compliance will not be in place and the SOX process will be at risk.

10.14   Key Takeaways

- In many ways, data protection and data security are similar, particularly in that they both protect data. The focus of data security has traditionally been to thwart man-made (either deliberate or accidental) attempts to threaten data, but with the rise of new business requirements, especially ones related to compliance, the definition of data security has to expand.

- Information assurance is a well-established discipline that focuses on the confidentiality, integrity, and availability of information. The processes of information assurance play a key role in data protection.

- Information risk management focuses on the management of risk. The concepts of IRM are very useful in analyzing risk in relation to data protection.

- If data is not preserved, the economic or legal impact may be unacceptable. Data security can protect against unauthorized modification or destruction of data.

- Confidentiality is a matter of public (i.e., governmental) concern when the private data of individuals need to be protected, whereas maintaining the confidentiality of its own intellectual property is a private (i.e., within a business) concern.

- Data security can play a key role in helping with two other objectives of data protection—data availability and data responsiveness—such as preventing or minimizing a denial-of-service attack.

- A traditional means of data security is to ensure confidentiality by limiting access to data only to authorized users. Identity management and access management are key to limiting access in this way.

- An emerging information-centric approach to maintaining confidentiality of information is to limit the use of information to acceptable purposes. This approach is called data loss prevention. DLP uses policy-based restriction, so those who set policy must do so carefully to meet compliance requirements without affecting necessary business use of information. DLP software now overrides user applications if necessary. The software must not affect performance, and the solution must scale to meet growing business requirements.

- Encryption renders unusable any information that falls into unauthorized hands. Encryption is likely to play a larger role in data security, since past issues with key management and performance seem to have been overcome.

Chapter 11

Where Data Protection Technologies Fit in the New Model

11.1 What to Look for in This Chapter

- Where active data protection technologies fit in the data protection framework
- What are the major categories into which data protection technologies can be divided
- What the base active data protection technologies are for active production data and for active archive data

In the preceding chapters on risk management in relation to data protection, eight data protection categories were identified and a framework was developed for characterizing data protection technologies according to the category to which they belong. In order to start deriving practical value from the framework, the eight boxes in the framework with the active data protection technologies will now be filled in (Table 11.1).

Many of the technologies (such as RAID and tape automation) will be familiar to most readers, but others (such as continuous data protection) may not be.

11.2 Categorizing Data Protection Products

Data protection technologies are not always purely for one task or function; there may be a lot of blending, morphing, blurring, and variations in the data protection functionality that any individual product may contain. The focus here is therefore on overall technologies and not on specific products. IT buyers should "extract the essence" in terms of what function is being performed, where the technology will fit in the framework, and

Table 11.1   Where Active Data Protection Technologies Fit in the Data Protection Framework

	Operational Continuity		Disaster Continuity	
	Active Changeable	Active Archive	Active Changeable	Active Archive
Physical	RAID Cloned point-in-time copy Tape automation* Virtual tape library* Continuous data protection Data protection appliance*	RAID Dated replication WORM tape	Synchronous remote mirroring Asynchronous remote mirroring Semisynchronous mirroring Dated replication Vaulting* Electronic vaulting*	Dated replication Vaulting
Logical	Point-in-time copy Tape automation* Virtual tape library* Continuous data protection Scheduled image protection Data protection appliance*	WORM disk Guaranteed uniqueness Electronic locking Dated replication WORM tape Compliance appliance	Dated replication Vaulting* Electronic vaulting*	Dated replication Vaulting

*Backup/restore software is or might be used in conjunction with this technology.

what it adds to the overall level of protection. Individual products can then be evaluated offline in terms of how they fit one or more of the organization's data protection needs.

The overview chapters that follow for the data protection technologies should serve as a logical sequence for understanding each technology—both standalone and in context with other data protection technologies. Data protection technologies are divided into five large categories for this purpose, as follows:

1. *Back to basics*—backup/restore software and RAID are well known, but what is the impact as today's backup/restore and RAID technologies change?

2. *"Supporting" technologies*—these technologies can actually perform key roles in the data protection drama even though they do not perform data protection directly (i.e., they are not active performers of data protection). These include *enabling technologies* that make other data protection technologies technically or economically feasible, namely, WAN acceleration and data reduction; *supporting technologies* that watch over or take care of data protection, namely, data protection management; and *facilitating technologies* that make data protection easier, namely, data protection change management and data classification.

3. *Disk and tape* as complements to and competitors with one another—the role of disk-based data protection is a current hot topic in data protection. Understanding the interrelationships between disk and tape data protection solutions can yield a better understanding of where each best plays a role.

4. *High-availability and low (or no) data-loss technologies*—these come in two flavors:

   - *Copy strategies*—point-in-time copy capability and its derivatives will play an increasingly important role in logical data protection.
   - *Replication strategies*—understanding the difference between replication for physical data protection (e.g., remote mirroring) and replication for logical data protection (e.g., dated replication that creates time-stamped copies) is essential for matching up the right data protection technology with the right need.

5. Special requirements for *compliance* and *governance*—the additional requirements that compliance and governance puts on data protection technology demand special technologies that organizations have to put in place.

The active (that is, not the "supporting") data protection technologies can then be integrated into a checklist for production copy and data protection copies of the data.

Table 11.2   Base Active Data Protection Technologies for Active Changeable Data

	Technology	Physical	Logical
Production Copy			
	RAID	X	
	Point-in-time copy Snapshot Clone	Secondary	X Primary
Data Protection Copy			
	Local (operational continuity)		
	Tape automation*	X	X
	Virtual tape library*	X	X
	Continuous data protection Scheduled-image data protection	Secondary Secondary (If appliance)	Primary Primary
	Data protection appliance*	X	X
	Remote (primarily disaster continuity)		
	Mirroring Synchronous Asynchronous Semisynchronous	X X X	
	Dated replication	X	X
	Vaulting*	X	X
	Electronic vaulting*	X	X

*Backup/restore software is or might be used in conjunction with this technology

11.3 Mapping the Base Data Protection Technologies to the ILM Version of the Data Protection Framework

The preceding chapters described many current and emerging active data protection technologies. Table 11.2 (for active changeable data) and Table 11.3 (for active archived data) show where these technologies fit in the information lifecycle management (ILM) version of the data protection framework.

Table 11.3   Base Data Protection Technologies for Archived Data

	Technology	Physical	Logical
Production Copy			
	RAID	X	
	WORM disk		X
	Guaranteed uniqueness		X
	Electronic locking		X
Data Protection Copy			
	Local (operational continuity)		
	Dated replication	X	X
	WORM tape	X	X
	Remote (primarily disaster continuity)		
	Dated replication	X	X
	Vaulting	X	X

Before the boxes in the ILM-version of the data protection framework can be filled in for each application in an application portfolio, users need to note and examine the technology choices available in each category. Application requirements have to jibe with available technologies and available budgets.

Replication is repeated at both the local and remote sites, to indicate that it is the primary technology for both.

11.4   Key Takeaways

- No one size data protection fits all; businesses have to select from a number of active data protection technologies that fit in the data protection framework.
- These data protection technologies can fit within a number of categories. Some technologies, such as backup/restore software, actually do data protection directly, but others are supporting technologies that do not do data protection directly, but rather serve in some kind of supporting role. Then the subjects of disk versus tape technologies, high-availability strategies, and special requirements for compliance and governance require an understanding of additional technologies.
- Businesses need to know their options for base active data protection technologies for active changeable data and active archive data.

Chapter 12

Back to Basics—Extending the Current Model

12.1 What to Look for in This Chapter

- What welcome change has come to RAID technology
- How backup/restore software is evolving to play a broader role
- What is happening with remote office data protection
- What is happening with backup consolidation
- What is the role of service suppliers

Technological change comes about not only by introducing new technologies and services, but also by modifying and morphing current technologies. Moreover, some things may very well stay the same while change comes about in other areas. A good place to start is with current RAID (Redundant Array of Independent Disks) capabilities.

12.2 The Move to Multiple-Parity RAID

RAID is the number-one means for improving the physical availability of a group of disks. As noted earlier, the original RAID technologies, while quite good, offer unpalatable choices: either hoping that a rebuild of a failed drive will complete before a second disk drive in an array fails, or investing in a costly extra mirrored array. Given that the wrong disk drive can be pulled from an array and cause an unexpected second failure, and that the disks in an array may be from the same batch of disks (and thus may be more likely to suffer from the same problem that led to the first failure), the organization's comfort level after a single drive failure should not be too high.

A concept called RAID 6 has recently come into favor. RAID 6 allows for up to two disk failures in a RAID group without even the temporary loss of data.

Typical RAID (excluding mirroring) is based on a single-parity protection scheme. Multiple-parity RAID requires the equivalent of multiple drives assigned for the parity function. Several companies that offer RAID 6 solutions appear to have solved most performance issues (within reason).

Alternative solutions to the traditional RAID categories are also coming to market. These solutions may use a parity-based algorithm of some kind or may simply ensure that multiple copies of data (at either the block or file level) are available. So RAID itself should not be used as a check-off box in an evaluation if a suitable substitute is available.

12.3   Evolving Backup/Restore Software

The one data protection technology that is common to almost all organizations is the use of backup/restore software to back up and restore sets of data. A backup can be called a dated duplication of a set of data. Backup/restore software copies the designated set of data from the data source system to a backup target—magnetic tape, magnetic disk, or optical media. A backup job is run at discrete intervals. Full backups are a complete copy of a source data set. Incremental backups are backups of only the changes that have been made to the data set since the last backup operation (either full or incremental) was run. (Differential backups, which backup all data from the last full backup, may be used as an alternative to incremental backups, but for simplicity, only incremental backups will be discussed.)

Incremental backups mean that a backup administrator has to run incremental restore, taking the original backup and then incrementally updating it, while full backups mean the administrator can just restore from one backup. Thus, the more frequent and massive the updates (e.g., online transaction processing), the more full backup becomes a "Good Idea."

Data on a backup copy is typically not "naturally usable," which means that the creating application cannot use the data (even on disk) until it has been restored (i.e., put on storage media where the creating application can use it). The restoration requires using a special process and software tool (which is typically the backup/restore software that created the backup in the first place). That means that the backup copy is not a replica—the data may be identical, but the format is not. Thus, the copy can only be restored, not restarted as a full replica could be. Failover to a full replica for restarting an application is fast; restoring data to storage media first before an application can be restarted takes more time (and sometimes much more time). Data protection solutions that use backup/restore software therefore inherently have "lower" availability than solutions that have a replica of the data.

Since a backup is typically done once a day, the inherent recovery point objective (RPO) of a backup copy is one day of potential data loss. RPO therefore is a parameter of the backup scheduling process and not a parameter that an IT administrator sets. Since an RPO of that magnitude may well be unacceptable, IT administrators have to apply other techniques, such as journaling, or employ other data protection technologies, such as remote mirroring, to bring RPO within acceptable levels. These technologies make sure that data is not lost between backups. However, this means putting multiple degrees of data protection in place, and understanding the implications of what a fallback to each lower degree entails is essential in the data protection planning process.

The backup/restore process implicitly assumes that all data changes at some point. The standard backup/restore process is therefore not "fixed-content-friendly." While daily incremental backups do not back up data unchanged since the last full backup, each full backup writes out all fixed-content information even though it is not going to change.

To get around this problem, a concept called *synthetic full backups* is gaining traction. Changes are only applied (on a "change forever" basis) to the original copy of the data set. If a full copy of the data is required, then the synthetic full backup fulfills the role of a standard full backup. A note of caution is to be careful not to wind up with just one backup instead of a series (i.e., one instead of multiple layers of data protection). The ability to dive deeper into the past is important in the event the original backup fails for any reason.

Despite its limitations on availability, RPO, and supporting fixed-content data, backup/restore software is still the backbone of most data protection strategies and is likely to remain so for the following reasons:

- No viable alternative solutions exist (except for a few emerging solutions) that can completely do away with backup/restore processing and still maintain sufficient degrees of data protection.
- Putting in place new policies, procedures, practices, and products is typically very difficult, no matter what the benefits.
- Data protection is so critical that IT organizations must think carefully through the risks of making any significant changes.

12.4   Recovery Management

A few backup/restore vendors are starting to recast their software in a broader context, acting as the *control center* for the entire data protection process as a *recovery management* strategy. This strategy will bring these vendors into conflict with other data protection software suppliers because they will be intruding on the snapshot, archiving, and storage resource management offerings of these other companies, but this approach is still likely to prove quite popular.

Offering a single management interface for an umbrella architectural platform that offers a broad sweep of functionality may be easier for IT organizations to swallow. That way, IT organizations can accept selected functionality as they become comfortable with the functionality and add more functionality as time goes on without having to learn a new interface. The approach also offers the possibility of things such as active archive management, which enables effective "replication management" of fixed-content information.

Backup/restore software vendors typically have focused on the scheduling aspects of the backup/restore process, not on management of the overall backup/restore environment. An IT administrator sets in motion one or more backup jobs that may or may not run to completion. Broader management reports for the backup/restore environment, to display information that can lead to a root-cause analysis for chronic problems, may not be in the purview of the backup/restore software. For example, backup/restore software may not report information that is important for managing the overall backup/restore environment, such as chronic network congestion and whether all critical information on backup "clients" has been successfully backed up according to a regular schedule. And that leads to the need for better management reporting and automation.

Still, what is happening is that backup/restore software is morphing to acquire the characteristics of other data protection technologies, such as continuous data protection, as part of an overall data protection package. This has several advantages: (1) the customer can continue a comfort-zone existence by continuing to deal with a trusted current vendor, (2) the customer can feel more confident that the new functions and features have been thoroughly tested, (3) the customer can start to use new capabilities at a measured pace, and (4) the learning curve is not likely to be high if using the new capabilities is simply using an extension to the existing software interface.

12.5   Moving Data Manually and Electronically—The Place of Vaulting and Consolidation

The old saw, "The more things change, the more they stay the same," applies to vaulting, which is the movement of tape cartridges physically from one site to another. For both operational and disaster recovery reasons, tape cartridges that are exported (which means that they are physically removed) from tape libraries have to be removed to a remote site. The transportation and storage of these pieces of tape media can be done within the resources of an enterprise, but typically they are outsourced to a third party for which vaulting is a core competency.

In an electronic age, physical transportation of a logical commodity—data—seems somewhat of an anachronism. However, the information packaged in a physically-small (about 4 inches by 4 inches by 1 inch) tape cartridge is already hundreds of gigabytes to a terabyte or more native (which means uncompressed), and trying to move that amount of data regularly could be a network bandwidth or cost challenge.

Nevertheless, electronic vaulting is making inroads. Small to medium business enterprises and branches of larger companies are among those that are able to take advantage of electronic vaulting, especially because the incremental amount of data that needs to be transferred each day is small. And with the increased adoption of synthetic full backups, large IT organizations may be able to take advantage of them for a wider range of purposes. Electronic vaulting over the Internet to a third-party service supplier, under such names as software-as-a-service, storage-as-a-service, and cloud computing, is becoming more and more a feasible option.

One of the primary uses of electronic vaulting today is to send data protection data from a production site to a remote disaster recovery site—a data center-to-data center movement of data. However, a key use of electronic vaulting that is attracting more and more attention is to consolidate backups from remote offices and branches into a central site. In order to make this new type of electronic vaulting more economically attainable, users can employ two enabling technologies—WAN acceleration and data transmission minimization (using data reduction and other space-saving technologies). Both enabling technologies work to get the most out of existing bandwidth without requiring a new investment in network technology (which could be a deal-breaker in any plan to use electronic vaulting).

12.6   Remote Office Data Protection

A significant portion of the critical data created, accessed, and used by an organization results from work performed at remote sites. This data requires the same level of protection that is granted to data of the same caliber at a central site. Yet most discussions of data protection tend to focus on individual large locations that have the scale to house corporate data centers. Data centers are optimized for large, local sites: A data center manages numerous backup streams for multiple applications across a large amount of data, features economies of scale, and includes professional IT staff to manage complex data protection processes.

Many remote locations do not have the scale to operate independent IT functions. Although the person who is assigned the part-time role of backup administrator is often not an IT professional, the real problem lies not in his or her skills or dedication, or the quantity of the data that needs to be protected, or even in the available backup software and backup media drives. The real problem is inherent in the backup process itself, which includes monitoring backups, swapping tapes, and performing restores.

Backup may utilize only a single tape drive or optical disk drive, but adequate backup processes require that multiple copies be available over time. A copy has to be sent offsite, say, on a daily basis, which, whether using mail or courier, tends to be relatively expensive. Moreover, at least one additional copy has to be kept onsite in case a restore is required and in case the last backup is on a defective piece of backup media. Importantly, the latest backup is likely to be that of the previous day, which may not be good enough. All in all, most remote backup qualifies as a manual process that should be automated.

12.6.1   Straightforward Backup Consolidation

The old dictum, "Think locally, act globally," applies particularly to data backup. Backup consolidation means that backup data is sent from remote sites via a WAN to a central site (which can either be an enterprise's own data center or that of a third-party service provider). The central site provides central control and automation of the backup process. Not only is the local backup drive and media infrastructure eliminated, but so are the cumbersome manual processes such as managing the offsite removable media.

Moreover, the recovery point (i.e., the time since the last backup) is likely to be greatly improved by such processes. Typically, a backup at a remote site is done once a day. In a central-site backup consolidation scheme, changes to data can be sent continuously, on an event basis, or on a scheduled basis (depending on the product used) to the central site. Typically, these changes can either be stored as incremental copies or reconstructed to provide a complete, up-to-date copy of a file. With products that have this latter capability, the ability to quickly restore a file that was accidentally deleted at a remote site is possible.

Moreover, the restore time for a full system may be faster in many cases with a local disk-to-disk transfer (taking into account the possible gating factor of the network) than with the old system. In having less data at risk and faster recovery times, the remote sites may actually have an advantage over their central office brethren in some cases! As a result, in one fell swoop, remote offices move from being insecure data protection backwaters exposed to the risk of loss to the forefront of data protection technology.

The technology for backup consolidation from hard disks at a remote site to hard disks at a central site over an IP network has actually been around for quite a while. However, today, the enabling technologies discussed previously—WAN acceleration and data reduction as well as other space-saving technologies—have made this process more cost-efficient and hence more likely to be economically justifiable.

12.6.2   Backup Consolidation as a By-product of Server-Storage Consolidation

A straightforward backup consolidation strategy does not touch the existing server-storage infrastructure, so the remote location can continue operating as before. Depending on the organization's business model, leaving well enough alone may be the right thing to do. Other organizations may want to consolidate remote server-storage infrastructure into a central site to take advantage of economies of scale from both an IT infrastructure and an IT organization perspective. Although backup consolidation may "sweeten the pot" in terms of justifying such efforts, backup consolidation is simply a natural by-product of the overall consolidation effort.

If remote office servers and storage are consolidated into a centralized data center, eliminating enough WAN latency to enable an acceptable response time to access the data now stored at the central site is critical if the solution is to be workable. A third technology, Wide Area File Services (WAFS), replaces branch-office file servers with a network appliance and adds a similar appliance at the central site. The appliance is, in effect, a surrogate file server to local applications that attaches directly to the LAN. The appliance maintains a cache copy of any file that a user opens. Meanwhile, since the central site stores the master copy of the file, standard backup practices and procedures can be implemented for the new data.

12.7   At Your Service—The Role of Service Suppliers

Of course, break and fix maintenance services have been around as long as there has been equipment that needed fixing. But other data protection services have also been around for a long time. Tape vaulting and recovery services are two examples.

Although still small, the numbers of professional services organizations that are dedicated to storage in general—and data protection in particular—are starting to grow. Of course, the large professional services organizations have skills in data protection (such as the design of disaster recovery sites) and so do storage vendors (such as planning and implementation of their data protection-related products).

The number of professional service opportunities for consulting, integration, project management, and knowledge transfer seems endless. Among them are site assessments, architectural planning, product and technology selection, project planning, installation, training, and troubleshooting.

Although the extended data protection category matrix is conceptually simple, applying the principles across a broad application portfolio, complex IT infrastructure, and a large number of existing and emerging data protection technologies can be a daunting task. Not surprisingly, many IT organizations are turning to third-party help for expertise that is not among their current skill sets.

Moreover, in a broader sense, new versions of outsourcing or facilities management, notably cloud computing, are coming onto center stage. These types of services will be examined later in greater detail.

12.8   Key Takeaways

- RAID 6 and new RAID alternatives increase the availability of groups of disks.
- Backup/restore software is evolving to include a broader recovery management perspective. This progress enables users to start to use new capabilities that can be run as separate and distinct products, such as continuous data protection, within the framework of an existing package. Moreover, monitoring and control capabilities can enable better management of the overall process, such as identifying backup job failures and their causes.

- Remote offices are participating more and more often in a backup consolidation process with a central site in order to improve the level of data protection that they receive.
- Specialized service suppliers are providing more targeted services, such as planning services for data protection, for businesses.

Chapter 13

When Supporting Actors Play Lead Roles

13.1 What to Look for in This Chapter

- What data deduplication and other space-saving technologies are really all about
- How WAN acceleration enables data protection
- Why data protection management is so important for the management of data protection processes
- Why data protection change management and disaster recovery testing should be included in a data protection plan
- How data classification is a facilitator of data protection

The data protection technologies already discussed (RAID and backup/restore software), as well as most of the ones discussed in succeeding sections, act in a direct fashion—that is, they either protect the production copy better (e.g., RAID) or they create a data protection copy (e.g., the backup process). Yet there are also management reporting and automation software tools that can play indirect—but vital—helper roles in data protection. They add value by reducing the chance for human error in very complex environments (such as backup/restore or a storage area network [SAN]), where error can lead to negative impacts on service-level agreements. For example, it is better not to have to restore at all than to worry about how fast you can restore. Preventing a disease is better than needing to cure it.

In essence, better data protection can be achieved through better management reporting and automation. Although it may seem to be splitting hairs at times, these helper technologies can be divided into three categories:

- *Enablers* make data protection possible, either technically or economically—e.g., WAN acceleration and data deduplication.

- *Supporters* watch over, guard, or take care of the data protection process—e.g., data protection management.
- *Facilitators* make the process of data protection in some way easier—e.g., data protection change management and data classification.

13.2   Data Deduplication and Other Space-Saving Technologies

The concept of data deduplication has a lot of merit. Data deduplication promises to require less storage space. The original areas targeted for data deduplication were backup data protection and archiving. In some cases, production data may also benefit from data deduplication. However, it is important to note that data deduplication is really only one approach in a broader category of data reduction technologies, in which other technologies also promise cost savings.

Typically, files and larger pools of data have a lot of redundancy. With the cost of both disk and tape continuing to drop, finding ways to save space by squeezing out the excess data due to inherent redundancies might not seem to matter—but, because of ongoing cost pressures, it does.

Redundant patterns of data can be "freeze-dried" to save space and then later rebuilt into the original information. As pointed out earlier, electronic vaulting for backup and replication solutions at a remote site is more likely to be affordable as bandwidth and storage requirements become smaller and less costly. In addition:

- Saving disk space defers acquiring more storage, thus freeing up IT funds for other uses.
- Backup performance can be improved. Since there is less data that needs to be backed up, the process can be completed faster—an especially important issue if an organization is "running out of night" for its backup.
- Network bandwidth can be allocated more efficiently when transmitting data, accomplishing more with less bandwidth and avoiding extra IT investments.

There are four techniques that companies typically use to save space or bandwidth.

1. *Compression*—An algorithm (such as the Lempel-Ziv algorithm for textual information) looks at the redundancy found in a stream of bits within a single file in order to condense the file. For business information a ratio of 2:1 reduction is considered reasonable. Information stored on tape cartridges is typically compressed to increase the capacity a tape can hold and to increase the ability to restore more data more rapidly.

2. *Single instancing*—This approach stores only a single copy of a file in a pool of storage. For example, content addressable storage (CAS) systems take a unique "signature" of each file and delete extra copies of files with the same signature. The reduction ratio is different for each organization, but it can be quite significant. Single instancing can be used for efficient storage of information in fixed-content repositories and for managing that information.

3. *File differencing*—This approach notices small changes in files via a byte-level scan and sends only the changes over a network from a target to a source repository. This approach improves the transmission of files over a network because only the changes are sent. The file differencing approach is useful in decreasing the time needed to back up files.

4. *Data deduplication*—This approach determines common sequences of data at a subfile level across a large volume of data. The key to effective data deduplication is the ability of the data deduplication software to reassemble the constituent parts that make up unique files. Vendor claims for how much data can be compacted are astonishingly high.

All four techniques have their place. However, a key principle is that the wider the scope of the data deduplication (i.e., beyond single files), the greater is the ability to eliminate redundancies. In other words, *interfile* techniques have greater capability to reduce the need for data storage and transmission than *intrafile* techniques.

Single instancing and data deduplication are the two approaches that look at redundancies across a pool of storage. Note that because of its unique signature approach, single instancing records each version of a file as a separate object, whereas data deduplication enables time-based recovery of a document (such as a Microsoft Word document) at each stage of its evolution. Also, single instancing does not detect redundancy within files, such as the Microsoft Word overhead that is necessary for using the Word processor, but that is not necessary for storing the file being processed.

Data deduplication techniques are useful in two other ways for backup. First, since multiple servers may use the same pool of backup storage, operating system and application files (in addition to data files) that have some commonality should benefit from data deduplication. Second, traditional backup processes involving full and incremental backups are likely to generate large redundancies over time. Data deduplication techniques can not only save space, they can enable the time-based recovery of information from an earlier stage than would have been stored without data deduplication.

Claims have been made for 20× data deduplication (and possibly much more). That may be the case in certain situations, but enterprises should check closely, as their "mileage" may vary greatly. Structured information (databases) is different in its ability to "reduce" from semistructured information (files such as word processing documents), and both are different from unstructured information (bitmapped information such as audio, video, and medical imaging).

The inclusion of metadata management capabilities is essential to providing efficient, dependable data deduplication, since the key result is getting data back together in a useful form. Since enterprises are dependent on those files for their business well-being, unordered bits of data are useless.

The bottom line is that data deduplication and other space-saving technologies are useful for electronic vaulting—and in many more ways in the world of data protection.

13.3   WAN Acceleration

Squeezing more effective performance out of an existing WAN infrastructure may seem impossible. However, there are two general categories of techniques that can—separately or together—get more out of existing bandwidth capability:

- Reduce bandwidth demand by sending only necessary bits of data (which is also part of the data reduction strategy). For example, eliminate redundancies by sending only one copy of a file or sending only the changes to a file that is already available at a remote site.
- Improve the efficiency of the carrier. For example, cut out the chattiness in the TCP protocol that slows things down, or

eliminate unnecessary actions that an application might take that increase latency.

These network and application efficiency improvements can be called WAN acceleration or WAN optimization or even application acceleration. The result is not more actual bits per second, but rather faster effective throughput of the bits available. That can be done by attempting to eliminate inefficiencies in the TCP protocol and individual application protocols that create unnecessarily repetitive WAN traffic. That may include shielding applications from intermittent network issues—such as bit errors, jitter, congestion, route buffer overflows, and packet loss.

13.4   Data Protection Management

The time that IT organizations spend on improving their backup/restore processes probably rivals the time that millions of individuals spend on improving their golf game—and with the same result. Although some improvement may be possible, a limit is quickly approached beyond which further investment is not cost-effective.

Given the number of available applications and inherently complex IT infrastructures, the problems associated with getting the backup/restore process to work effectively are enormous, including:

- Not having time to run a backup job
- Failure to schedule backup jobs to protect all the data that needs to be protected
- Failure to notice that backup jobs failed or to take corrective actions to rerun those jobs
- Not noticing alarming disparities in output from backup jobs that appear to have succeeded (such as noticing that the data written for the backup is much smaller than the size of the original data)
- Not noticing that the file system is going to run out of space if no corrective action is taken
- Not detecting, *before* attempting the restore, mechanical or other physical errors that will cause a restore *to fail*

No technological *deus ex machina* exists to solve all these problems. IT organizations may expect their own backup/restore software to help (and in some cases, some assistance is available), but typically, solving these problems is not the focus of the backup/restore software. As a result, IT organizations may want to examine other software products that support monitoring and reporting, as well as real-time operational analysis, to provide information that can help address these problems.

IT organizations still depend on traditional software-based processes as the backbone of the backup/restore process. As we have noted before, the more things change, the more they stay the same. And the fact that a virtual tape library (VTL) may front-end a physical tape library does not alter basic backup/restore processes.

In a large number of organizations, however, these processes are at best frayed and at worst broken. In order to determine how well protected their data is, companies must answer two questions about the state of the processes:

- Can IT guarantee that all data that needs to be restored after a production data loss is backed up all the time?
- Can IT guarantee that all the data that needs to be restored will be able to be restored in a timely manner that is consistent with the capabilities of the data protection technologies that are used?

If the answer to both questions is not an unequivocal yes, then the company's data protection processes (and investments) are not delivering the necessary level of service.

The usual culprit in poorly performing data protection processes, primarily backup/restore, is complexity. One simple source of complexity is the never-ending growth of data. Even when backup/restore processes have been fully optimized in terms of performance, if additional data is added to a backup job, it will take longer to run. Additionally, requirements to keep applications up longer (a growing necessity among increasingly globally focused businesses) shortens the logistical time available to do backups. So, while an organization's "days" are getting shorter, the amount of work that needs to be done each "day" is increasing. In addition, delays due to restarting a failed backup or coping with network congestion that prevents a running backup job from completing in the allocated time must be addressed as quickly as possible. The trade-off between having an application up that is not fully protected or having unplanned downtime for an application while a backup job runs is unpalatable.

A second cause of complexity is the common mixing of heterogeneous products (more than one type of backup/restore software, operating system, or storage hardware). The amazing thing is that—despite all the problems inherent in such environments—backup/restore processes continue to run.

To deal with all the problems of data protection processes, many companies need additional help. Data protection management (DPM) is the name for that category of products that help manage these environments. DPM products *do not perform* data protection, but do enable better management of the production processes that perform the actual data protection. These include backup/restore software and continuous data protection (CDP) appliances, as well as the other elements of the IT infrastructure that make up the data protection "ecosystem."

The word *ecosystem* implies interrelationships among the various components—or domains—of the IT infrastructure, including servers, networks, storage, applications, operating systems, file systems, and databases. For example, if a network is congested and backup I/O traffic cannot transverse the network in the allocated time, a backup job may not be able complete within the planned backup time window. This example illustrates the need for IT management to have both timely and actionable information to either prevent service-level-impacting events or, failing that, to minimize the damage of the service-level-impacting events that have already occurred. Actionable means that the problem can be alleviated—either on a one-time basis or permanently. DPM delivers the reporting, monitoring, and troubleshooting capabilities that IT needs to manage data protection processes more effectively.

Issues that data protection management products are designed to address include:

- *Ensure completeness of data protection coverage*—by determining if any servers have not been backed up successfully or if there are servers for which backup has not been attempted at all
- *Speed up response to real-time data protection problems*—by facilitating the troubleshooting process to identify and rectify potential or actual data protection service-level-impacting events.
- *Carry out long-term backup window problem analysis*—by performing a pattern analysis (e.g., determining from historical information the slowest, fastest, and most unreliable components of the data protection infrastructure) in order to see if any systemic issues, such as repeating problems or bottlenecks, need to be addressed.
- *Perform preventive maintenance through predictive analysis to prevent unnecessary negative service-level impacts*—by using historical information to perform a trend analysis to determine when elements of

the data protection environment will exceed a predetermined threshold, such as when pieces of tape media will run out.

Monitoring and reporting are the first steps to achieving efficient data protection management, so absorbing and making use of DPM capabilities is the first task for IT. Then IT may very well want to turn to a deeper analysis of the information to be able to proactively find and resolve fundamental issues that cause real or potential problems (rather than having to deal with a set of cascading alerts where the causal needle is hard to detect in the infrastructure haystack).

13.5   Data Protection Change Management

From a storage perspective, changes in the storage configuration of a storage area network (SAN) at the primary site must be reflected at the remote disaster site in a consistent and timely manner. The user should put a change management process in place that ensures that alterations at one site are validated and synchronized at the other site. Remember that, if or when a disaster should occur, the staff handling the disaster may be different from the staff that managed the original production site. Along with facing extreme technical demands, they will be under a tremendous amount of emotional stress and time pressure. Disaster recovery time is not the right time for them to have to figure out what should have been done to synchronize the storage requirements at both sites. That is the responsibility of the original production site staff.

Production-site staff can perform site storage synchronization manually or with the aid of software tools, but keeping configurations up to date through a change management process is critical to success. And with the complexity of modern SANs and the criticality of the data, use of software tools may be literally essential.

13.6   Disaster Recovery Testing

One of the most neglected areas in data protection is disaster recovery (DR) testing (which may build off data protection change management). The result may be a serious problem in the event of a disaster because a business faces a threat that it cannot recover all its data, the data may take much longer to recover than planned, or even that it may not be able to recover at all.

However, DR testing is typically difficult. A business does not want to have to take down existing applications for the time needed to test a restore. Second, disaster recovery is typically costly in terms of times and people. Third, there is a risk that something might go wrong during testing and create additional problems, such as the loss of data. Consequently, DR testing is often done partially to reduce cost and risk and is done very infrequently, which increases the risk of exposure.

Fortunately, software automation is now available that can help identify DR vulnerabilities. These can identify gaps between what should be and what is for disaster recovery protection. For example, changes in a production environment may not be reflected on the DR side, that is, the remote site may get out of synchronization with the primary site. DR test technology can be useful not only for risk management, but also for governance and compliance, because data completeness, data inconsistency, and data tampering can be examined.

13.7 Data Classification

Data classification is the process of separating data into different piles (i.e., categories) to which different policies, such as data protection policies, apply. Identifying and ordering data according to business and regulatory requirements requires tools that use a policy-management engine based on essential business rules, as well as metadata and content knowledge of files and/or databases. By using such solutions, organizations can more easily classify data according to value or requirements such as compliance or availability.

Data classification can reflect and bolster the benefits of ILM: more efficient use of the storage infrastructure through the use of tiered storage solutions (e.g., for archiving), greater productivity for storage management, enabling or simplifying compliance management and eDiscovery governance processes, and enabling information that was lost to be found and used effectively. Developing greater knowledge of information allows querying across broader sets of data, identifying new relationships between data for competitive advantage, easier programming at a higher (business metadata) level, better governance (legal discovery can find the information needed), enhanced data quality (if you use extract, transform, load [ETL] tools), and better administration across data stores.

A couple of terms that have popped up to cover the data classification space are "information classification and management" and "intelligent information management." Both are good attempts at product categorization, which attempts to organize products not only for comparison purposes, but also to help IT organizations understand what they need to get their hands around data classification and define what solutions they can buy for that process.

13.7.1   Looking at Data Classification Through Different Lenses

Enterprises can use two different perceptual lenses to help them clarify which data classification solution may serve their needs.

The Management Lens

The first filter is to determine which types of management functions IT staff performs: storage, data, or information. The three types (derived from the Storage Networking Industry Association [SNIA]) are

- *Storage management*—discovers, monitors, and controls physical storage assets
- *Data management*—deals with the non-data-path control and use of the data itself, from creation to deletion, such as migration, replication, and backup/restore processes
- *Information management*—manages the content and decision-making relationships of information as it moves through the lifecycle of a business process, such as records management and content management

What are the differences among these three functions? Storage management covers tiering (ensuring that data resides on media that reflects its value), data management focuses on data protection (such as employing different types of data protection for different classes of data) and migration, and information management is about content awareness (where what is contained in the data influences management processes), such as applying eDiscovery.

In a broader sense, information management is the enterprise-wide administration at the metadata/business level across all vendors/data types. There can also be a mix of management types working in harmony and integration. File metadata (a data management function) may be mixed with an index of information (a content-aware information management function) to classify data. That classified data can then be migrated (a data management function) to the appropriate tier of storage (a storage management function).

Storage management is at the block level and uses primitive metadata tags, such as when the block was last accessed. Data management can use file and database metadata (it is at the level of the file or the database "record," but it does not understand the content of the file or record). Information management is content-aware in that the contents of a file or database can be examined and that information can be used (either directly or in the form of an index) for classification purposes.

The Data Lens

The second way of looking at data classification is through the data lens, examining the types of data that the data classification process manages. Data classification does not have to be universally applied; IT can select one application at a time or even a series of interrelated applications. However, data classification typically involves only one data type or a mix of data types (Table 13.1).

The most common differentiation that businesses utilize is between structured and unstructured data. What users typically consider to be structured data—data in databases—is essentially correct. What is frequently considered unstructured data—for example, where word processing documents are commingled with video files—is not a correct categorization. There is an essential differentiation between semistructured and unstructured data in

Table 13.1   Differentiating Among the Different Types of Data

Type	Structured	Semistructured	Unstructured
Common forms	Database	"Text" documents, such as e-mail, word processing, presentations, spreadsheets	Natively bit-mapped data, such as video, audio, pictures, and MRI scans
Key differentiator	Sort	Search	Sense
Examples	OLTP systems, such as CRM and ERP Data warehousing	Personal productivity, such as e-mail and word processing Websites using HTTP	Entertainment, such as video and audio Imaging, such as digital photography and bit-mapped medical tests

that semistructured data can be searched more effectively. For example, one can search for all e-mails or word processing documents (i.e., those supported by content-aware applications) that contain a certain word. That is why there is a need for the semistructured category.

That same search capability does not apply to *native* unstructured data (note the use of the word *native*). For example, questioning when a certain word was spoken in a movie is unanswerable in native mode because video cannot be searched but only sensed (viewed or heard). Speech recognition might be used to determine whether and when a word was spoken, and this information could then be put into a searchable, semistructured format. For many businesses, the goal for unstructured data is to increase its structure (and value) by pairing it with complementary structured or semistructured searchable information.

The term *semistructured* is most often used to refer to e-mail, while other semistructured data is erroneously relegated to unstructured status. What probably separated these classes of documents is the mistaken impression of vendors associating unstructured data with Microsoft Exchange, a composite application that can contain multiple data types. However, to achieve optimum data classification success, organizations must focus on the nature of the data. There is nothing intrinsic in an e-mail that gives it more "structure" than a word processing document.

Since the word *unstructured* tends to be used gratuitously (and often inaccurately), determination has to be made between unstructured and semistructured data. That distinction is important. True unstructured data cannot be used natively by content-aware applications. Unstructured data is typically stored in BLOBs (Binary Large Objects), which are changed and, of course, administered less often. This close link between administration and classification highlights the critical importance of accurate data classification.

Note that no one product has to or even can encompass all types of data. The only proper measurement is whether universal data classification is an appropriate goal for the enterprise; if so, then all types of data within the organization have to be covered. This is a classic *caveat emptor* example for IT customers, who must look and consider carefully the types of data supported by the software tools under consideration.

13.8   Key Takeaways

- Data protection is not only about technologies that do data protection directly, but also about those that aid, i.e., enable, support, or facilitate data protection. These technologies may be as essential and as important as the technologies that do data protection directly.

- Data deduplication promises to save a lot of space, but other data reduction technologies, notably compression and single file instancing, can also play important roles.
- Surprisingly, many data protection technologies, such as backup/restore software, are used in a managerially blind manner. This means that administrators do not have the monitoring, reporting, and analysis capabilities to determine if a data protection technology really worked as advertised. The important role of data protection management is to eliminate those limitations.
- Change management and disaster recovery testing are important to ensure that data protection, especially for disaster recovery, is really in place and will work as expected.
- Different data requires different levels of data protection (such as availability). Data classification separates data by policy into different pools that meet different business and regulatory requirements. Data classification can be looked at through two lenses—a management lens, which filters data by the type of functions the data is involved with, and a data lens, which examines data type as a differentiator.

Chapter 14

Disk and Tape— Complementing and Competing with One Another

14.1 What to Look for in This Chapter

- Why disk-based backup is attracting so much attention
- What a virtual tape library adds to disk-based backup
- What value idle disks bring to the table
- What data protection appliances are all about
- What the ongoing role is that data automation is likely to play

From a risk management perspective, the heart of data protection involves disk and tape. The data protection role of both has been changing recently, so it is important to understand how disk and tape complement and compete with each other. The "flashpoint" for how disk and tape complement and compete with each other is in how they interact with traditional backup/restore software. Disk and tape can interact with the traditional backup/restore process in a number of ways.

- *Disk-based backup* substitutes disk for tape as the target for backup or data restoration. Although the possible consolidation of tape automation systems may means that disk and tape compete with each other, the fact that backups on disk may be copied to tape also means that disk and tape complement each other.
- *Virtual tape,* which is often confused with a virtual tape library, makes more efficient use of tape with the help of a front-end disk cache. Disk is a necessary addition to the solution, so tape and disk are strictly complementary.

- A *virtual tape library* is a particular disk-based backup strategy, so disk and tape have the same relationship as in the overall disk-based backup strategy.
- *Massive Array of Idle Disks (MAID) and removable disk drives and media* are strictly competitive with tape, as they represent direct replacements.
- *Data protection appliances* are dedicated hardware/software combinations whose sole purpose is data protection. The appliance may be a disk array (which means possible competition with tape) or an integrated disk array and tape automation solution (in which disk and tape complement each other).
- *Tape automation* is the traditional starting point for discussing backup/restore applications. If there are any substitution effects between disk and tape, disk tends to replace tape, so what the role of tape will be after all the assaults from disk is the key question.

14.2   Disk-Based Backup

Using disk-based backup in conjunction with traditional backup software, backup jobs copy data to a disk array rather than to a tape drive. A set of disk drives has to be reserved for this process. The cost of the disk system as well as any software that is necessary to process the data is an incremental cost to an IT organization, since the existing tape automation infrastructure is typically not replaced. Moreover, some change in operational procedures as well as retraining of staff may be necessary. The question, then, may be why so many IT organizations are so interested in disk-based backup.

The answer lies in two words: reliability and speed. *Reliability* refers to improving the reliability of the data restoration process, and *speed* refers to shortening the length of time that a backup or data restoration job takes.

14.3   Speeding up the Backup/Restore Process—Your Mileage May Vary

A key justification for inserting disk as an additional layer in the backup/restore process is to reduce the time to create a backup copy and the time to restore a given set of data. Although there are ways to do backups at any time (such as from a point-in-time copy of the data), many backup jobs are still run after a production application has been shut down at night. The problem is that the ever-increasing amount of data with which many enterprises have to deal takes longer to back up, but the number of hours in a night have not changed. This is the "running out of night" (a.k.a. "shrinking backup window") problem. On the restore side, improving the time to restore data in order to meet quality-of-service objectives may be equally important.

So, how much faster is using disk instead of tape? A publicly available major-storage-vendor claims to cut backup time by 30% to 60% using a single process, and to cut restore time by 90% using a virtual tape library (VTL), one of the two approaches for disk-based backup. (A VTL is generally regarded as having better performance characteristics than straight disk-based backup.) Another reputable VTL vendor claims a doubling of both backup (which is a write-only process) and data restoration (which is a read-only process). The results held true for both large and small files.

These results are useful for IT organizations trying to relieve the pressure of a shrinking backup window for, say, 1 to 3 years. On the restoration side, disk can help with partial restores, in which only selected files (down to individual files) have to be restored. And since partial restores are much more common than full restores, this can be very helpful indeed.

However, while disk-based backup and restore lead to higher availability, the result is still low availability, not high availability. Hours may be cut in half, but hours are not minutes or seconds. Keep in mind that tape emulation means that the disk cannot be used natively to run an application. The data has to be copied from one set of disks to another set of disks. That process is a restore, not a restart. IT organizations have to set their expectations for disk-based backup and restore accordingly.

14.4   Improving Restore Reliability

Another justification for disk-based backup that many IT organizations offer is improving the reliability of restore. Many IT organizations are concerned that the potential failure rate on data restorations with their current tape automation infrastructure is higher than they find acceptable. Physically, a RAID (Redundant Array of Independent Disks)-protected disk array can survive the failure of a single disk without loss of data, so the array has a much greater mean time between failures (MTBF) than a single disk. Generally, tape does not have this advantage (a mirroring technique for tape does not seem to have attracted a great following), as each piece of tape media has to stand on its own MTBF. (Although the aggregated set of tapes resulting from using multiple generations of tape delivers greater overall reliability than an individual tape, each deeper dive into the past to restore from tape takes additional time.)

Keep in mind that the data must be available on disk (not staged off to tape) for the restoration process. Disk space should be able to accommodate, say, a weekly full backup as well as all the daily incremental backups for a week. This should suffice for most circumstances.

Note that, with data deduplication, businesses have the ability to keep data for much longer periods of time. A side benefit of data deduplication is that data can be made available from farther in the past with very little need for additional storage to house the additional data. That is because data deduplication leaves only one copy of the data, whereas tape leaves multiple copies of at least most of the data. Remember, though, that with data deduplication, only one physical copy of the data is stored and therefore there is only one layer of data protection. In contrast, all the old magnetic tapes offered additional copies of the data if necessary and therefore additional layers of protection.

Moreover, recall that if a backup copy was not created in the first place, no data restoration process can take place. Note, however, that not creating a backup data set may be a process problem and not a physical problem. This process problem can occur for a number of reasons, including scheduling errors, failure of backup jobs to run to completion (e.g., because of network congestion), or failure to notice that not all the critical data is being backed up. Disk-based restorations today cannot rectify policy and process errors.

14.5   Keep in Mind

Note that the disk-based backup and restore process is for operational continuity, not disaster continuity. For operational continuity, the disk-based process adds a layer of physical *and* logical data protection.

Often data still has to be moved from tape to disk. There are two primary methods for doing this. The first is to send the data from disk through the server that ran the backup job in the first place (the server may be called the media server or the backup server) and then to tape. The reason for doing this is that the media server can keep track of where the data is, so that the media server (which is also responsible for the restoration process) can restore data from either disk or tape.

The second approach is to allow the VTL to write directly to tape as a secondary media manager, without going through the original media server. If this is done, there is a risk that the original media server may not be able to restore from tape. (Restoring to the backup disk first and then to the target array for the restoration would add an unnecessary and time-consuming step.) Vendors get around this potential problem by using the common technique of electronically writing barcodes on pieces of tape media that can be read by the original media server.

14.6   Virtual Tape

The terms *virtual tape* and *virtual tape library* are frequently bandied about as if they were the same, and that can cause confusion, because they are separate and distinct terms. *Virtualization* makes a disk appear as something that it is not naturally. Virtual tape refers to the virtualization of a piece of media rather than virtualization of the tape drives that go into a tape library.

Virtual tape has a longer history than virtual tape libraries, and the use of virtual tape is a common practice on mainframe systems. On the mainframe, the process of writing data sets to tape often left the tapes with a lot of empty space. With virtual tape, multiple data sets are concatenated on disk and then written to tape. Open systems typically have not had the same issue with empty space, but some efficiencies can still be achieved with open systems tape, so virtual tape is now available for open systems as well.

Virtual tape is primarily an asset utilization and ease-of-management benefit play. Virtual tape achieves indirect benefits for data protection by minimizing the number of tapes that have to be restored, which leads to fewer chances for restoration problems.

14.7   Virtual Tape Library

Today's backup/restore software is designed to minimize the impact on the existing policies, processes, procedures, and practices of an IT organization. Standard backup/restore software packages can target disk as well as tape. A virtual tape library is software that runs on a disk array to emulate a tape library.

A VTL adds the cost of the virtual tape library software to the cost of the standard backup/restore software. However, simply retargeting standard backup/restore software from tape to disk requires that each backup job be manually retargeted to disk. That is not true of a virtual tape library. If the number of backup jobs that have to be changed is manageable, straight disk-based backup may be a feasible alternative. A second concern is that there might be a file system size limitation, which would apply to straight disk-based backup but not to a VTL. The two primary issues are integration and scaling.

A more complex backup environment and/or large-capacity backup requirements (say, 6 TB or greater, as a rough measure) tend to favor a VTL. Otherwise, straight disk-based backup may be a reasonable choice.

14.8   MAID

If nothing else, the acronym MAID catches the eye. In a MAID, the disk drives are powered down, individually or in groups, when they are not needed. The premise of MAID is very simple: Why spin disks continually if access to the data on those disks is very infrequent? By not spinning disks, savings are accrued on environmental costs (air conditioning and electricity), even though the disk drives may be packed more densely. In addition, reducing the power-on time for the disks means that lower-cost disks targeted for lower-duty-cycle applications can be used, such as *Serial Advanced Technology Attachment* (SATA) disks. These lower-cost disks have a shorter MTBF than the higher-cost disks used in high-performance, always-on arrays. There is also a "green" benefit, because idle disks do not require the power and cooling that always-spinning disks require.

MAID is a middle ground between "online," always spinning disks and tape. "Online" disks not only have random access, which means that they can access specific information quickly when needed, but are always spinning, whereas tapes are idle until accessed. MAID is a middle ground where the benefits of random access can be used when an I/O request is actually made, but the benefits of idleness are also taken into account when the information is not needed.

MAID occupies the ground in active archives where the archive is still "active" in the sense that the data has to be "online," but the need for that access is infrequent. MAID therefore acts as the step in information's lifecycle before deep archiving. That long-term archiving lifecycle stage may contain pools of infrequently accessed production data, such as old customer histories, old CAD/CAM files, and old camera surveillance data, but may also contain compliance data, such as medical test data. This is the type of data that is written once and only occasionally ever read. When it is needed, however, the expectation is that it will be easy to find and can be accessed relatively quickly, at least when compared to the same data archived on tape.

From a data protection perspective, MAID uses idleness to extend the operational reliability of an array. MAID is therefore suitable for use as a bulk compliance information repository, extending its usefulness to the logical operational side, if the proper software is used to ensure that data cannot be modified improperly.

In the long-term archive space, MAID competes with tape on a bulk cost space basis and with "active" disk on a cost basis.

The term *spin down* is sometimes used to convey the functionality that MAID provides without using the term MAID directly. The implication, however, is that individual drives can be spun down rather than having to trying to manage a large array. This is useful for targeted applications which do not require the capacity that the term MAID, in the sense of a massive disk array, conveys.

14.9   Removable Disk Drives and Disk Media

A few vendors are now reintroducing removable disks. One approach is to bundle a RAID group of Winchester disk drives and associated disk media into a removable magazine that is comparable in form factor to a similar magazine of tape cartridges. The second is to actually decouple the disk media from the disk drive. Both approaches enable the transportability of disk-stored information for offsite storage. Since the first approach embeds the drive along with the media, the key transportability issue is shock resistance; no one wants to lose data because the magazine was dropped! In the second case, each piece of media has to be put in a protective case to prevent environmental damage.

The direct removable disk media approach may be useful for small businesses (or units of large businesses, such as branch offices), for which having even a single tape drive introduces a level of expense and complexity that may be difficult to manage. Moreover, these organizations have to manage their own data protection. The challenge is to provide media management without having the formal tools—for example, managing movement of data to and from an offsite location while at the same time ensuring that no disk is lost, misplaced, damaged, or has the wrong version of information.

The bundled group of removable disk drives approach also requires media management, but, since this approach is more likely to be used in larger IT environments, the media management approach that is already used with tape may be employed.

The magazine may represent a backup copy in tape format or a replica in disk format. If the magazine represents a backup, this is an example of a disk-based backup, and using the magazine for restoration constitutes a disk-based restoration. If the data is in disk format, the data will be for a single point in time. Although restoration may be fast (especially important at a disaster recovery site), administrators must find and apply all the changes since the disk copy was made.

Removable disk drive and disk drive media approaches are likely to be useful in selected applications, but they are unlikely to unseat established mainstream tape solution infrastructures in the near future.

14.10   Data Protection Appliances

A data protection appliance is a dedicated, self-contained bundle of software and hardware that serves a specific data protection function, such as acting as a VTL. A standalone VTL appliance may consist of a disk array whose disks serve only to support the VTL and a VTL software package. An integrated VTL appliance may couple a tape library to the disk array, either logically through software or physically. Three interrelated questions arise when discussing data protection appliances:

1.   Where should the "intelligence" for a data protection function reside?

2.   When should an appliance solution be used rather than a general-purpose solution?

3.   If an appliance is used, should it be standalone or integrated?

The first question is where software intelligence for data protection functions should reside: on an application or database server, in the storage network or on its edge, or on the array—either a general-purpose array or a dedicated appliance array.

The answer should not depend on philosophical arguments, but rather on business needs. If an enterprise expects to have to scale a data protection function beyond the capabilities of what an individual array might be expected to provide, or wants the ability to shift between heterogeneous storage platforms over time, intelligence in the network may make sense when it is generally available. Otherwise, having the data protection capability at the array level may make sense, as that is a familiar level for managing intelligence for data management-related functions.

The second question, whether to use special-purpose appliance servers or general-purpose computing servers, goes well beyond their applicability for data protection functions. The answer may well be that both will continue to flourish. An appliance is a "black box" in which the inputs and outputs are well defined but, if there is a problem, only vendor technical experts can solve the problem. Maintenance support is therefore critical. General-purpose solutions may also have problems, and although the problems may not be related to the data protection function, they still may affect it. If more than one vendor is involved in a general-purpose solution, this can lead to "finger pointing" and a possible delay in finding a solution. In contrast, with an appliance solution, the appliance vendor is clearly responsible for addressing a maintenance problem.

The third question, regarding standalone versus integrated appliances, really comes down to whether the value of improved ease of use through integration outweighs the risk of proprietary lock-in for all parts of an integrated solution.

In summary, IT organizations have to decide how they want their data protection functional intelligence to act: either alone as software that is independent of a particular physical implementation or embedded in a specific physical implementation. Solving an immediate problem by improving manageability compared to what was done before has to be weighed against whether the new solution will scale to meet future demands.

14.11 Tape Automation

Frequently, IT organizations are not in love with large, complex electromechanical tape automation systems, both for perceived reliability reasons and because of these systems' drain on administrative resources. Moreover, having a very large number of pieces of tape media increases the risk of not being able to easily restore data when it is most needed. When you add in the inherent lower availability of tape versus disk, and top it off with declining disk prices and the rise of a large number of disk-based backup alternatives, you may leap to the conclusion that tape's days are numbered.

However, that is very unlikely to happen. To paraphrase Mark Twain, reports of tape's death are greatly exaggerated. To see why, look carefully at Table 11.1, "Where Active Data Protection Technologies Fit in the Data Protection Framework." Tape is solidly entrenched in each of the eight boxes in the table (because vaulting typically refers to tape). Although disks can have a role in each of the eight boxes, disks are not as established as tape in all eight boxes, because in many cases the use of disk depends on emerging software technologies. Moreover, a single piece of tape media can fit into each of the eight boxes if necessary. That is not true with nonremovable disks. The removability and transportability of tape creates flexibility that may prove vital. For example, tape can be used to re-create data at a third site if the planned disaster recovery site also fails.

Recall the discussion of degrees of protection. Three degrees of protection are probably the minimum safe number of layers of protection. For a time- and revenue-sensitive application, three layers of disk may very well be necessary, but even then, tape is probably sensible. The reason is that if all the disks fail there may be a significant revenue loss (and consequent loss of market valuation), but if the enterprise can never recover its data, it may be out of business—period.

Three sets of disk arrays may seem extremely unlikely to fail physically. However, deliberate external or internal threats or even inadvertent human error (such as pulling out the wrong disk in an array, compounded by cascading procedural errors) may cause unexpected problems. Tape automation delivers "biological diversity" for extra degrees of protection.

Tape should continue to provide a relative cost advantage over disks. This is not true in all situations, of course, because it may depend on how many pieces of tape media are used for each tape drive in a tape automation system. However, the decline in absolute cost of storage (as a result of the continuing price/performance improvement of more than 30% a year for disk drives) means that using disks for disk-based backup has become more affordable. That absolute drop in cost also applies to tape media, however, so strict head-to-head comparisons between tape and disk still tend to favor tape.

A tape automation system consists of pieces of tape media, tape drives, and a robotic automation system. Significant advances have been made in all three areas over the last several years in reliability, manageability, and capacity; and the roadmaps of leading vendors indicate that these trends will continue.

The introduction of new technologies does not always lead to displacement of existing technologies, but rather may lead to a change in the portfolio of functions that they perform. Tape has a long history of adjusting to disk—tape's primary role in batch processing (with extensive sorting of tapes to produce reports) has been replaced by its role in data protection.

Tape will continue to serve as the last line of data protection defense for time-sensitive critical systems and will be employed closer to the front line for not-so-time-sensitive applications. On the active changeable side, these applications will include both the traditional backup/restore processes (although perhaps on the back end of disk-based backup) and continuous data processing applications (where tape will contain copies of the data). On the active archiving side, copies will need to be made, but replicas of ingested fixed content may not be performed with traditional backup/restore processes.

Tape may very well play a role in active archives for storing primary copies of very large amounts of compliance data, such as medical records, rights management data, such as videos and music, and bulk data, such as seismic data. The key determinant of disk versus tape should be the frequency of access and the required response time once the data needs to be retrieved.

IT organizations should focus on how disk and tape can best complement each other, because tape will be here for the foreseeable future.

14.12   Key Takeaways

- Disk-based backup is attracting a lot of attention for its promise of improving the reliability and speed of the backup process. Remember, though, that on the restore side, the data has to be available on disk.
- Virtual tape library software, as a disk-based backup/restore technology, can manage more complex and larger-capacity backup/restore environments than can "plain vanilla" disk-based backup/restore approaches.
- Infrequently accessed data that still has to be available online can be put on a Massive Array of Idle Disks (MAID). That improves the operational life of those disks and is more environmentally friendly.
- A data protection appliance is bundle of software and hardware that serves a specific data protection need. That permits a business to enjoy "one-stop shopping" for that particular data protection function, such as having a virtual tape library that combines both software and disk, but may represent more of a lock-in than some businesses are willing to commit to.
- Despite continued pronouncements of its death, tape is still viable for many businesses and is likely to be so for the foreseeable feature because of cost reasons as well as removability and transportability reasons.

Chapter 15

Technologies for High Availability and Low (or No) Data Loss

15.1 What to Look for in This Chapter

- What copy strategies do for high availability and low data loss
- How point-in-time copy, continuous data protection, and scheduled-image data protection work
- What replication strategies do for high availability and low data loss
- How the various mirroring technologies—synchronous remote mirroring, asynchronous remote mirroring, and semisynchronous remote mirroring—work
- How dated replication technologies differ from mirrored replication technologies

Recall that one of the basic objectives of data protection is data availability. Ensuring data availability is the goal of some data protection technologies. The purpose of these data protection technologies is to deliver low or no data loss, that is, a recovery point objective (RPO) of little or no data loss; and high availability in terms of only seconds or minutes per year of unplanned downtime, that is, a recovery time objective (RTO) where little or no downtime occurs. These technologies work by first making a copy or replica of the original data. A copy or replica is an imitation or reproduction of an original.

This chapter divides low-data-loss/high-availability strategies into copy strategies and replication strategies. In data management theory, the distinction between copying and replication is that *copying* simply copies the original data, whereas *replication* carries out an identical transaction on two copies of the data in sequence.

Three key principles to keep in mind throughout this chapter are the following:

- A full physical copy (or replica) of the data needs to be made if physical data protection is to be provided.
- The copy (or replica) needs to be dated (i.e., time-stamped) if logical data protection is to be provided.
- The copy (or replica) needs to be natively usable. That means that an application has no difficulty in using the copy (or replica) directly when the original is unavailable.

The key to low-RPO/low-RTO (i.e., low-data-loss/low-downtime) solutions is the ability to restart rather than restore. *Restart* means the ability of an applications to switch quickly to a data protection copy that is natively usable (although with a possible degradation in performance if the data protection copy is not on media that can equal the performance characteristics of the original). *Restore* means that no copy is natively usable, and so a copy must be migrated from another set of media. (For example, data written in tape format, which is sequential in nature, cannot be read by an application that expects the data to be in a random access format without the data being migrated to a disk in a random access format that the application can use. Note that this applies whether the data in tape format is written on tape *or* disk.) Restart (or switching the application to use the new copy) is typically much faster than migration.

15.2 Copy Strategies

For purposes of classification, a copy is a reproduction of data either on an array that is logically (if not physically) local or on the same array as the original. (For low-RTO/low-RPO purposes, disk—not tape—must be used.) Point-in-time copy capability was the first disk copy capability. Continuous data protection is a newer copy capability that is attracting a lot of attention. However, a new category of copy capability that does not adhere strictly to the definition but still provides low-RPO/low-RTO solutions is emerging. Although there is no standard term for this category yet, we can think of it as scheduled-image data protection, to distinguish it from continuous data protection.

15.2.1   Point-in-Time Copy

The ability to create a point-in-time copy of a pool of data has had—and will continue to have, through ever more ingenious uses—a major impact on data protection. A point-in-time (PIT) copy is a "copy" of a pool of data at a chosen instant in time. The advantage is that the copy is frozen in time. Although there is no guarantee that the copy itself does not suffer from data corruption, there is a guarantee that changes after the time of the copy will not change the original pool of data; thus a point-in-time copy provides logical data protection.

Since a PIT copy is considered to be a fully usable collection of data, some vendors offer the capability of writing to a PIT copy. Although a PIT copy can be a starting point for adding in changes, the moment that changes are made, it ceases to be a PIT copy. The ability to use the PIT copy as a foundation for change is valuable, but the protection offered for logical data protection requires that a PIT copy be read-only.

The two basic "flavors" of PIT copies are PIT clones and snapshots. A PIT clone is an exact *physical* copy of a pool of storage. A PIT clone delivers both physical (as of the time of the cloning) and logical (from cloning time onwards) data protection. The price that is paid (other than the cost of the software) is a doubling of the amount of disk storage required by a storage pool. The cost of such a doubling (as well as manageability) severely limits the number of clones to only one or a few. The advantage is that use of the clone for such purposes as serving as the basis for backup to tape or for production testing does not affect the performance of the production disk array.

A snapshot is a software image of data as of a predefined instant. A snapshot is taken on the original disks where the data is stored, and at the time the snapshot is taken, the original production data and the snapshot are identical. This means that no additional physical space is required at that instant. The original production data and the snapshot data diverge as writes change the original production data. The approach taken is typically a copy-on-write technique that creates temporary blocks and updated blocks of data. When changes are made, additional physical disk space has to be available and allocated. The process requires the management of index tables.

The key differences between a clone and a snapshot are that:

- A clone is an offshoot of mirroring technology, whereas a snapshot uses an indexing strategy.

- A clone requires space for a full physical copy of the original data, whereas a snapshot requires only enough additional space to accommodate all the changes since the snapshot was taken.
- A clone is a real *hardware* duplicate or replica; a snapshot is only a *virtual* duplicate or replica.

PIT copies can serve many roles, including as a starting point for making a backup copy or for application production testing, but a key role is in providing high-availability logical data protection.

15.2.2   Continuous Data Protection

With continuous data protection (CDP), an enterprise can create a data protection copy (typically on a disk-array-based data protection appliance) that can recover to *any* point in time. Typically, changes are recorded continually by the CDP appliance, which uses a noninvasive journaling technique that does not require even the momentary halting of an application's I/O processing (which has to occur when creating a snapshot point-in-time copy). The journal can be rewound to any point in time as the basis for creating an any-point-in-time (APIT) copy of the data, without having to know at what point in time a copy should have been taken.

When offered on a data protection appliance, CDP offers today's only up-to-the-moment logical data protection and physical data protection with high availability. CDP is not a new backup approach; CDP is an alternative (or, more likely, a complement) to the traditional backup software approach. CDP provides fine granularity over the data restoration process in that logical unit volumes (LUNs) or individual files can be restored.

CDP can be used natively as a temporary alternative to the original array (although with performance degradation, if one is using capacity disks instead of performance disks [for cost savings] in the array that holds the CDP copy of the data). CDP can also serve as the basis for business intelligence analyses or production application testing without disturbing the performance of the production disk array.

CDP is an operational continuity approach when implemented in a data protection appliance locally (which integrates both the CDP software and the necessary storage hardware in a bundle). However, CDP can be made available over a distance, as a disaster continuity approach. In this case, it would fall into the dated replication class, where the changes that are made all have a time stamp associated with them (i.e., the system knows the time each change was made).

One issue that has been raised is how well a CDP system can handle consistency groups. An application may use data that is spread across multiple physical disks. The entire data makes up a consistency group—a set of data that has to be synchronized for restoration purposes. This may not be an issue (because frequently data is not spread across multiple disks), but it is a question that IT managers should raise when reviewing CDP products.

The concept of CDP is still sinking into the collective consciousnesses of IT organizations, but it is likely to be one of the technologies that make a major difference in how enterprises design their data protection infrastructures in the future.

15.2.3   Scheduled-Image Data Protection

That might seem to be the end of the low-RTO/low-RPO story. However, there is a new class of products that does not adhere strictly to the definition of CDP (i.e., it cannot guarantee rewinding the data to any point in time) yet provides low-RPO/low-RTO solutions for logical data protection.

Since some of these products use tight-interval snapshots (i.e., multiple snapshots taken within a short period of time), one school of thought has been to name the class as a form of snapshots. There are two problems with this. The first is that using frequent snapshots is only one of the technologies that can provide this type of solution. The second is that naming the category as a subclass of snapshots can lead to further confusion in mixing up standard uses of snapshots with specific low-RPO/low-RTO uses. Also, a CDP solution may use snapshots as long as they can be created after the fact.

The other school of thought is to ignore the distinction and lump them into CDP anyway. The problem with this is that if an organization really needs to capture every last I/O (and some do and some do not), trying to determine which are *pure* and which are *near*-CDP solutions may be very difficult.

This new class of products can be called scheduled-image data protection (SDP) rather than near-CDP, as it is sometimes called. "Scheduled" means that an image—such as a snapshot—is taken at a predetermined time. The frequency with which the images are taken varies by product. As the interval between snapshots decreases, the risk of data loss becomes less.

As with CDP, SDP products may be on an appliance, which, as a separate hardware copy, then provides both physical and logical data protection. However, SDP products may also run on the array where the production data is located (especially if SDP is carried out via a series of multiple snapshots). That does not afford extra physical protection, but the combination of RAID (especially multiple-parity RAID) and SDP can provide both the necessary physical and logical redundancy for a low-RTO/low-RPO solution without having to go "outside the box." Note that a CDP solution can be constructed to run within the production-data system; but typically CDP solutions have been designed to run on an appliance.

15.3   Replication Strategies

Replication technology is one of the strong suits in an IT data protection strategy, because of its promise of "high" availability for both operational and disaster continuity.

Although technically it does not have to be, in practical terms, a replica is a remote copy. For data protection purposes, a replica has to be a separate physical copy. A replica also has to be natively usable. A replica can either be a dated replica, which means that it has a stamped time of creation, or an undated replica.

A backup/restore copy is not a replica, since the copy is not natively usable without undergoing a transformation using the restore functionality of the backup/restore software. A PIT clone to a remote system is a replica, since the clone is a separate physical copy of the data. A snapshot on a production copy is not a replica, since there is no additional physical copy on a remote system. However, snapshots that are copied to a remote target either individually or in the context of continuous data protection result in a replica.

One of the big discussion topics in replication is where the software intelligence to manage the replication process should be located. The three choices are host-based, storage network-based, and disk array-based. The different choices can be examined on the basis of cost, scalability, manageability, performance, and use of IT resources. The decision in favor of a particular product depends on the application requirements and budget of the IT buyer, but the basic principles of replication apply to all three choices.

One key distinction in replication is between mirroring, which is a form of undated replication, and dated replication. Mirroring is valuable for physical data protection in disaster recovery. Dated replication is useful for data protection in all aspects of disaster continuity as well as in active archiving for operational continuity. If CDP is also considered a replication technology (and it is certainly possible to design a CDP solution that operates remotely from the original production data), then dated replication is the only type of data protection technology that covers the entire data protection category matrix.

15.3.1 Mirroring

The job of mirroring is to create an exact copy (also called a replica or duplicate) of data on a source disk to a target disk. Mirroring is a continuous process. That means that the mirroring process does not take time off—whenever the source data is online, the mirrored copy should be as well. This also means that mirroring provides physical data protection but not logical data protection, since data corruption may be copied to the target disk.

Mirroring is a process to provide protection for active changeable data, not active archive data. In fact, an active changeable data store will typically have some (a little or a lot of) fixed content data in it. From a mirroring perspective, the fixed data is copied only once (unlike full backups of data, in which fixed data is copied each time the backup is made), so there is no real overhead. Thus, after the initial copy has been made, there are no network demands from the fixed data. The only burden of mirroring is that the remote array is weighed down with the cost burden of larger and therefore perhaps more expensive disks than would otherwise be the case, because of fixed content that is never accessed.

However, mirroring is not appropriate for an active archive. Granted, inflows to the archive are changes, but other replication techniques are sufficient for one-time changes, without introducing the costs and management requirements of mirroring.

One exception to these rules occurs when the mirrored copy is split off, which means that updates from the source no longer take place. At that point, the mirrored copy is now a point-in-time clone. The clone offers both logical and physical data protection and can be used for making a backup. When the clone is put back into service as a mirror, a resynchronization process has to take place.

Although mirroring can be done locally, local mirroring is typically synchronous and goes under the name of RAID 1 (and variants). When mirroring is typically mentioned from a replication perspective, the discussion is really about remote mirroring. The three "flavors" of mirroring are *synchronous remote mirroring, asynchronous remote mirroring, and semisynchronous mirroring.*

Synchronous Remote Mirroring

A *synchronous remote mirror* maintains an exact up-to-date copy of the data located on part or all of a local (also called primary or source) disk array with that of a remote (also called secondary or target) disk array. Every write I/O on the local array is immediately sent to the remote array. No further I/O write actions are performed on the primary array by an application until the remote array acknowledges that it has also written the I/O to one of its disks. Thus the source and target are always identical, which is why this approach is called synchronous.

The big advantage of synchronous remote mirroring is that its RPO and RTO are (or can be made to be) zero. An IT organization does not have to worry about loss of data (from a physical perspective only), so the data preservation objective is met; and failover can avoid loss of availability, so data-availability service-level requirements are met. This seems like the best of all possible worlds, so it is no wonder that synchronous remote mirroring has done so well.

However, synchronous remote mirroring does not supply all the answers. It provides physical data protection, but no logical data protection. That is fine for its basic purpose of providing physical data protection in case of a disaster, or for a secondary purpose of helping recover from hardware failures at the primary site. IT simply has to not ask synchronous remote mirroring to do a task (logical data protection) that it was not designed to do.

A second issue has been cost—for software, for storage network hardware to connect both the local and remote arrays to a WAN, for a separate remote array and surrounding IT infrastructure, and for having a private dedicated network line with sufficient bandwidth. Depending on the nature of sunk fixed costs (such as for storage networking hardware) and variable costs (such as the size of an array), an IT organization may find that it cannot economically justify synchronously mirroring applications for other than time- and revenue-sensitive, mission-critical applications. This means that synchronous mirroring does not protect non-mission-critical applications (which might be the bulk of the application portfolio in terms of storage requirements).

A third issue is the latency inherent in remote communications resulting from the fact that the speed of light is finite. (Other latencies, besides the speed of light, are also involved in the process, but the other latencies are fixed, whereas the latency due to light is variable based on distance.) Latency in acknowledgment of writes at the target site to the source site introduces delays in the ability of an application to continue to do new transactions. This problem is not noticeable at "short" distances, but it becomes a problem at "long" distances. Although the longest distance is entirely arbitrary (because the effect depends not only on the latency, but also on whether that latency actually noticeably degrades the performance of a particular application), a common rule of thumb is a *maximum* distance of 100 km (about 60 miles).

This distance seems reasonable for disaster recovery purposes until the organization realizes that these distances may still put both production and disaster recovery sites at risk in the same disaster (a hurricane, for example). Although arguably somewhat arbitrary, the *minimum* distance between disaster recovery sites is likely to be 500 km (roughly 300 miles). And that argues for the need to have another replication technology that either complements (for those enterprises that can afford it) or supplants (for those that must have the longer distance and cannot afford both) synchronous remote mirroring.

Asynchronous Remote Mirroring

The purpose of *asynchronous remote mirroring* is to maintain a copy of data on a source data array at a distant target disk array. However, in asynchronous remote mirroring, an application does not wait for an acknowledgment of an I/O write request from a remote target array before moving on to its next task. This means that the data at the source and target arrays are not necessarily identical, since there is no guarantee that the remote site has actually received and written the I/O request successfully.

Asynchronous remote mirroring can take advantage of lower-speed (and, if necessary, less reliable) networks, in contrast to synchronous remote mirroring, which requires a high-speed, highly reliable network. In synchronous remote mirroring, an application is tightly coupled with the remote site from a performance perspective, so a high-speed network is necessary even if the volume of information sent is relatively low. In asynchronous remote mirroring, an application's processing performance is independent of the target site, so it does not depend as heavily on the speed of the network.

An asynchronous remote mirror runs the risk of having a nonzero RPO. Depending on the particular implementation, the RPO may be 15 seconds, 30 seconds, or minutes. An IT organization may thus face another unpalatable choice: Business conditions (such as financial processing) may require a zero RPO, but the need to have a disaster recovery site at a distance greater than necessary for guaranteed synchronicity physically forces a nonzero RPO.

A possible solution is to accept an emergency nonzero RPO in case of a disaster. Disasters do not occur very frequently, and for such a situation a nonzero RPO might be tolerable even if not desirable.

Another possible solution is a "workaround"—for example, having three sites, one for production, one for asynchronous mirroring, and one for synchronous mirroring. The assumption is that the synchronously mirrored site will have time to transmit the necessary changes to the asynchronously mirrored site before it too goes down. (In the case of major disaster that affects both synchronously linked sites simultaneously, the loss of RPO data will probably be of small relative concern.) This solution is expensive and should probably be used only for time- and revenue-sensitive, mission-critical systems.

However, less expensive workarounds that enable recovery from the asynchronously mirrored target disk array without loss of data are available—for example, journaling all unconfirmed transactions to a single disk somewhere within synchronous-mirroring range, even if the technique used to synchronize is not mirroring. Buyers should pay attention to how particular data protection suppliers deal with this issue.

Semisynchronous Remote Mirroring

Another technique for helping to resolve the trade-off between small data loss and the safety of having a remote site outside the same potential disaster zone is semisynchronous remote mirroring. Using a log file for active remote write commands, two or more transactions (instead of just one, as in synchronous remote mirroring) can proceed before waiting for acknowledgment of receipt of the I/O from the remote site. This reduces write latency. Implementation can also provide a consistent copy at the remote site in case of a disaster, since write-order fidelity is guaranteed. What is not guaranteed is that every last transaction will get through, but, when balancing cost of solution versus risk of lost data, semisynchronous remote mirroring may be an option that needs to be examined.

15.3.2   Dated Replication—Pay Close Attention

Dated replication—a time-stamped copy of data—is a new term, but the phrase is necessary to separate dated from nondated replication and mirroring. Mirroring in general—and synchronous remote mirroring in particular—has been the glamorous replication technique, but it provides physical data protection only. Dated replication is important in that it provides both physical and logical data protection.

That does not mean that dated replication is better than nondated replication, because synchronous remote mirroring—a form of nondated replication—may provide better RPO and RTO for physical disaster recovery. However, dated replication may provide a competitive alternative to asynchronous remote mirroring for disaster recovery of active changeable data, as well as serving as a technology to be used in conjunction with the inflows and outflows that are associated with active archives.

Again, a dated data replica is a natively usable remote copy of data, which means that the application that created the data should be able to read the copy without difficulty. A backup copy is not a dated replica, because typically a backup copy is not natively usable.

A snapshot is not a dated replica, because it is not a physically distinct copy of the data that is separate from the original pool of data. However, a snapshot can be used as the basis for creating a dated replication on another set of storage media.

A PIT clone is a dated replication, but it is also a full copy, and one of the advantages of many dated replication techniques is that the replica can be updated with changes over time. The dated replication is then dynamic and not static, which is useful in an active archiving world.

Dated replication is quietly infiltrating the replication market and will continue to do so. There are multiple approaches and strategies for dated replication. Apart from snapshots, the following are some techniques that can be used.

- *I/O journaling*—all I/Os (including both volume and file-level I/Os) are copied and time-stamped, so that one replica of the full data pool can be restored ("rolled forward") to many different times.
- *Periodic replication*—a process whereby the original data pool is synchronized with the replica data pool on a periodic basis.
- *Copy-on-close*—a copy is made of a file (typically not a database) when an application finishes writing the file.
- *Copy-on-insertion*—the requisite number of copies are made upon ingestion of data into an active archive; this is a "once and done" approach.

Dated replication can be divided into "local" and "remote," where local solutions are on a LAN or SAN (for help with operational continuity), whereas remote solutions might be over a WAN (for help with disaster continuity).

IT organizations can use the term *dated replication* to help them classify and examine a number of data protection techniques that may have other names. IT organizations should pay close attention to dated replication approaches to see where they fit in the data protection framework, and if they match an organization's particular requirements.

15.4   Key Takeaways

- Low-data-loss/high-availability technologies can be divided into copy and replication technologies. A copy technology simply copies the original data, whereas a replication technology carries out an identical transaction on two copies of the data in sequence. Each type deals with "copies" of the data, but the distinction is how each type of technology goes about performing its tasks.
- There are three principal forms of data copy technology. A point-in-time copy takes a picture of a set of data at a designated moment. Continuous data protection, in effect, takes a picture at every point in time. This is in contrast to scheduled-image data protection, which takes many snapshots but may leave intervals in which a small amount of data may be lost. Copy technology is about logical data protection except when another full physical copy of the data is made.
- There are three principal forms of data mirroring replication technology. Synchronous remote mirroring guarantees that both a local and a remote copy of the data are always up to date. If a failover has to be made to a remote site, the failover can occur very quickly (high availability), with no data loss. For latency reasons, this type of mirroring is not likely to work at distances that are necessary for proper disaster recovery protection. That job is left to asynchronous remote mirroring, in which transactions may not always be quite up to date, risking some data loss. Workarounds are possible for businesses that cannot afford any data loss. Semisynchronous mirroring is an infrequently used technique, but it may help limit some of the problems of asynchronous remote mirroring.
- Mirroring techniques can be expensive and they only provide physical data protection. Dated replication technologies, which make time-stamped copies of data, can perform periodic replications that provide both logical and physical data protection. However, applications such as high-speed online transaction processing systems may need mirroring replication rather than dated replication.

Chapter 16

Special Requirements for Compliance, Governance, and Data Security

16.1 What to Look for in This Chapter

- What WORM (write-once, read-many) technology is all about
- Issues to deal with when physically destroying WORM media
- How WORM tape and WORM disk are used
- What is the role of electronic locking
- What techniques can be used to perform encryption
- What a compliance/governance appliance is, and what it does
- How should data shredding be done

Each type of compliance/governance request requires extensive individual attention to policies, processes, procedures, and practices. However, the basic principles of compliance and governance remain constant across all requests.

Enterprises should not look at compliance/governance as just a one-time task, but rather as an ongoing activity. Moreover, other types of information management can benefit from a compliance effort. For example, many of the same principles apply to a digital rights management program for the control of digital assets, such as data preservation and controlling who is allowed to have access to the information. Protecting trade secrets and monitoring intellectual property offered for sale over the Internet are important to the business, and both types of information must comply with internal requirements, even though they are not likely to be subject to regulatory compliance requirements.

16.2   The Use of WORM Technology

Compliance data must be immutable (i.e., guaranteed unalterable at least until the expiration date for retention has been reached). One way to do this is to write the data on a piece of write-once, read-many (WORM) storage media. Some optical media technologies are physically WORM. By contrast, neither magnetic disk nor magnetic tape is inherently physically WORM media; but both can be made so logically through the use of software or firmware (which is software physically captured in hardware).

Some enterprises are concerned that they need physically WORM media to ensure regulatory compliance. This is generally not the case. Regulators try to specify functionality (e.g., immutability) rather than a particular technology that delivers that functionality.

16.2.1   Issues with Physically Destroying WORM Media

A physical device can be destroyed, either according to a set policy or not according to policy. If it is according to policy, destroying a piece of physical media means that all of the data is destroyed, so it is critical that all of the data be expired—i.e., formally certified as no longer expected to be used. If all the data has not expired, policy should not authorize the physical destruction of a piece of storage media.

However, this presents a problem. When data reaches its expiration date, the change in status does not necessarily mean that the data has to be destroyed, but rather that it is eligible to be destroyed. In many cases, no problem exists if the organization chooses to retain the data beyond the end of its "freshness date." This may not be true for all data; policy may require the deletion of some data immediately after the data is eligible to be deleted.

WORM disk may have the option to delete the data through a software process, but WORM tape probably does not have that option. The alternative to destroying the data physically is to have the data encrypted, which, of course, occurs at the one and only time the data is written to a particular part of a piece of tape media. The data can be logically deleted by the simple process of disposing of the encryption keys. However, IT organizations then have the burden of putting into place a "key management program" for managing encryption keys. In that case, the IT organization must ensure that encryption keys are not lost accidentally, but it may need to have procedures in place for disposing of certain keys deliberately.

Encrypting creates another management burden besides key management. The content of encrypted data cannot be examined without decrypting the data first, which requires time and resources. A comprehensive

metadata repository may provide an index that can facilitate the search process without the burden of decrypting some entire data sets, but not in all
cases. For example, a business intelligence query or eDiscovery analysis may
need to search each file or document in its entirety.

Despite the burdens of managing encryption, IT organizations may
have no other choice than to put an encryption key strategy in place for the
management of compliance data. This is particularly true when only some
parts of a WORM tape archive must be stored indefinitely, and other parts
must be deleted.

Physical destruction can also occur outside of policy, whether this
destruction is unintentional (such as a head crash) or willful, malicious, and
illegal. To counter out-of-policy destruction, data protection copies have to
be made. Those copies need to be direct copies, and they must be only
WORM-enabled. Otherwise, a non-WORM-enabled copy could be altered
and then rewritten to a WORM copy. The WORM copy would appear to
present the data correctly, but it would not be correct. As with other areas of
compliance, while software and hardware can help, the responsibility is for
IT management to put in place the proper policies, processes, procedures,
and practices to ensure that the duplication process is done correctly, which
includes making sure that the necessary data auditing capabilities are available and invoked.

16.3   WORM Tape

Typically, WORM tape refers to tape cartridges, not to the tape drives that
read the tapes. Electronic keys or unalterable firmware on the tape cartridge itself turn that piece of media into a WORM tape. Data on a
WORM tape cannot be rewritten or reformatted but can be appended
(until the tape runs out).

Depending on the vendor, a WORM tape cartridge may be a purchasable stock-keeping-unit (SKU) item, which comes only in WORM format,
or may be initialized as a WORM tape cartridge at the time of first use. In
either case, visual identification of a tape cartridge (color of cartridge for a
permanently designed WORM tape cartridge or color of label for a tape cartridge that is initialized as a WORM tape cartridge) can help prevent manual mishandling of tapes after removal from a tape library.

Using WORM tape in conjunction with WORM disk is logical from a
data protection perspective, because the data protection copy on tape also
has to retain the compliance characteristics that were required on disk.
However, remember that moving data from WORM disk to WORM tape is

a one-way, one-shot replication process and cannot double as part of a backup/restore process involving disk or tape reuse. Thus, WORM disk/tape cannot be used for the traditional weekly full backup, because a rotational scheme involving multiple generations of tape implies that the tapes are reusable. (Tapes from an expired generation are put in a pool of "scratch" tapes to be reused.) Although a synthetic full backup approach might be used, data probably would be copied from disk to tape by a periodic replication method.

16.4   WORM Disk

The nonerasable, nonrewritable functionality that enables WORM disk capability comes from software at the operating system (OS) level of a storage system—at the network-attached-storage (NAS) "head," or at the storage controller/server level. When WORM capability is invoked, no one—not even a system administrator with superuser privileges—is allowed to rewrite or modify data. Building in the necessary WORM software functionality requires the storage system vendor to have the ability to change the operating system kernel itself, which means that a proprietary or Linux-based OS would most likely be the chosen OS.

WORM disk is actually a misnomer (but the term can stand), because the actual disk drives themselves have nothing to do with the WORM functionality. Theoretically, "WORM-protected" disk drives could be removed from a system and moved to another system which does not offer WORM protection, thereby invalidating WORM's protections against data tampering, but that type of event should be detectable and is extremely unlikely.

One advantage that WORM disk may have, and that the current generation of WORM tape does not have, is the ability actually to delete expired data (assuming that each piece of data is managed on a file basis, although blocks of data on a logical volume may also have expiration dates). This functionality is important because organizations need to be able to reuse disk space as well as allow the use of encryption if desired.

WORM disk may present a planning problem that does not affect WORM tape. If data that is subject to compliance rules grows much more rapidly than anticipated from a WORM tape perspective, the only requirement is additional WORM-enabled tape media. If the compliant data overflows a disk array, that could present a problem. In a non-WORM environment, an IT organization might migrate data from an older, smaller-capacity disk array to a newer, larger-capacity disk array. The older array would either be repurposed or sold. In a WORM case, the data might be migrated to a new array (with suitable precautions), but then the older array would be rendered unusable and unmarketable, because data cannot be deleted until at least the expiration date.

One solution is to select an array that can start small but can expand if necessary to meet future requirements. Another solution is to select WORM disk functionality, where the disks assigned for the storage of compliant data are *virtual* disks that can be changed (i.e., migrated) to other physical disk drives as the need arises.

16.5   Electronic Locking

The ability to put an electronic "lock" on a piece of data for a prescribed period of time is a key piece of functionality that a WORM disk can provide. A time-based lock might be used on non-compliance-related data in an active archive to deliver an easy method of logical data protection, since no write I/Os can tamper with or destroy the data. The time lock need not be very long and might be automatically renewable if the decision is made to retain the data.

16.6   Guaranteeing the Authenticity of Data

With compliant data, the question of data authenticity may come up. The uniqueness of a particular document may be guaranteed by a combination of software and hardware called *content addressable storage* (CAS). Uniqueness does not guarantee authenticity, but, if the creation date and the date put in a protected storage state are incorporated as part of a document, then the genuineness of the document is much closer to being verified.

16.7   Encryption Techniques

Encryption can take place in software on a host, on a device, on a switch, on a router, or on a dedicated encryption/decryption appliance. The trade-offs are the usual ones—performance, scalability, and manageability versus cost. Simple encryption (or no encryption) of data is useful when an organization feels that the level of surrounding security is adequate by itself—for example, when transmitting data over a virtual private network (VPN).

16.7.1   Software-Based Encryption

A server host is usually used for software-based encryption. Depending on the software chosen, host-level encryption can perform either database-level or file-level encryption Database encryption is typically performed on one or a few of the most sensitive records ("columns") in a database. Because the encryption is software-based, it is slower than hardware-based encryption and may result in significant overhead for transactions and resultant performance problems with business-critical applications. However, by combining encryption with compression, host-level encryption can sometimes actually improve transactional performance, because the smaller database size and resulting querying speed-up can counteract the processing overhead from encryption/compression and the reverse. File-level encryption may have the same type of performance issues. File-level key management may be a headache because of the need to manage separate keys for each file directory on each system.

16.7.2   Encryption Appliance

The appliance approach, which couples the necessary hardware and software for encryption/decryption, is the industrial-strength approach to encryption—either disk or tape or both, depending on the appliance. The advantages of an appliance are advanced encryption management for key management, tighter integration between IT tasks and security, and significant reduction in the latency caused by the encryption/decryption process (i.e., improved performance). The disadvantage is cost, especially since one appliance is needed on each side of the network for data-in-flight protection.

16.7.3   Full Disk Encryption

The availability of disks that have hardware-based full disk encryption (FDE) has overcome two of the apparent concerns that might prevent the adoption of data-at-rest encryption technology on a broad basis. Those two concerns were performance and whether the data was natively usable. Performance effects of encryption using hardware-based FDE disks are said to be negligible. On top of that, the data is natively usable. Natively usable means that processes accessing the data do not need to be changed to handle the encrypted version of the data. That is important for eDiscovery and search functions, especially full content search capabilities such as an SQL (Structured Query Language) search of an entire disk for business intelligence (BI) reasons (as well as for data deduplication). The problem, however, is that using hardware-based full disk encryption requires that existing disks be replaced.

Software-based FDE is an alternative that can be applied to existing disks. When businesses must protect sensitive data now, such as on laptops, and cannot afford to replace the existing disks, then software-based FDE is preferable. However, retrofitting the encryption software is an additional cost and requires considerable administrative effort. By contrast, hardware FDE is relatively low-cost (becaue the extra hardware cost on each disk may be subsumed into the overall cost of the disk at no charge or only a small charge to the user) and the central administration process is easier (more specifically, it is faster, because encryption has been built in and need not be added).

16.7.4   Drive-Based Tape Encryption

Tape-drive-based tape encryption provides simplicity and performance for tape encryption. Standard practice when backing up to tape is that the data on the tape media is compressed. Compression has to be performed before encryption (as compression takes out the redundancies in intrafile data, and encryption would mask those redundancies). Tape-drive-based encryption processes the data in the proper order and is hardware-based, so there is no performance loss. However, as with hardware-based FDE, these drives may be added only during a replacement cycle.

16.7.5   Router-Based Tape Encryption

Routers often connect to tape drives. Tape data encryption on a router has an advantage in performance versus, say, an appliance-based tape encryption approach, because the low-latency, high-performance stack in a router is faster than the standard I/O stack that an appliance has to use in its server—in other words, the encryption itself may be no faster, but the data transmission tasks before and after are shortened. A router-based solution also offers a cost advantage over a tape appliance. With respect to drive-based tape encryption, a router-based approach allows existing tape resources to be able to take advantage of tape encryption without upgrading.

16.7.6   Switch-Based Encryption

From a logical perspective, putting encryption in a switch box may seem to make sense, because this will minimize the number of boxes of equipment and network connections to be managed. A practical consideration, however, is whether a particular switch-based encryption will solve the interoperability issues to work in a particular enterprise's network environment. A business question is whether you want to put all your eggs in one basket. Should the fabric have additional functionality if breakdowns for any reason could bring everything down?

16.8   Compliance/Governance Appliance

A compliance/governance appliance is an intersection of a production copy of the data and a data protection appliance. Whereas a data protection copy's sole purpose is to serve as the basis for restoring or restarting access to data, a compliance/governance appliance is also a production version of the data, in the sense that applications that need access to the data can access it immediately, without a restore/restart process. For example, the appliance may contain data that is on litigation hold.

The debate between advocates of a general-purpose storage system that contains compliance/governance data along with other data and those favoring a dedicated appliance storage system for managing only compliance or governance data does not have the same level of intensity that it has in the case of a data protection appliance. A need to isolate compliance or governance data from the rest of the information infrastructure tends to favor the use of a dedicated compliance/governance appliance. The software that manages compliance or governance can work in conjunction with the appliance's operating system without conflicting with other requirements. This might be important if two opposing demands—the need to keep a revenue-producing application running around the clock and the need to satisfy a regulatory request—come into conflict on a general-purpose storage system that does not have sufficient performance to satisfy both. A general-purpose system can still be used, but the requirements have to be thought through carefully.

An active archive can serve as a dedicated compliance/governance appliance as long as controls are in place to prevent legitimate noncompliance or nongovernance uses of the compliance/governance data from tampering with the data.

16.9   Data Shredding

Businesses may need to make sure that data is really physically destroyed or is guaranteed unreadable, for two reasons. First, logical deletion of information as part of the enforcement of a data retention policy does not mean that a forensics expert could not recover the data. Second, the movement of storage devices outside an organization's direct control, such as the disposal of laptops/desktops or storage devices or the remote maintenance of storage devices from a disk array, could expose a business to the loss of confidential information. The process for permanently erasing the data may be called data disposition, data shredding, or data destruction, but it also goes by the gentler name of media sanitization, because storage media are where the data is erased

How should organizations go about the data shredding process? Logically, the process is easy. Encrypting data and then losing the encryption key makes the data unreadable (theoretically!). Another simple way (in principle) is to overwrite any part of a disk or tape on which data was written with all zeros for every bit on, say, a particular track or cylinder. Practically, that destroys the data so that it cannot be recovered even by a forensics expert. The key is to find software that performs that zeroing function in a guaranteed manner.

Of course, overwriting is not possible with WORM tape, so "losing" the encryption key is the only WORM tape deletion option. However, overwriting may be possible with WORM disk for data whose retention period has expired, because WORM disk is software-based, so theoretically the software could permit overwriting.

However, while data shredding is apparently simple, many organizations may want to ensure that they follow proper standards. Until recently, the National Industry Security Program (NISP) Operating Manual (DoD 5220.22-M) gave U.S. governmental guidelines for media sanitization, which is the public-sector term for data destruction. However, the new "Guidelines for Media Sanitization" (NIST Special Publication 800-88) list the recommendations (from the National Institute of Standards and Technology) that government agencies should follow. While private organizations need not follow these guidelines, the recommendations are logical and straightforward.

A large number of electronic storage media are covered, including hard disk drives (HDDs), mobile computing devices, and memory devices, but the publication does not (and recognizes that it cannot) identify all current and future devices. For example, Fibre Channel (FC) drives are notably absent. As a result, organizations need to follow the guidelines with both common sense and best practices.

The NIST guidelines describe three levels of media sanitization: clearing, purging, and destroying. *Clearing* is designed to prevent robust keyboard attacks. That is, the data must not be able to be retrieved from data, disk, or file recovery utilities by keystroke recovery efforts from standard input devices or more sophisticated data scavenging tools. Overwriting media with nonsensitive data is a recommended practice for clearing.

Purging is designed to protect data against a laboratory attack, in which highly trained people and sophisticated signal processing equipment are used to recover data from media outside their normal operating environments, such as stand-alone Winchester disk drives. Winchester drives, the solution commonly used today, encapsulate the disk platters, with the read/write mechanisms enclosed in a sealed unit.

Purging ranks as the highest level of security that does not involve actual physical destruction of the media. This means that even with purging, the hard drives can be reused with new data, so the investment in the drives is protected. When the drives have been removed from their normal operating environment, the guidelines recommend that data be purged with a SecureErase command. Firmware-based SecureErase can be executed to destroy the data (and in the process perform both the clear and purging functions) for most ATA drives over 15 GB that were manufactured after 2001.

Another purging process, degaussing, uses a strong magnetic field to destroy data on magnetic media such as HDDs and tape. Naturally, degaussing cannot be used on optical media, such as CDs and DVDs. Degaussing a hard drive typically renders inoperative the firmware that manages drive processes. Thus, the drive can no longer be used to read and write data even though it has not been physically destroyed.

Finally, *destroying* is typically reserved for circumstances where absolute destruction of the data is required. In these cases, physical storage media are altered physically beyond the point where any data could be recovered by either a keyboard or a laboratory attack, no matter how sophisticated. Disintegration, incineration, pulverization, and melting are processes that completely destroy the data along with the physical media.

Clearing, purging, and destroying are implemented at the level of individual pieces of media rather than at the level of selected pieces of information, such as files. In cases of planned data destruction (unplanned data destruction, such as sending a hard disk back for unplanned warranty work, cannot be predicted), an organization has to plan in advance to try and make sure that sensitive and confidential information is confined to as few pieces of media as possible. At the same time, an organization should try to ensure that the end of a data retention period is as close to the same as possible for all the data on a given piece of media. Otherwise, the nonexpired data must be migrated in a permissible fashion to another piece of media before the piece of media targeted for media sanitization is actually purged or destroyed.

16.10   Key Takeaways

- WORM technology is used to guarantee that data cannot be changed until at least the expiration data.
- The use of WORM media presents some challenges when trying to dispose of the data. If the data is encrypted, then the encryption key can be lost. Otherwise, the media has to be physically destroyed, which may not be easy. The other challenge is how to manage data protection copies of the WORM data.
- WORM tape cannot be used in a traditional rotation-of-tapes strategy, because the tapes are not reusable, so managing the process of writing to WORM tape requires some planning.
- WORM disk can be used for compliance data. However, the use of WORM disk should be planned very carefully, especially if there is a need to migrate data to another storage array.
- Electronic locking is the ability to prevent data from being altered or deleted for a period of time.
- A number of encryption techniques—software-based, encryption appliance, full disk, drive-based for tape, router-based for tape, and switch-based—exist, and each has its advantages and disadvantages.
- A compliance appliance is a dedicated hardware/software appliance that manages a compliance copy of the data.
- Data shredding, which is a process that ensures that deleted data can no longer be read or used in any way, can simply be done by overwriting the data if it is not encrypted or "losing" the encryption key if it is encrypted. A more formal approach allows several levels of media sanitization: clearing, purging, and destroying.

Chapter 17

eDiscovery and the Electronic Discovery Reference Model

17.1 What to Look for in This Chapter

- Why eDiscovery is going to become more and more important
- What the Electronic Discovery Reference Model (EDRM) is
- What the eDiscovery information management process is, and why records management and data mapping are important components of that process.
- What the different steps in the EDRM model are, and how each step contributes to fulfillment of the eDiscovery process

Recall that governance, as one of the three pillars in the governance, risk management, and compliance (GRC) model, concerns itself with the processes and systems that ensure the proper accountability for the conduct of an enterprise's business. Data governance, as part of IT governance within the overall governance framework, is required to ensure the preservation, availability, confidentiality, and usability of an enterprise's data. These are all mandates that relate to data protection. And a major responsibility of data governance is to help with civil litigation.

Previously, the subject of civil litigation with respect to governance was explored in depth using the changes to the Federal Rules of Civil Procedure (FRCP) as a focal point. The role of eDiscovery was touched on a number of times, but it was not explored in depth.

Understand that the importance of eDiscovery is going to increase as more and more as businesses realize the implications of those changes to the FRCP and as litigation demands continue to mount. However, recognizing the importance of eDiscovery is only the first step. Doing eDiscovery right is the next step.

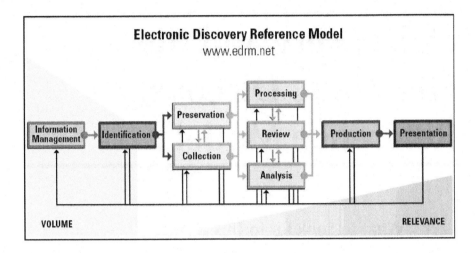

Figure 17.1   Electronic Discovery Reference Model

Civil litigation is already a heavy burden on many businesses and that burden is only likely to grow. Doing eDiscovery right is a tough balancing act between the financial risks of lost lawsuits as well as court-imposed financial penalties in the case of a failure to do things right and trying to keep the expenses of doing eDiscovery within as reasonable bounds as possible.

Doing eDiscovery right is not easy, because eDiscovery is much more than the simple search of electronically stored information (ESI). Rather, eDiscovery is a set of processes that can be integrated with evolving technologies to serve the purpose of managing ESI for civil litigation.

Fortunately, an existing framework covers the steps in eDiscovery. This very useful framework is the Electronic Discovery Reference Model (EDRM) (Figure 17.1), which is part of the ongoing valuable work of the EDRM group (www.edrm.net). The EDRM can serve as a useful base to reference in exploring the concepts of eDiscovery. The EDRM group has created specific focus groups that constantly address the relevance of the model and how organizations can pass information in a standard way between the various steps—for instance, when they choose to outsource part of the process. Individual organization may interpret the sequence of events and/or the process differently, but the EDRM serves as a useful basis for comparison.

17.2 Information Management—Getting eDiscovery Off on the Right Foot

Recall that information management manages the content and decision-making relationships of information as it moves through the lifecycle of a specific business process or cross-functional workflow. In this case, the business process/workflow is eDiscovery. Given the nature of this type of workflow, which touches multiple different areas of business information, the general approach lends itself to a more proactive rather than reactive approach.

Treating an eDiscovery event as a one-off ad-hoc incident is likely to be very costly and invariably does not achieve the desired results. Trying to complete all the set of complex tasks that doing eDiscovery right entails is hard to do in a fire-drill hurry-up mode. That is especially true when there is a steep learning curve in trying to put together the complex process. The result is that an eDiscovery process may complete within the time constraints allowed, but it is not done well and creates obvious litigation risk. One reason is that all the time is spent in gathering the information, so no time is left to evaluate it properly. Or the process may result in unacceptable delays. Or inadequate preparation may lead to adverse inferences or spoliation claims. Finally, the lack of processing around collected information often leads to lengthy and unnecessary content review that causes further delay. Whether it is done on time or late, the net result may be unnecessarily high legal costs, higher-than-estimated internal IT costs (such as for more storage than necessary), and legal penalties for not complying on time or correctly with the rules. On top of that, since an enterprise is not likely to put its best case forward, it may lose a case that it might otherwise had won. And that costs money, since civil litigation is about money—who wins and who loses.

Consequently, incumbent on enterprises is the responsibility to plan in advance what needs to be done for eDiscovery. That requires establishing the necessary policies, processes, procedures, and practices ahead of time.

17.2.1 The eDiscovery Information Management Process

Assume that the hide-the-head-in-the-sand, *tabula rasa* approach of welcoming each new civil litigation event without any real learning from past ones is not a real process model for eDiscovery. Then, consider two possible models for managing the repeatable information management process for eDiscovery. Call one the informal model and call the other one the formal model. A business may actually be somewhere on a continuum between the two extremes as far as process methodology, maturity, and complexity is concerned, but for the sake of discussion, the two models can be treated as discrete extremes.

In the informal model, experience, knowledge, and working relationships among key constituencies (such as members of the general counsel's office and the IT organization) all play an important role. Organizational learning takes place (at least to some extent), so that what is learned from one civil litigation event can be applied to the next one (insofar as is possible). The basic processes for doing key tasks are put in place, such as conducting litigation holds. Key data sources, such as e-mail systems, may be recognized as a common source for litigation holds. Key constituencies develop guidelines and a general understanding of what needs to be done and can then apply them on a case-by-case basis.

In the formal model, a rigorous process management program, including both a records management program and a data mapping program, need to be put in place. In addition, these tie into the data retention management process. An organization has to defend its position on the exclusion of records that have expired as part of the everyday policies of the business. The good news is that a records management program may already exist, so the foundations are in place. In general, however, a lot of time, effort, and money have to be expended to make eDiscovery a rigorous repeatable process.

It is no wonder, then, that the informal model predominates. The eDiscovery jobs get done and the apparent out-of-pocket costs are less than with the formal model. But how efficient is the informal model? The cost of eDiscovery is already high in many cases and is likely to grow higher. Moreover, can businesses win more cases and reduce the financial awards in the cases they lose? That also represents costs.

The formal model is also no panacea. How much the costs of eDiscovery can be cut is likely to be very uncertain, and eDiscovery is still likely to be expensive (although hopefully not as much so). Whether the win/loss ratio in civil litigation can be improved may simply be speculation and conjecture.

Still the road less taken should be examined to see what it brings to the table. Two examples will serve to illustrate some of what needs to be done: records management and data mapping.

17.2.2 Records Management—Back to the Future

Records management traditionally dealt with paper records, not electronic records. However, eDiscovery is only about eRecords, so a records management program also has to encompass eRecords if it is to be of any assistance to the eDiscovery process. Among the objectives that a records management program bring to the table are classification, retention management, guaranteed document authenticity, and the ability to establish litigation holds—all previously identified as key issues.

Putting together a robust records management program requires a team of knowledge workers who can carry out the complex and time-consuming task. Data stewards include business unit personnel who are familiar with the different types of eRecords in the business, how they are used, and what value they have in the organization. Specialist data stewards include lawyers and compliance personnel who are familiar with the legal requirements for specific types of eRecords, such as retention policy and confidentiality. Data custodians include IT personnel who understand the types of eRecords that the company generates or receives, understand the IT capabilities of the company, and should know where eRecords are stored and how to retrieve them.

But wait—there's more. The team must also include records management specialists. These are the people who manage the records management process. Note that records management is a business function, not an IT function, so the records management specialists are a type of data steward, not a data custodian.

The records management team should be part of the data governance approach for the business.

17.2.3 Data Mapping—Carrying Out the Data Knowledge Imperative

Although data mapping can logically be put in the Identification node of the EDRM model, the concept of data mapping is generic to all eDiscovery requests and not just particular requests. Therefore, for purposes of discussion, data mapping will be examined as part of the Information Management node.

Recall the data knowledge objective that was added to the list of data protection objectives to accommodate governance. A data map that gives a complete and accurate picture of a company's data sources is essential to achieve that objective for governance and is an essential requirement for a formal eDiscovery information management model

The data mapping challenge can be overwhelming. The first challenge is the discovery process of simply trying to understand what is available, and that includes trying to understand from a variety of perspectives:

- Structured, semistructured, and unstructured information in all its various forms and permutations, including databases and e-mail archives
- Active changeable production information and active archive information for legacy systems
- Data stored on business systems—direct attached storage (DAS), networked-attached storage (NAS), and storage area networks (SAN)
- Data stored on desktop computers and mobile devices, including laptop computers, personal digital assistants (PDAs), and cell phones
- Data stored on both nonremovable media (such as on disk arrays) as well as on removable media (tape, external disk drives, and flash memory drives)
- Data protection information locally on disk and tape
- Disaster recovery information, either offsite at a company site or at a third-party site

And that is just the beginning. There are other issues with trying to pin down what information is available, where it is, and how to access it. Information is dynamic in nature in that it can move around from place to place—and perhaps may do so unpredictably. All information is not under the central control of an IT organization. Information is often in fragmented application silos, where information is isolated from one another. Finally, knowing just what type of information is where is not enough. Further granularity is necessary. Knowing that there are word processing documents on a system does not distinguish the value of them from a business use perspective, nor does it classify them from, say, a sensitivity perspective.

On top of everything else, the process of data mapping is likely to be expensive. No wonder, then, that when faced with the mind-boggling challenge of data mapping, most enterprises would like to take a pass.

Unfortunately, taking a pass is becoming less and less an option, as data knowledge is becoming more and more a "have to do" requirement that may very well become mandatory, and data mapping is a means to accomplish that requirement. Now, eDiscovery alone is not necessarily the reason, although governance requirements are a major impetus. However, when the need for compliance is added, further weight is given to the need for data mapping. For example, classifying information for sensitivity purposes may be difficult, but it is necessary to satisfy data privacy requirements. And the third pillar of the GRC framework also has to be taken into account: risk management. Where are the risks and rewards in not doing things properly? Moreover, information is an asset to a business, and businesses use it for other purposes than transactions of one kind or another. Mine the value.

Frankly, data mapping is never likely to be complete or perfect, and it does not have to be. Some type of triage approach needs to be taken in order to determine priorities. The methodologies of information assurance and information risk management may play a big role in determining the risk/rewards that have to be taken into account in order to assign priorities. Naturally, the low-hanging fruit, such as legacy systems and e-mail systems, are targets for data mapping, but even there a formal analysis process is likely to be important in helping to determine the granularity of what needs to be done. And not developing a data map is becoming a less-than-viable option.

17.2.4   Again a Return to the Need for Data Governance

Note that data knowledge is not the only data protection objective that a formal eDiscovery information management model can help with. Data preservation now has a data quality attribute for ensuring the completeness, accuracy, and consistency of information. The data auditability objective requires the authentication of information for reporting and evidentiary purposes.

However, a formal eDiscovery model does not have to—and should not be—developed in isolation. The concept fits nicely into the data governance function. Using the data governance concept within the GRC frameworks creates leverage (funds used can serve multiple purposes simultaneously, except for specific extensions for particular needs) and synergy (combined actions can yield greater benefits for a smaller overall investment). Project teams that are working on somewhat similar requirements separately will not only spend more money, they will have to reinvent the wheel in many cases, and they may come up with inconsistencies that have to be resolved at additional cost. So, once again, data governance plays an essential role in data protection, this time eDiscovery.

17.3   Overview of the Steps of the EDRM Model

The specific steps of the EDRM model are roughly divided into information collection, information analysis, and information delivery steps for carrying out a particular eDiscovery event process. In summary form, these steps are as follows:

- Information collection
  - *Identification*—locates all the information that may be used in a pending or prospective legal proceeding
  - *Preservation*—protects the necessary information against deletion or alteration that would result in spoliation
  - *Collection*—gathers the information that will be used in the electronic discovery process
- Information analysis
  - *Processing*—reduces the volume of information to only that necessary for legal processing and then converts, as appropriate, to a more manageable format for the review and analysis steps
  - *Review*—examines the information to determine what is relevant to the matter at hand and what can be excluded as privileged information
  - *Analysis*—evaluates a collection of electronic discovery materials from which relevant summary information can be determined
- Information delivery
  - *Production*—delivers information that is required and relevant to a legal proceeding in the proper format and with the use of the appropriate means of delivery
  - *Presentation*—occurs when electronically discovered information is displayed at proceedings related to the case

The workflow steps are not necessarily linear from left to right. Iteration of the steps may be necessary to refine the process. For example, suppose that during the course of the process, some additional ESI is now thought to be relevant. The steps of identification, preservation, and collection have to be repeated for that information.

The process can be seen as more cyclic, given the repetitive nature of requests from legal to IT for eDiscovery information. As an enterprise moves to a more proactive model, IT and legal can come together to enable a more seamless cyclic model that reduces the need for repetitive activity. That takes place through the proactive management of ESI content across the whole process, regardless of its role.

17.3.1   Identification

Identification is the discovery process that locates all the information that can conceivably be used in a pending or prospective legal proceeding. As such, the identification step is the data mapping step. If the data mapping has not already been done as a result of an established and ongoing formal data mapping process, this is the step where it has to be done.

However, this step is more than just data mapping. A litigation response plan also has to be put together. As part of that process, key witnesses and data stewards, who have administrative control of the data, have to be identified. In addition, a meet-and-confer meeting with representatives from both sides of the dispute should take place in order to define terms and scope of discovery based on what is reasonable effort.

In the actual EDRM model, the term *data custodian* is used for the person who has administrative control of a document or electronic file. That is a reasonable definition in that this person is the source for information. However, the definition conflicts with previous usage in this book. We shall substitute *data steward* (an agent who administers the data on behalf of the data owner) for *data custodian*, to distinguish the meaning of data custodian as one who physically guards the data (and is essential from a preservation perspective).

The key witnesses and data stewards help identify what information is relevant to a particular litigation. If a data map is already available, this becomes a subset of the overall map. If a data map is not already available, a targeted data map process has to be followed to find only the information relevant for this particular situation.

17.3.2   Preservation

Preservation results in saving information that may be relevant in a contested matter, whether that is a litigation or a government investigation. A company has the affirmative duty to preserve that information and produce it as necessary to an adverse party, even though the information may be detrimental to a company's legal position.

Preservation may come after collection, depending on the methods of identification, collection, and processing. Traditional approaches identify documents and then preserve them, collect them, and then process and review them. Newer technology enables proactive identification and collection of all data across the enterprise, which can subsequently be searched, processed, and placed on preservation, depending on the required responsiveness and scope.

Preservation may result in an enterprise retaining a lot more data than is absolutely necessary. This could become a major problem for organizations that do not take a proactive approach. Without a prescriptive approach to legal hold, backed by a process of authenticity, many organizations face large amounts, if not all, of their corporate data being retained indefinitely due to a preservation order. Without the application of a formal deletion policy, the cost and management implications are significant, especially as data volumes grow.

However, prior to full implementation of the preservation process, a meet-and-confer meeting between the adversarial parties (as mandated by the FRCP) should take place (if it hasn't already, as discussed earlier). (Some information may have had to have been put on litigation hold in reasonable anticipation of requirements beforehand.) The meeting is an attempt to reach agreement on the scope and responsibilities related to the discovery process.

The meet-and-confer meeting may or may not take place before one of the parties issues a preservation letter to the other party. The preservation letter is designed to request only the information that might be relevant or important to one's case. Asking for everything but the kitchen sink, even though much of the information may be patently irrelevant, can be considered a bad-faith litigation tactic by the courts. However, honest disagreement may arise. If so, a written counter-offer can be sent, or, if one has not already taken place, a meet-and-confer meeting can be suggested.

Litigation Hold

A litigation hold letter has to be distributed to everyone, including key witnesses, data stewards, and data custodians, who are part of the preservation process. All recipients have to formally acknowledge (by signing a certification) that the recipient not only has read the hold, but understands the obligations that the hold contains and will fulfill those obligations.

When information is put on litigation hold, the normal data retention policies that might enable the deletion (i.e., destruction) of the data have to be halted. Recall the earlier discussion that this information is subject to chain-of-custody management to establish the causal time history of events that affect the information so that it can be considered to be authentic and therefore eligible to be used as evidence. That work is necessary to avoid any possible spoliation of data claims.

Data on hold is not just a point-in-time copy of the information at that time, i.e., a historical copy of the data. Data on hold is also all the new relevant data that is created during the time that the litigation hold is in place. People who are involved in the preservation process should be given clear instructions on how to preserve the new data.

One of the issues is whether the data is in a production copy of the data or in a data protection copy of the data. If it is on data protection copies that reside on backup tape, the question arises as to how to manage the process when a rotational scheme is used that involves periodic recycling to a scratch pool of the oldest tapes in the rotational scheme. There are a number of options, but essentially, some tapes have to be identified as relevant to the litigation hold process and taken out of circulation (at least until they have been copied) so that they cannot be recycled.

Another issue is metadata. Metadata is data about data that accompanies the data and is used for tracking, understanding the history of, or managing the data. Recipients of the litigation hold letter should be given specific instructions about the preservation of metadata that is associated with the relevant material as well as the data itself. This is especially important when ESI is produced (i.e., given) to the requesting party in native format. Native format requires that the application that uses the data accompany the data. For example, in order to understand a spreadsheet, the underlying formula for a cell must be known, as well as the actual value that was calculated in a specific instance of the spreadsheet. Understanding the metadata is even more important when trying to understand a database application.

Note that a process also has to be in place to enable data to be taken off litigation hold and normal business processes (including data retention policies) to resume.

Winnowing Process

A number of factors contribute to the cost of eDiscovery, but the amount of data that has to move through each step in the EDRM model is at or near the top of the list. The more data is involved, the more time of more people is spent and the more support infrastructure, such as software tools and storage, is needed. Without managed processing or winnowing, the full collection set, regardless of relevance, is passed on to legal, which then incurs wasted time and costs associated with reviewing obviously irrelevant material. It is thus no wonder that attempting to limit the scope of what has to be preserved is important.

Trying to reduce the amount of information at each step, consistent with good practices, is a major determinant in being able to keep the costs of eDiscovery within some kind of sensible bound. Winnow down the amount of data from what might be relevant and so has to be considered as such at the preservation step to what is really relevant, which is what is delivered in the production step. That difference may be substantial. The difference between what information needs to be preserved and what information needs to be produced could be two orders of magnitude (i.e., 100 times) less.

Winnowing down the amount of data that might be relevant at the preservation step to what is really relevant in the production step is essential for controlling the overall cost of the eDiscovery process.

Note that the amount of data and the relevance of the data are somewhat inversely proportional—i.e., as the amount of data falls, the relevance of the remaining data increases.

Starting off at the preservation step by minimizing the amount of data that has to moved on to subsequent steps can make the subsequent steps faster and less costly.

17.3.3 Collection

In the collection step, the information that will be used in the electronic discovery process is gathered. Note that not only the content of the data, but also the activity of the user, may have to be taken into account.

Auditability, Completeness, and Accuracy Are Essential

The data auditability objective must receive paramount attention in order to establish the chain of custody that is necessary to satisfy the authentication requirements to be able to use any collected ESI and its associated metadata as evidence. Part of the security procedures should be to identify privileged work product so that it is not part of the other data that is collected or produced.

Whoever acts as the collection agent needs to be able to prohibit unauthorized access to the data as well as being able to track all attempts to access the data as part of the requirements for establishing the chain-of-custody process.

Ensuring the completeness and the accuracy of the collection can be a challenge. For example, transformations to the metadata of a file may change during a file's lifetime, either as a result of an action by an end user or automatically by an operating system or other software, such as encryption or migration of the file. Those changes may make it difficult to determine that a file was actually created, modified, or viewed by a particular person. Consequently, the processes for determining how to collect a complete and accurate collection are important.

The Collection Process

Data is typically collected from a piece of storage media—either fixed, such as a hard disk on a laptop or storage array, or portable, such as a magnetic tape cartridge or a flash memory drive—or over a network, such as from a third-party service supplier's storage at a remote site.

Two questions arise: how to collect the data, and where to store it. They are interrelated. One approach is to collect data by freezing it in place. This is possible in an active archive if the archive management software can handle the process, such as guaranteeing the data retention of the information. However, no guarantee exists that all the data is on an active archive.

However, if the data is not already in an active archive and is available on fixed storage, the collection process in essence creates an archive, since the data collected is by definition fixed—alterations or deletions are not acceptable. This archive could be on tape and collected via a process called the supervised tape archive process. Alternatively, everything might be written to disk on a standalone governance appliance. The advantage of this method is that the appliance has server capability to run the application software that can present the data in a useful manner. However, the tape method can still be used, because copies can be made for both offsite and onsite processing and analysis.

Portable media can be handled in one of two ways. One is simply to impound the media and store them in a physically secure facility. However, the media might be needed for some business purpose, such as a backup tape. Also, no mechanisms exist for ensuring chain of custody, because someone who obtained unauthorized access to the supposedly secure facility could alter data, say, on a flash memory drive. Moreover, processing and analyzing the data may be difficult, as it hasto be done piecemeal.

So a catch, copy, and release strategy is more appropriate. *Catch* means to acquire the piece of media, *copy* means to faithfully duplicate the data and secure it for chain-of-custody purposes, and *release* means to return the original piece of media for its originally intended purpose.

For backup tapes, native-environment restoration requires the original backup/restore software to be used in copying (which is the purpose of this particular restoration) the data to an eDiscovery-process-managed piece of media, i.e., a piece of media that is chain-of-custody- and auditing-compliant. Non-native extraction is an alternative method that is typically used by third-party vendors who specialize in backup tape processing. This approach is seen as faster and less expensive than native-environment restoration.

Getting data back from a third-party vendor depends on the use of the data, but the third party may not allow an onsite visit. If the data is a backup copy, then a native-environment restoration will work, because that process has already been put in place. For an archive or an active changeable production database (such as when using a software-as-a-service application), collection may require some help on the part of the third-party service supplier.

17.3.4   Processing

The processing step attempts to cull the volume of information before the review and analysis steps start. The decisions made in the prior steps of the lifecycle—identification, preservation, and collection—somewhat determine the requirements and activities that have to be undertaken during the processing step. That is, the types and amounts of data preserved and collected as well as the time frames for the production step have already been determined.

The processing step gets the data ready for review. Agreement is necessary on both what data needs to be processed as well as what should be the input and output format of the data. These attributes shape the scope of the processing effort, which, in turn, affects the timeframe as well as the cost of processing and reviewing the ESI.

Processing Methods

Automated processing of datasets to cut them to an easier-to-use subset reduces the cost of review, because attorneys will not have to review what is not there. Overall, the technical approaches or processes that are used to reduce a large amount of data to a much smaller set are called *data culling*. One technology that is helpful in this process is deduplication, such as the single-instancing data reduction technique to get rid of multiple copies of the same file. Contrast traditional and new technologies in this area. eDiscovery technologies that have to "grab" documents for preservation, collection, and processing need to deduplicate to drive efficiency from that point on. Technologies that already have data management under control and are deduplicating content at the source are more efficient through all the steps of EDRM. The latter approach is obviously about being more proactive (and is an illustration of how a particular data protection technology may be useful for more than one purpose).

File-level filtering using selected metadata criteria, such as selected time stamps that are associated with the file, can cut down the size of the datasets to be reviewed. Moreover, the collection process may grab a lot of unnecessary files—say, when copying a whole disk. Various file types, including those of an operating system, may safely be exorcised from the files that need to be reviewed as part of the litigation process.

Of course, an electronic search is a familiar way to filter the data. Specific words that are likely to be relevant to the matter at hand, whether they are in the text of a document itself or in the metadata, can be used in the search process. Or the process may be as simple as finding the names of key individuals on the "from" or "to" lines of e-mails.

The search may employ the familiar full Boolean logic in a search engine. This type of search allows more than one key word to be used in the search process (using such search operators as AND, OR, and NOT). Proximity operators can be used to determine words that are close to one another in a document, which is useful in a context search.

A newer method of searching is called *concept searching*, which is used to identify content that is conceptually similar to the search terms. No standard method exists for doing concept searching. Concept searching is currently not an accepted means for eliminating data from a collected set, probably because a concept search cannot sufficiently conclude the presence or absence of data that may serve as evidence. However, concept searching may be very helpful in defining and refining search terms in the processing step and in helping to navigate the data in the review step.

Other Processing Considerations

A key question is whether or not to convert the data for review. One way of converting is to convert to quasi-paper format, such as PDF (Portable Document Format) or TIFF (Tagged Image File Format). However, the conversion process is expensive, and most of the large amount of reviewed material is likely to be deemed irrelevant to the matter at hand anyway, so an initial review of the documents in native form (i.e., opened with their native application) may be a better first step. Then, if it is necessary to convert only nonprivileged information that appears relevant at this step (obviously, non-relevant ESI can be excluded from further review). Note that a quality control process, both automatic and manual, needs to be in place to ensure auditability. Reporting, especially when a third-party service supplier is involved, is part of the control process.

One example can illustrate the difficulties. If e-mail is converted to TIFF or PDF format, a lot of the embedded metadata is lost. The internal e-mail distribution list at the time that the e-mail was sent would be part of that lost metadata. So the original ESI (native-format e-mail) has higher evidential integrity, because it would show who was on that distribution list.

Processing documents for electronic discovery can be very expensive. The process of converting and indexing data into a common searchable and usable format can be a very complex and difficult activity. Depending on the situation, the process may be a very labor-intensive specialized activity. No wonder that innumerable options exist to process the data, from internally with an investment in software tools and infrastructure to the use of outside services.

17.3.5   Review

Once the data has been processed, it is ready for review. The review process determines what documents are responsive. A *responsive* document is one that meets the established parameters of the document request that led to the search process in the first place. Response documents then have to be produced, which means that those documents have to be delivered to other parties in the legal matter in appropriate forms through the use of appropriate delivery mechanisms. Note that the word *document* is used broadly to include not only any file produced by a software application, such as word processing documents, but also e-mails, databases, spreadsheets, and graphic files. The review process also excludes documents that are seen to be privileged, such as attorney work product and certain client–attorney communications, from having to be disclosed.

The scope and objectives of the review have to be determined. Reviewing each and every piece of documentation may very well be infeasible, so limiting the scope of the review through the use of carefully selected technology or other means is likely to be necessary. Key issues need to be documented, and a clear distinction needs to be made between issues of fact and issues of law. The review team needs to know what it should be looking for in the documentation.

Choosing Between In-House and Online Litigation Tool Support Technologies

Often a business may not have all the skill sets nor technical capabilities in-house to carry out the review process in its totality. Therefore, the business has to turn to an outside third-party vendor to fill in the gaps that it cannot provide internally. In fact, trying to build a litigation support system internally is probably not a good idea.

Two basic options exist for vendor selection: in-house or online. An in-house review is conducted using an application that is executed and maintained on an internal network. An online review is performed over a network, such as the Internet, to a site hosted by a third-party vendor.

An online tool gives less direct control but increased flexibility. If an in-house tool is selected, a business will want to leverage its investment over multiple legal matters. However, using more than one online vendor over time enables the business to have the flexibility of being able to select the right mix of review functions and features to be able to address each particular legal matter in the best way possible. That approach takes more evaluation time, does not leverage the learning curve in using one set of tools (whether in-house or out of house), and raises the overall cost.

A combination solution may be the answer. Some vendors have partnered with others to provide a combination in-house solution and an online solution or an online solution that involves different tools to meet different needs. One approach is to have on-premises eDiscovery archiving, capture, and data management solutions that integrate with hosted (out-of-house) case management solutions for the support of eDiscovery review and process analytics across multiple outside counsels. The passing of preserved and processed content for further review and chain-of-custody analysis with the resultant work product information finding its way back into the in-house environment are features of this approach.

The review process then has to be carried out by the lead attorney and the review team. Productivity and quality control metrics need to be in place to help manage the process.

17.3.6   Analysis

Analysis is the process of sifting through a collection of electronic documents and other materials to find context and content that is important for the legal matter at hand. Analysis helps to find key patterns and topics within the ESI, identify important people, discover specific vocabulary and jargon, and target individual documents. Effective analysis requires a blend of good technology and techniques. The goal is not only to obtain key information quickly and easily, but to do so in a less costly and more accurate manner than could be done using an exhaustive manual review. Note that analysis is not a separate step in the EDRM model, but rather part of another step—the review step.

Analysis uses the body of documents that have been output through the processing step as its input. The ESI therefore has had to be put into analyzable form, such as being indexed, as a precursor to the search process.

Sample Types of Analytical Tools

A number of analytical tools are available. Search (as previously discussed) in its various incarnations is a primary analytical tool. Clustering technology groups together items of ESI on the same topic, such as documents including e-mails. However, clustering is not an exact approach, so it may include items that should not be included and exclude items that should not be excluded.

Guided navigation is an analysis tool for examining a collection set or the result of a query, where the data items have been categorized in a number of ways. This is a drill-down approach (which has been employed in business intelligence tools for years) in which one can start at a high level and then drill down to successive levels of details (from category, find key person; from key person, find another person with whom the first person has exchanged e-mails; from the e-mails exchanged between the two people, find the e-mails most relevant to the legal matter at hand). This helps with not only gaining an overall understanding of what is going on, but also to be able to find specific issues of importance.

Visualization tools create a visual output to help create a better understanding of the relationships among the items available for analysis, using the famous principle that a picture is worth a thousand words. One type of visualization is a social network analysis that shows the most important people in an analysis and the communications links between them. A context group structure is another technique. This technique depicts the actions that are taken in an electronic e-mail discussion over time, such as replies and forwards of e-mail.

Topical cluster analysis presents visually the interrelationships and internal structure among groups of documents and messages. These are just some of the tools, and their strengths, limitations, and applicability in a particular situation all have to examined before a decision can be made on whether or not to use any of them.

17.3.7   Production

According to the Federal Rules of Civil Procedure, "a responding party must produce the information in a form or forms in which it is ordinarily maintained or in a form or forms that are reasonably usable." The four basic choices are paper, quasi-paper, quasi-native form, and native. Paper is of course self-explanatory.

Quasi-paper is a little trickier. Quasi-paper is an electronic version of paper, such as immutable PDF of TIFF files. The only difference is that some metadata may be incorporated with the text.

Quasi-native means producing ESI electronically in a format that can be read by an application other than the native application that was used to create the information in the first place.

Native form means the document is produced using the file extension for the information of the application that created it. For example, a spreadsheet file would be in a particular file format with a particular file extension and would require a copy of the spreadsheet program to be able to read the file. Keep in mind that an original copy should be preserved for production and a working copy should be used for review purposes, as any interaction is likely to change the metadata associated with the document. The application typically has no means for freezing any changes to the metadata of a document as part of a litigation hold.

Produced documents should be run through a quality control process prior to release. Managing the redaction process may be a problem. *Redaction* is the process of removing privileged information from documents prior to producing them. Although rule changes allow the ability to retract privileged information if it has been inadvertently produced, it is best not to produce privileged information if at all possible.

The production process has to be carefully managed for the ESI that it sends to another party as well as for the produced ESI that it receives. Checking for completeness, making sure that the ESI is safely stored, and making sure that only authorized people have access are all essential.

17.3.8 Presentation

The respective attorneys have to decide what ESI they will display at various events during a legal matter, such as depositions, hearings, or trials. They need to be equipped with the technology that enables this to be done, such as a computer with a native application on it, such as a spreadsheet application, and an overhead projector, which can display images from the computer to all the people at a legal event. The selection of a relatively small set of ESI that has reached this stage for presentation is correct based on the best judgment of the legal team for each party involved in the legal matter.

17.4 Key Takeaways

- Civil litigation requirements are only likely to increase; eDiscovery is essential to civil litigation where ESI is used; therefore, eDiscovery is going to become even more important.
- The Electronic Discovery Reference Model is a generally accepted model for understanding the eDiscovery process.
- Information management manages the content and relationships of information as it moves through its lifecycle; eDiscovery needs to be managed not as a one-off ad-hoc process, but as an established

process that is repeatable. A formal information management process for eDiscovery benefits from employing methodologies that have been developed for records management and data mapping that is necessary to show what data is available and where it is located within a business.

- In addition to the information management step, the EDRM model can be divided into roughly three categories: information collection (which includes the steps of identification, preservation, and collection), information analysis (which includes the steps of processing, review, and analysis), and the information delivery steps (which include production and presentation).

Chapter 18

Cloud Computing, SaaS, and Other Data Protection Services

18.1   What to Look for in This Chapter

- What services are all about
- Why data protection is important when using a third-party services provider
- What the key distinguishing characteristics of cloud computing are
- What software-as-a-service and storage-as-a-service are
- What the drivers are for the services model
- What the numerous data protection requirements are when using a third-party supplier
- How a business should handle the issue of control when deciding whether to use a third-party services supplier

18.2   Growth in Services Raises Questions for Data Protection

From a business perspective, the dictionary definition of the word *service* that is most apropos is "the supplying or supplier of utilities, commodities, or other facilities that meet a public need." However, the word *services* has many other connotations in an IT context. *Professional services* here means the consulting provided by a third party, which might be project management or knowledge transfer or a number of other activities that we have mentioned. Although a professional services engagement could go on forever (or at least it seems that way to the hiring organization!), the engagement is supposed to end when specified services are delivered.

When the word *services* is used in the context of *service provider,* however, an end point is *not* specified. The expectation is that the service provider will provide an ongoing permanent service, where *permanent* simply means that there is no planned, definite end point for delivery of the service.

Commonly, a service provider is thought of as a third party—a supplier of services that is neither the primary vendor (such as the supplier of servers or storage hardware) nor the purchaser. However, IT organizations actually provide self-service; and primary vendors often offer services along with the solution.

A simple way of understanding what service is about is to look at it from a historical perspective. Traditionally, if the service provider provides a task on the basis of a long-term relationship (typically defined in a contract), then the service task is a form of *outsourcing*. This will be the starting point for future discussion.

Keep in mind, too, that there is another common meaning of *service* in an IT environment. This meaning comes from client-server days, when the tasks that a hardware-type server carried out through software were called a service. The latest incarnation of this other meaning is a *Web service,* which is software with a standardized interface that carries out tasks when invoked through that interface. The whole superstructure of passing invocations to Web services and sending task results back is known as a *service-oriented architecture* (SOA). In fact, many software-as-a-service (SaaS) implementations use both meanings: They provide services to customers primarily via off-premises Web service applications built to run on an SOA over the Web. And SaaS serves a key role in the growing service provider market.

Another way of looking at service is as all-encompassing offering in whch key components may be invisible to the user of the service. The use of these services is purchased on an ongoing/recurring basis. The key distinction is that the cost of the outsourced service is typically booked as an operating expense (OPEX) rather than a capital expense (CAPEX). So a user faces two choices. The user can provide the server/storage infrastructure and the necessary software on top of that infrastructure (CAPEX) and then provide the staff to integrate everything. Or the user can buy SaaS from a third-party service provider, and all of the underlying infrastructure components needed to run the application are invisible to the service user. Moreover, they are no longer CAPEX.

18.2.1 Service-Related Data Protection Issues

Why are services so important from a data protection perspective? With a third-party service provider, a number of data protection issues have to be taken into account for both production data and data protection data. For example, suppose that online backup is done at an off-premises site that is managed by a third-party service provider. What happens if onsite production data is destroyed in a disaster and the only available data protection copy, which is the offsite backup, fails? Not only is this a risk management issue, it could be a compliance issue. A company subject to Sarbanes-Oxley rules (as discussed in Chapter 7) will not be able to faithfully re-create financial data. Moreover, it might also be a governance issue. An eDiscovery attempt might also fail. The service-buying company remains responsible (because tasks, such as service-related ones, can be delegated, but responsibility cannot be). What legal recourse does the service-buying company have if the service provider can be shown to be at fault?

Questions like these become more important as services become a bigger piece of the IT budget. And that may well happen, as we will see.

In order to understand these and other service-related data protection questions, we need to go into some detail about services in general before again delving into data-protection-specific issues.

18.2.2 The Off-Premises Third-Party Services Food Chain

Although all off-premises third-party services can be considered to be at least some form of "managed services," the services provided tend to be provided at one of four levels (Table 18.1).

Table 18.1 The Off-Premises Third-Party Food Chain

	Service Provider Provides	Customer Provides
Colocation	Data center services including space, bandwidth, and power	Hardware and software
Colocation plus hardware platform	Data center services plus servers, routers, network storage, etc.	Software
Managed services	Onsite support and specialized services that may include shared or dedicated SAN and NAS storage options and data protection options, ranging from data backup management to disaster recovery	May or may not provide hardware, but does provide the software (although the service provider may monitor the process)
Managed hosting	In addition to managed services, automated on-demand provisioning and configuration for an IT infrastructure, plus may offer software (and/or storage) as a service	May or may not provide some of its own software

The first, and simplest, service level is *colocation.* A third party provides space and data center services such as power, and the customer provides its own hardware and software, which it administers itself. In other words, the customer is operating as if the service were still physically in its own data center.

At the next level, the third-party services provider provides not only the colocation services but also the hardware infrastructure, including servers and storage.

The next layer of service provision is *managed services,* where the service supplier provides onsite support and administration services and sometimes the hardware to run the software on (as well as specialized services), while the customer provides the software. In other words, the provider now adds to colocation the task of administering the service (backup/recovery, etc.).

Managed hosting provides the highest level of off-premises service provision, in which the service provider may take over all tasks to do with the service, as well as providing the software that carries out the service. Thus, managed hosting services may provide other capabilities, such as on-demand provisioning or software-as-a-service. The distinction between managed services and managed hosting is not precise, and the terms are often used interchangeably.

The customer therefore has a range of options to consider in choosing a service provider. In many cases, customers can begin with colocation and move to higher service levels as the provider proves reliable.

18.2.3   Services Point Toward Utility Computing

A key goal for IT organizations is to make their IT operations more like a fully-automated "electricity-like" utility, whether that be achieved internally (self-service or third-party-provided service), externally (third-party service), or using a mix of the two. Of course, that has been a goal for at least two decades, but once-fashionable ways of achieving "computing utility" such as the lights-out data center have not proved out in practice.

Utility computing requires improvements in both efficiency (doing things right) and effectiveness (doing the right things). (Thanks to late management guru Peter Drucker for the definitions of efficiency and effectiveness.) These twin concepts are critical in helping deal with the complexity of modern IT operations. Effectiveness should come first (because optimizing the wrong things makes no sense), followed by doing the right things as well as possible.

Much progress is being made (using consolidation and virtualization, among other things) in transforming the data center to be more effective and efficient. But in the near future, services are likely to play a larger role in this process—and that is where cloud computing comes in.

18.3   An Introduction to Cloud Computing

The latest trend in IT service provisioning is *cloud computing*. In a broad sense, cloud computing is the delivery of any IT resource as a *networked service*—that is, as service plus networked platform. Cloud computing can be provided publicly, i.e., through a hosted third-party service provider, or privately, i.e., IT provides self-service. A hybrid model, a combination of public and private services, is also a possibility. Thus, the point of cloud computing is that it unlinks service provisioning from a specific data center to deliver IT services, such as software-as-a-service (SaaS) or storage-as-a-service (STaaS), "in the cloud."

Since the definition is broad, looking at some of the key characteristics of cloud computing should bring cloud computing into clearer focus (Table 18.2).

18.3.1   Common Characteristics for Hosted or On-Premises Cloud Computing

As noted above, cloud computing can be delivered either externally, internally, or as a hybrid. A key characteristic of all of these delivery types is *on-demand* resource delivery.

One of the notable problems that IT organizations have long faced is that demand for resources (such as CPU cycles or storage) may fluctuate widely on a daily, weekly, or monthly basis, even though the long-term trend is increasing. There are sometimes periodic spikes in demand for resources. For example, retail stores may have higher requirements during the December holiday season. Monthly, quarterly, and annual financial closings may cause spikes in demand, as can periodic business intelligence (BI) query analyses.

The process of dealing with resource capacity spikes while delivering resources on demand is called *peak shaving*. The aim is to balance the resources of one application that has temporary high demands with one that has lower demands or less urgency. An external supplier has an advantage in doing this, as it typically has many more clients through multitenancy (i.e., more resources and more slack capacity) that it can balance.

Internally, there has to be a large enough pool of applications that their peaks offset each other. If not, then the cost of the cloud infrastructure becomes fixed and the internal provider has to "size the church for Easter

Table 18.2   Selected Key Characteristics of Cloud Computing

Characteristic	Comments
Hosted or on premises	
On-demand resource delivery	May or may not use virtualized resources, such as thin provisioning, but some form of automated provisioning needs to be provided.
Simple management	Installation and ongoing management should require little or no specialized IT support, as the need for end-client physical interaction with the physical infrastructure should be completely removed (off-premises) or greatly reduced (on-premises).
Scale-out performance and capacity	The service provider has to be able to expand quickly, linearly, and transparently without hitting a ceiling. Various terms—such as grid computing, distributed computing, and horizontally scaled computing—and various interpretations have been bandied about to account for this capability.
Highly automated	Self-healing and automatic load balancing are necessary for high availability without a lot of manual intervention.
Hosted	
Networked	Typically networked through the Internet, but some companies may need to use leased public lines.
Usage-based pricing	Customers pay only on a usage basis, but that may be on a monthly basis, with a minimum monthly floor, on a long-term commitment basis.
Multtenancy	Applications and resources may be shared among multiple customers while maintaining confidentiality.

Sunday" for a private or internal cloud. Then the private cloud is really only a standard IT infrastructure with virtualization on top, and the potential benefits of cloud computing vanish.

Administration of on-demand resource delivery should be easy. Obviously, this is an aim of all management, but in cloud computing it is a necessity because of the complexity of the balancing act. Note that simple management is not possible without a high degree of automation, but automation alone does not guarantee simple management. And, of course, all vendors claim that their product delivers simplicity, so claims of easy cloud on-demand resource delivery management should be examined carefully.

Scale-out performance and cost-effective capacity expansion are also necessary, in this case to make on-demand resource delivery economically feasible.

18.3.2   Characteristics of Hosted Cloud Computing

Obviously, users of hosted cloud computing have to access the cloud over an external network. (Internal cloud computing may very well have users that access over the Internet, such as remote and mobile workers, but local area networks [LANs] are mostly likely to be the focus of networking.)

The Internet is widely touted as the appropriate access vehicle for hosted cloud computing, and, indeed, the availability of the Internet makes a good deal of cloud computing possible—especially when the network costs are borne by someone other than the purchaser of the cloud computing service. However, the service provider still has to build some network costs into its price, e.g., for internal networking and for connecting to the Internet. Moreover, some large enterprises may opt for private leased lines to the hosted services provider in order to achieve higher bandwidth, security, and guaranteed service levels in such areas as response time and availability.

The Pricing Model Is Right for Cloud Computing

Although long-term contracts may be negotiated as part of a deal to use cloud computing, cloud computing typically uses a usage-based, pay-as-you-go subscription model.

Usage-based pricing has a big advantage over the long-term capital expenditure process that is typically used in-house for acquiring IT infrastructure resources. Usage-based pricing allows the buyer to classify expenditures for the service as operational expenses (OPEX) instead of capital expenses (CAPEX). OPEX represents a variable cash flow: Payments go down when fewer resources are used, and they go up when more on-demand resources are required. (Regular managed-service hosting can accomplish this as well.) There is every incentive to keep these expenses down on an ongoing basis, and these expenses tend to increase or decrease in line with other operational expenses, making the reason for in-contract increased expenses clear to all.

The biggest potential disadvantage of usage-based pricing is if ambiguous metrics are used to calculate charges (and there is no industry standard).

That could lead to an inability to predict costs before committing to the service. So service users have to be sure that they understand what they are getting into up front and be able to plan their costs within reasonable bounds.

With CAPEX, a large sum of money is allocated and committed up front to pay for expected demand for resources over a period of time. There is little incentive to cut resource usage (such as figuring out what data can be deleted to reduce storage capacity requirements), since the money has already been committed. However, if during the period of the contract an unexpectedly large increase in resources occurs, a business has to go back to the capital budget well (i.e., hat in hand to a capital expense-approving committee), which is likely to be an unpleasant experience.

Another risk of usage-based pricing is that the cloud computing supplier could raise prices at any time. Any business considering the use of a cloud computing supplier should aim, if possible, to negotiate a deal in which prices will remain stable for a specified period of time, and can rise only by limited amounts thereafter.

Sharing May Be Equal, but Sharing Must Be Separate

One way a cloud computing supplier can achieve cost savings is through economies of scale, such as by sharing resources, such as a storage array, among multiple clients. Sharing resources while giving each user the impression that it has sole use is called multitenancy. For example, the supplier can maintain an "executive" for each business customer, identifying the unique data and "state" of application processing of all end users from that company, while using code and data shared across customers for all other purposes. Multitenancy is a typical difference between SaaS suppliers and the older Internet (application) service providers.

A key issue for users of multitenancy cloud computing is security. Sharing resources in a compartmentalized manner is fine; unauthorized sharing of data is not. One client should not be able to view, corrupt, delete, or change in any way another client's data. Not only is this a confidentiality and business-risk issue, it is also a data preservation issue. Moreover, one client should not be able to affect the availability or responsiveness of another client's system by flooding an infrastructure component. If that were to occur, one client might be able to deny service to everyone else sharing that infrastructure component with it.

Today's requirements for long-term storage of business data mean that customers must handle archiving of shared data in concert with the supplier, in such a way that security and the data are preserved as necessary.

Supplier encryption of shared data, while a good idea, is not the only way to achieve adequate multitenancy security. Other approaches may focus on multitenant "firewalls" or access controls. Internal security personnel should be able to closely scrutinize how the supplier is carrying out its security mandate.

18.3.3   An Introduction to Software-as-a-Service

Software-as-a-service (SaaS) is a variation on an existing IT theme, namely, application service providers (ASPs). The basic premise in both cases is that a client business uses a software application that is accessible over a network at a third-party site. A key difference between SaaS and ASP, however, is that SaaS applications are designed to be accessed over the Web. That means that typically they are built from the ground up for Web access, and include Web service provider code and other aspects of a service-oriented architecture.

A SaaS application can very easily be offered as part of a cloud computing environment. SaaS shares the same basic characteristics as a hosted cloud, i.e., networking, usage-based pricing (although per-seat rather than transaction pricing may be used), and multitenancy. Consequently, the questions for data protection that need to be addressed are similar to those for cloud computing:

- How is multitenancy security of information handled?
- What kind of disaster recovery mechanisms are in place?
- How are governance issues with respect to legal holds, eDiscovery, and data retention policies, handled?
- How are compliance issues addressed?

Note that SaaS is only one model for delivering cloud services. Two other ways of delivering cloud services that are emerging are infrastructure-as-a-service (IaaS) and platform-as-a-service (PaaS). IaaS, such as servers and storage, is provided from the premises of a third-party services provider directly, as an on-demand service. In PaaS, the service provider hosts application development platforms and middleware. Client developers can code and deploy without have to interact with the underlying infrastructure. Whether these two terms and their definitions will catch on to match the acceptance of SaaS is debatable, as they are simply distinctions within managed hosting.

18.3.4 An Introduction to Storage-as-a-Service

Storage-as-a-service (STaaS), as its name implies, is a hosted services model for storage services and storage capacity. Although STaaS could theoretically be used as an alternative to a company's own entire storage infrastructure, often the data stored is targeted information. Thus, STaaS could be used for backup data, where the hosted target is either the primary site for backup or a disaster recovery site for backed-up data. Alternatively, the data could be a copy of "hold for legal purposes" information that could be used for eDiscovery purposes, or an alternative archive for old but still potentially useful information.

STaaS might be considered to be a variant of software SaaS, as the data only gets to the outsourced hosted site with the aid of software, such as backup/restore software; and supplier software often mediates between the business and the "servicized" storage. Moreover, STaaS can be provided as a cloud computing service, as part of an overall cloud computing environment. Therefore, the data protection challenges common to cloud computing and software SaaS also apply to STaaS.

18.4 Where IT Services Are Headed

The services model (in either the currently fashionable terms or in some evolutionary incarnation that has some different characteristics from existing models) is likely to become the dominant model for IT operations in the long term. Note the use of the words *dominant* and *long term*. Long term means that the dominance will not arrive in the next 2 to 3 years.

In particular, the "utility" model of providing services will prevail, in some form such as self-service (provided internally in a formalized manner), third-party services (either on premises or off premises), or a hybrid. Each business will move at its own pace in implementing a utility, and it is not clear yet what the long-term mix of in-house and third-party service will be. However, because of today's energy considerations in designing data centers, it is likely that most services will be to some degree centralized, localized, or regionalized at points of minimum energy consumption and/or energy costs—and some cloud computing suppliers appear to be farther along on this path than many businesses' in-house operations.

18.4.1 The Drivers for the Services Model

The perceived reason for moving to the services model is lower costs—whether measured by direct purchase costs, total cost of ownership

(TCO), or return on investment (ROI). If that were the only differentiator, then IT operations would have to compete with third-party services on the basis of cost and, except for the largest enterprises, the third-party services provider is likely to have an economies-of-scale edge as well as enterprise-caliber infrastructure that the individual client may not have.

An interesting short-term concern is the drive toward reduced energy consumption and/or reduced carbon footprint in the data center. One effect of this may be to drive services toward less capacity-bound, less regulated, less scrutinized, less centralized, sunk-cost hardware, such as off-premises, off-shore, line-of-business PC farms. In the long run, however, a level regulatory playing field will mean that services-provider economies of scale will apply to energy consumption as well.

The driving business dynamic for third-party services such as cloud computing is the core-versus-context concept, promulgated and brilliantly articulated by Geoffrey A. Moore, starting in his book, *Living on the Fault Line* (Harper Business, New York, 2000). Moore argues that core tasks are those whose outcome can directly affect the competitive advantage of the company; everything else is context. In most enterprises, context tasks chew up too much of the resources. Moreover, failure to do context tasks typically results in punishment of the personnel involved, but performing them better than necessary does not generate any rewards, especially competitively.

Consider payroll, for example. Not meeting payroll on time or experiencing payroll errors can have serious negative consequences, but doing payroll exceptionally well has no positive payoff (other than perhaps some small cost savings for efficiency improvements).

Moore argues that context tasks should be outsourced whenever feasible. An alternative is to create a "business within the business" to carry out the task in competition with third-party suppliers. Thus, for example, if the self-service cloud computing model is chosen and IT "governance" (software to allow the business to treat IT as a business unit) is implemented, this is really a form of context outsourcing, as the IT operations unit essentially becomes a business unto itself.

18.4.2 IT for Competitive Advantage Is Still Important

IT can still perform tasks that yield a competitive advantage, even with a fully deployed services model. IT competitive advantage once revolved around unique software code, such as the first airlines reservation system. And although code differentiation may be important in some cases, such as a Web-based company with unique software, one key to competitive business advantage today is better management use of similar software tools. Whether those tools are sales force management, customer relationship management, supply-chain management, business intelligence, or some other application, the policies, practices, procedures, and people that one company uses in contrast to another company—business process management—may still make a world of difference in terms of competitive advantage. Where those applications run is likely to be totally irrelevant. (Yes, there are some latency-dependent applications for which responsiveness is a key issue, but with ongoing increases in bandwidth and performance, these are becoming a vanishingly small part of the overall picture.)

Second, each company has a unique set of data, whether it is customer history data, CAD/CAM information, or some other unique set of information. Once again one company may do a better job of taking advantage of its information heritage than another company does. If so, competitive advantage typically results, such as when a company uses its unique customer data to identify customer buying patterns, uses these patterns to proactively suggest other products to its customers, and achieves major add-on sales and customer loyalty increases as a result.

Note that, from an IT perspective, core tasks themselves (such as running a business intelligence application to help set up a marketing campaign) are most likely to be retained in-house, but where an application runs, where data resides, and who owns physical servers and storage systems may very well be outsourced.

18.5   Data Protection Considerations in Using a Services Model

Although there are a number of potential inhibitors (business ones, such as control, and technical ones, such as security) to a services model that have to be addressed, no structural business or IT infrastructure barriers stand in the way of moving to a services model. (That the IT infrastructure is very complex is a description of what is, not what should be.) This is not to say that the transfer will take place, only that no fundamental structural barriers stand in the way of doing so.

Even though data protection services have specific needs compared to an overall services model, many of the key perceived inhibitors, such as security concerns, third-party "trust," and difficulties of migration, are the same. For some organizations, these inhibitors are nonexistent today; for others, these inhibitors will dissolve over time as new processes and technologies are put in place. The goal is to determine how to handle the inhibitors, so that a decision to go to a services model can be based on only truly fundamental decision criteria and so that, if a services model is deployed, the requirements for data protection will be met.

18.5.1 Data Protection Requirements When Using a Third-Party Supplier

One lens through which to view data protection requirements when using a third-party services supplier, such as cloud computing, is what Rudyard Kipling called his five serving men—who, what, how, where, when. These are the five basic questions that have to be answered to the satisfaction of a potential purchaser of third-party services before a contract is consummated (Table 18.3).

Table 18.3   Kipling's Five Serving Men Put to Work on Managed Services

Serving Man	Key Issues
Who	Ownership, security, confidentiality
What	Preservation, discovery, retention
How	Infrastructure, people
Where	Location
When	Availability, responsiveness

18.5.2 Businesses Cannot Abrogate Responsibility

Who owns physical assets (such as networks, servers, and storage) or the logical assets (such as software applications) is irrelevant from a data protection perspective. Who owns the *responsibility* for the data and the processes surrounding the use of that data is extremely relevant. And that responsibility remains with the business that purchases the outside services.

The principle to be followed (as has been stated previously) is that a business can *delegate tasks;* a business *cannot abrogate responsibility.* That means that a business cannot end its fiduciary and legal responsibilities simply by asking a third party to do its tasks (such as perform backup/restore functions).

Sarbanes-Oxley will once again serve as an illustration. The accuracy of financial statements has to be confirmed by the CEO and CFO of businesses that are subject to this compliance law. If production data fails, the financial data has to be restored to a verifiable true state from a backup copy.

If the third party backup supplier fails to do this, the CEO and the CFO are still on the hook.

Does this mean that a business should never entrust tasks to a third party? That is not true by any means. The CEO and the CFO are still also on the hook if the internal IT organization fails to perform as required. What needs to be done is that the business needs to ensure that the third party can perform its tasks at least as well as (if not better than) they can be performed internally.

And the results of that comparison may very well turn out to be in favor of the third-party supplier. Consider, for example, site infrastructure. Except for large businesses, a third-party service provider may have a more advanced data center. The Uptime Institute (www.uptimeinstitute.org) has defined four tiers for a data center infrastructure. Tier 4 is the highest level and is deemed to be fault-tolerant. No single point of failure exists. For example, electrically, two uninterruptible power supply (UPS) systems must be in place. This provides extra availability (99.995% uptime or less than half an hour of downtime per year), but at a cost. A large third-party services company that serves many clients can spread out the costs of Tier 4, but anything less than a large enterprise cannot afford the expense.

What businesses must do is exert *due diligence*. They must examine their internal capabilities and compare them to potential external options. They must keep records of what they have done. Courts are likely to be reasonable about a failure (such as the ability to restore information) if a business can demonstrate that it did all that any business could reasonably be expected to do to prevent the failure.

Businesses also have to make sure that the third-party supplier has the necessary controls in place for security and confidentiality. Internal data security personnel need to make sure that they are confident the necessary authentication, access, auditing, and any other necessary security mechanisms are in place, especially where confidentiality is an issue.

18.5.3   Businesses Must Get What They Need Done for Their Data

What data the third-party supplier manages for a business client, and the requirements for use and protection of that data, determine the level of capabilities that a third-party services provider has to deliver.

Data that may be considered to be put in the hands of a third party for managed services can have many characteristics, such as (but definitely not limited to):

- Class (production, protection, or test)
- Type (structured, semistructured, or unstructured)
- Scope (from a single application to all applications)
- Sensitivity (say, from publicly available to "top secret")
- Criticality (from "nice to have" to mission-critical)
- Timeliness (from relevant to "too old to apply")
- Service-level requirements (such as availability and responsiveness)
- Legal requirements (from not needed for compliance and governance reasons to mandatory for compliance and governance requirements)

Businesses have to group data into sets that have the same characteristics and then determine *what* has to be done from a *preservation, discovery, and retention* perspective. The business has to prepare the proper questions to ask the third-party supplier, and make sure that it gets the answer it needs. Some sample questions that illustrate what a business could ask include:

- What steps will be taken to ensure the complete recovery of any data within the specified service-level requirements?
- If eDiscovery is necessary, can the service supplier accommodate the use of software tools that are supplied by the client, or does the client have to use a tool supplied by the service supplier?
- Can the client business manage the retention process, such as for litigation holds, directly? This means applying fine granularity (specific records or files) retention policies rather than just specifying a retention period for an entire data set, as well as being able to change retention periods (subject to auditing constraints) as necessary.

18.5.4 How Does the Third-Party Supplier Deliver Its Capabilities

How a third-party services supplier delivers its brand of managed services is through its infrastructure and its people. Except for "help desk" support, the infrastructure is the most well-known element. However, the people are the key element—in design, implementation, management, and support. Definitely check out the people. On average, do they have the necessary skill sets to do the job, and does an acceptable customer service attitude permeate the service provider's entire organization? Note that customer service tends to be thought of as responsiveness to problem requests and a results-focused problem-resolution mentality. That is true, but equally important is what the provider is doing behind the scenes to make sure that a problem does not occur in the first place. The capabilities of all third-party suppliers are not equal, nor do they have to be the same.

The concept of a capability maturity model (CMM) is useful in understanding what level of infrastructure/people a business should seek. Although maturity models have proliferated in recent years, the concept was clearly promulgated first in the software arena by the Software Engineering Institute at Carnegie-Mellon University in Pittsburgh. A maturity model describes the maturity of the capabilities of selected business processes. The software model is divided into five levels: initial (chaotic), repeatable (process is repeatable), defined (institutionalized as a standard business process), managed (quantified process management and measurement takes place), and optimizing (deliberate ongoing process improvement).

The general rule is that the higher the level of maturity, the more sophisticated the process management and measurement capabilities are of the service supplier. The purpose is not to go only with a purported level-five supplier. For a business to consider a managed services supplier, the business has to answer two questions: (1) Is the external supplier at least at the maturity level that the in-house supplier of services is? (2) Is the external supplier at a maturity level to deliver the necessary capabilities that the in-house service is incapable of delivering?

The business has to develop questions that it can ask itself as well as the service-supplier candidates as to the level of capability maturity, such as what is the data center tier level and why are you at that level? The "why" question here is relevant, as an organization may not be at the highest level (because it cannot afford to be), but does understand its limitations and still has good processes in place.

Typically, a business will not consider a service supplier at a lower level of maturity than its own internal IT organizations, because that might expose the business to charges of irresponsibility if something should go wrong. However, exceptions for special situations might be made. For example, a business may need to back up data to a disaster recovery (DR) site through electronic vaulting, but it cannot afford its own DR site. A third-party supplier can be considered, if the service is good enough to meet the business's DR needs.

When in-house and third-party providers have equal levels of maturity and internal service levels are good enough, an assessment needs to be made between the financial trade-offs of the two approaches. When the outside supplier is superior, assurance has to be obtained that the level of

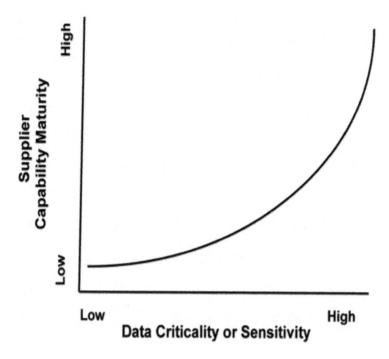

Figure 18.1   Match Supplier Capability Maturity with Data Requirements

outside-supplier capability maturity meets the business's data requirements (Figure 18.1).

Capability maturity is not just a matter of assessing the supplier's process management, but also what the supplier is able to agree to in terms of service-level agreements (such as availability and responsiveness), its ability to accept the use of customized software applications, and the like.

Smaller businesses are likely to be able to accept lower levels of capability (because those levels are better than what can be achieved internally) and use managed services more broadly, whereas larger businesses are likely to consider a transition to managed services (if appropriate) in a more staged manner.

18.5.5   The Need to Know Location for Data Protection Purposes

Someone once said that technology should be "mundane and opaque." *Mundane* here means that the technology should be easy to use, while *opaque* implies that someone else has to fix it if it breaks. But opaqueness has another dimension with regard to data managed by a third-party supplier, and that is location.

A third-party supplier may believe that *where* it keeps the data and how it moves it around is its business and not the client's. Unfortunately, that is not so. The supplier and the client have to agree on the transparency of the data's location in a physical/geographical sense, at all times.

The supplier has custody of the data, but it has no insight into the content of that data, i.e., what makes the data *information*. What information resides where, and where it is made available, is subject to government regulation. Note the data privacy (or data protection!) requirements of the European Union, for example. Also, some governments may not want certain data available in other governmental jurisdictions (because the other country might be able to seize the data).

Transparency is also necessary because, in the case of disaster recovery sites, a business needs to know that its managed services supplier maintains the necessary distance separation between primary and disaster-recovery sites. More generally, a client business may not want to bear the risk that its data is stored in a particular physical location, for whatever reason.

Encryption is not a magic bullet that can get around these constraints. So location may not be as important as in real estate, but it is still an important consideration for data protection that relies on third-party services.

18.5.6   The Need for Formal Service-Level Agreements

Some businesses may not need service-level agreements when dealing with a third-party services supplier. A cloud computing supplier may simply offer processing cycles and storage, with no guarantee of performance. As long as the business understands and can accept the risks it is taking (and the risks might be minimal for certain types of data), that is fine.

Many businesses need to know *when* their data will be *available* and *that it will meet* their needs. For that, formal service-level agreements (SLAs) are necessary—even though a business may never have formally specified them internally before (although SLAs may have been informal or implicitly understood).

The argument that utilities such as telephone, cable, and electrical service providers do not give service-level guarantees, so why should a managed service provider, does not hold up under examination. These utilities are regulated and are generally held to have achieved a high degree of "trust" from their users. Service providers have not yet reached that nirvana.

One reason for insisting on SLAs is that the services supplier that can offer an SLA is more likely to have the processes necessary to meet that SLA in place:

- To determine whether the agreements are likely to be met (4 nines availability cannot be met in a 3 nines data center)
- To measure actual versus expected results
- To proactively predict potential SLA-impacting events and fix them before the event occurs
- To be able to respond swiftly to minimize the damage from an SLA-impacting event should it occur

SLAs, and the processes to deliver on the SLAs, are therefore about the ability to monitor, report, analyze, and act in three time frames:

- *Real time* (technically "pseudo-real-time," for computer science purists)—the ability to detect issues and act while an event is happening
- *Ad hoc*—the ability to query over any time period and to be able to drill down on a number of dimensions to better understand what has happened and why
- *Longitudinal*—reporting over specified time periods, such as a week, month, quarter, and year

Note that some of these capabilities may be reserved for the service supplier for its own use, but the supplier should be able to communicate the type of capabilities that it has available.

The bottom line is that service suppliers that are able to commit to SLAs are higher up the capability maturity curve, because they have the more sophisticated processes needed to manage SLAs. SLA-impacting events can occur anyway, due to circumstances beyond the control of even the best suppliers, but having an SLA is like having an insurance policy. An insurance policy doesn't mean that no loss will ever occur, only that some remedy is in place to help alleviate the loss in one way or another.

And that remedy is, effectively, *best-effort* attempts by a capable organization to fix the problem. Suppliers that do a good job of solving problems that may occur (and that do an even better job making sure that they do not occur) are more likely to be trusted suppliers, because "best effort to correct a problem" is not just lip service, but ingrained in the supplier's way of doing business.

What about compensation? Skipping a monthly fee is not going to be very helpful for a company whose December holiday sales were cut in half by data availability and responsiveness problems. Still, a supplier's willingness to waive a fee is a useful gesture.

Suppliers are unlikely to risk larger amounts, however. A business may want to specify the conditions (such as the supplier not living up to expected and agreed-on processes for reasons that the supplier could have controlled) under which stronger penalties might apply. That would be a harder sale, but it might be necessary in certain cases.

18.6   Confronting the Issue of Control and Third-Party Services

The overarching issue regarding the use of third-party services is the perceived loss of control. *Control* means regulating, commanding, or directing the operation of a function subject to regulation by government bodies. *People control* is said to be about the ability to use rewards (such as bonuses or pay raises) or sanctions (such as no pay raise, suspension, or termination). *Resource control* is about the ability to allocate budget dollars.

From the perspective of whether to engage a managed services partner, these control issues are more or less irrelevant. Internally (and externally), hiring selection practices to find qualified people and the professionalism that those people bring to an organization are more important than short-term rewards and sanctions. Control measures cannot provide short-term fixes if the problem is that the wrong people were hired in the first place. As far as resources are concerned, the existing IT infrastructure cannot be "turned on a dime" even if (and that is unlikely) a large amount of budget dollars were made available. Turning a large oil tanker in a harbor takes a considerable amount of time, whereas a speedboat can turn very quickly. The IT infrastructure is much more like the large oil tanker.

Whenever the word *control* arises, this issue is usually really about *fear*. Control is about avoiding the nightmare scenarios that a business could conceivably face in dealing with its third-party services supplier when things go wrong:

- Proprietary lock-in if switching costs (to another supplier or back in-house) are too high
- Lack of responsiveness to perceived issues (from intermittent to sheer incompetence)
- Unexpectedly going out of business (including a sudden shutdown)
- Lack of ability to meet specialized needs, including customized software functionality

- Lack of transparency as the client loses the visibility to what is going on in the IT infrastructure that supports it, especially where IT components are shared with other clients.

These are serious concerns, because the data of a business and the ability to access and use that data for business purposes with the necessary application software is necessary for business continuity and the other issues relevant to data protection.

The first step in allaying these fears is to make sure that a trusted supplier is chosen. The word *partner* is often thrown around in these cases, and it's a fine sentiment, but remember that the trusted "partner" does not have the final responsibility.

A relationship of trust should be a necessary condition, but it is not a sufficient condition, for dealing with supplier risk. No matter how financially sound, functionally capable, and honest the trusted supplier is, risk always exists. For example, a trusted supplier may be bought out by another company that replaces management with people who do not have the same values and beliefs in service to the clients.

Therefore a business should develop a contingency plan and determine under what conditions it might be invoked. This plan is not likely to be perfect, and invoking it may be very painful. However, the service supplier might be involved in some way. For example, if service levels fall below expectations for a certain period of time, the supplier might be required to arrange for free migration of applications and data to an alternative supplier selected by the client. Suppliers will be reluctant to agree to something like this, but if they really want to be trusted, they have to demonstrate their trustworthiness in any negotiation process.

The important step here, however, is to honestly assess the business's risks and rewards from third-party service provision. A business that understands what its risks are may find that the risks are small and that the rewards (financially, and hopefully in service levels) of using a managed services supplier far outweigh the risks. And by taking this step, the business will have faced its fears and can no longer use the control issue as a smokescreen or as an excuse to dismiss the use of third-party services without exploring them.

Overall, control versus breadth versus scale are the key trade-offs. If a client is not large enough to duplicate a third-party provider's scale and breadth of capabilities including skill sets, then giving up control, including the ability to customize, may be worthwhile. If the client is large enough, then it may decide that giving up control, as well as the ability to customize, may not be worth giving away a function even though it is classified as context.

The business's evolution into a user of managed services, including cloud computing and both SaaS and STaaS, therefore depends on a careful analysis. And at the heart of that analysis is how the objectives for data protection will be met.

18.7   Key Takeaways

- A key use of the word *service* is that it is what a third-party service provider delivers. However, the use of the word in the context of Web services is also important—it is the software that third-party suppliers use to deliver services more automatically and cost-effectively.

- Putting custody of data and ownership of IT resources in the hands of a third-party service provider raises a number of questions related to data protection that have to be thought through carefully, including trust, security, and whether the service is "core" or "context."

- The real key to understanding cloud computing is that it can handle on-demand provisioning of resources with usage-based pricing. To deliver the expected cost advantages, however, a cloud computing supplier has to deliver for scale-out of performance and capacity and has to be highly automated.

- Software-as-a-service and storage-as-a-service are two specialized services that may be especially attractive parts of an overall cloud computing environment—but they are not the whole of cloud computing.

- Tasks that are important to a business, but are not core to its competitive differentiation, are candidates for being done through a services model. Those tasks are cost-based and not profit-based, so the services model must demonstrate cost advantages over the *status quo* approach.

- Data protection requirements with regard to the use of third-party supplier services must be considered carefully, because a business retains responsibility for data protection requirements even if carrying out those tasks has been delegated to a third-party service supplier. Service-level agreements and the capability maturity of the services provider must be taken into account.

- Businesses may be reluctant to relinquish control to a third-party services supplier. Businesses have to face their control concerns directly and make a decision on the use of third-party services on the basis of the risk–reward ratio of in-house compared to third-party.

Chapter 19

Other Considerations in Data Protection

19.1   What to Look for in This Chapter

- What the role of tiering is in data protection
- How each of the common tiers of storage differ in what they offer from a data protection perspective
- Why server virtualization raises some challenges for data protection
- What has to be done to achieve high availability in a virtualized environment
- What needs to be understood to backup/restore effectively in a virtualized environment
- What needs to be done to do disaster recovery properly in a virtualized environment
- What is master data management and how it reinforces the need for effective data governance
- How data can be protected while at the same time helping the process of "going green"

19.2   From Flash Computing to Tape—The Role of Tiering in Data Protection

Recall from the discussion in Chapter 6 on information lifecycle management (ILM) that tiering is the separation of storage devices into classes according to the characteristics of the storage devices themselves. The performance of different classes of storage devices (in the sense of speed) tends to correlate with the cost per unit of storage. That makes sense: All other things (such as availability and reliability) being equal, higher-performance devices would otherwise drive lesser-performing devices off the market if the cost per unit of storage were equivalent, because the extra performance would be "free."

One implication, then, is that different business needs require the use of different tiers of storage. Otherwise, one tier of storage would predominate over the others.

Note that although tiering may be used in conjunction with ILM, tiering and ILM are not synonymous. During different periods of its lifecycle, a piece of information is put into a logical pool of storage in which all the other pieces of information are homogeneous from a quality-of-service (QoS) perspective. Recall that the logical pool is then mapped to a physical tier of storage device for actual placement. Multiple logical pools of storage may reside on the same physical storage device. Even though the performance (in this case, speed and availability) are the same for different pools, each pool has one or more characteristics that differentiate it from the other pools—for example, one pool may be data-retention-managed while another is not.

Numbering schemes may vary, but we will consider four tiers of storage—0, 1, 2, and 3—as an illustration. Tier 0 consists of solid-state *drives* (SSDs) (alternatively, solid-state *devices* or solid-state *disks*). Although variations are available, there are basically two basic types of SSDs. The first type is based on random-access memory (RAM) using Dynamic Random Access Memory (DRAM) chips. The second type is based on NAND (for "not AND" Boolean logic elements on gate array chips) architecture for flash memory. Tier 1 consists of the highest-performance (speed and availability) hard disk drives (HDDs), i.e., Fibre Channel (FC) and serial SCSI (SAS) drives. Tier 2 consists of serial ATA (SATA) drives. Tier 3 consists of tape. Although the tiers have been discussed before (without assigning them tier numbers), reviewing their strengths and weakness in concert should help put each in overall perspective.

A business may also have optical drives and may consider optical as Tier 3 and tape as Tier 4. Or a business may have a MAID platform and consider that a tier as well. However, a simple set of four tiers will serve to illustrate the points (see Table 19.1).

The obvious question is why start with Tier 0? Why not consider that Tier 1? The reason is that Tier 1 storage early on was seen as the HDD storage where the information that supports the most important business applications resides.

19.2.1   Tier 0 SSDs

Although both SSD products are relatively high-performance and high-cost devices relative to the other tiers, each product is architecturally (and therefore data protection-wise) different from the other.

Table 19.1   Sample Set of Storage Tiers

Tier	Type	What It Delivers	Key Benefit
0	SSD—DRAM-based or flash-based	Low latency and high transaction rates for performance-sensitive data	Responsiveness in high-IOPS environments
1	FC, SAS	A blend of performance and capacity deigned to meet the needs of traditional business applications	Balance of performance and capacity
2	SATA	Online high-capacity storage for non-performance-sensitive business applications	Online storage at the best per-unit cost
3	Tape	Nearline or offline bulk capacity storage	Both logical and physical preservation naturally for bulk storage at lowest cost

DRAM-based devices provide higher performance but at higher cost than equivalent-capacity flash-based drives. The trade-off is that DRAM-based drives are volatile; if the power goes off, the data goes away. Since that is not good from the perspective of preserving data, battery backup has to be provided as an electrical life-support system. If main power (and yes, the supposedly uninterruptible power supply [UPS]) fails, the battery backup has to provide power long enough for the DRAM-based drive to stage (i.e., migrate its data) to another storage device. If that other device is a Tier 1 HDD, the cost is not particularly high, but the time to restore may not meet high-availability service-level agreement objectives. If the other device is a flash drive, the cost will be higher, but the restore time will be much more acceptable. Actually, what is becoming more popular is that DRAM-based devices are being used as front-end caches to flash drives.

However, flash drives often operate independently. Although flash drives can have a high mean time between failures (MTBF), some concern has been raised about wear mechanisms—i.e., too many writes wearing out particular cells. Methods generally referred to as "wear leveling" have been developed to deal with this potential problem. Wear leveling is an algorithm internal to the SSD that distributes writes more evenly; this means, for example, that a revised file may be written to less frequently used cells rather than being rewritten (mostly) to cells that had stored the previous version of the file. In addition to wear leveling, error-correcting techniques that have long been used with HDDs are used to correct bit errors that are inherent to NAND flash. Finally, "bad block management" algorithms isolate bad "blocks" (blocks with so many worn-out bits that they cannot be corrected with error-correction software) from further use. These drives that focus on supporting business applications are often called enterprise-class flash drives, to distinguish them from the garden-variety flash memory devices.

RAID can be used by using multiple flash drives as a RAID group. RAID 5 is likely to be the chosen RAID. Rebuild times are likely to be fast (i.e., less than an hour) so the risk of a second failure is minute; thus RAID 6, which provides for two drive failures, is overkill. So is RAID 1, since the mirroring that is RAID 1 doubles the number of flash drives needed and hence doubles the cost.

SSDs can serve as independent drives or as part of an array.

Flash Drives in an Array

Flash drives that are in an array are treated exactly like any other random access disk drive and may very well coexist with Tier 1 and Tier 2 drives. This means that flash drives fit smoothly into the management of the existing storage array environment. The customer is not forced to make changes or add things to the environment.

From a data protection perspective, this is invaluable. The same backup/restore software that protects other drives in the array can also protect flash drives. The same remote mirroring software that is used to protect at least selected drives in the array can now use flash drives as a source for the data that is to be mirrored. The only caveat is that the target drives should also be flash drives, in order to prevent significantly degraded (and likely SLA-breaking) performance in the event that the target devices have to be used because the remote site is required to take over production responsibilities.

Independent SSDs

SSDs can be located independent of any particular array. This strategy creates flexibility, such as being able to manage data from two or more applications that might have resided on two or more arrays. However, from a data protection perspective, a couple of challenges arise. With flash drives in an array, the decisions as to what backup/restore software to use and what should be the target of the backups (say, a VTL or tape library) have already been made for Tier 1 storage, and flash drives can piggyback on what Tier 1 storage uses. For independent SSDs, the decision has to be made on which backup/restore software to use and what should be the target for backups. Implementing the backup/restore process may therefore require some more work (because IT may have to choose between two existing software products, and the existing target for backups may not be able to handle a new, unanticipated workload).

This work is much harder when disaster recovery is taken into account. With an array, one can simply add an enterprise-class flash drive group at each of the source (local) and target (remote) sites and, through a storage software management console, include the new devices and tell them what to do from a mirroring or replication perspective. The array-based software already exists, and flash drives are simply a variation on a theme.

The same is not true for independent drives. Software to manage mirroring or replication between two sites has to be evaluated, selected, paid for, installed, and then managed. Not only is that expensive, it is a lot of work—and work that cannot take advantage of what has already been learned (since it is unlikely that the array software can be used, a whole new process and a whole new user interface have to be learned).

As a side note, secure data deletion on a flash drive takes only a few minutes, compared to much longer on a HDD. This factor has only specialized applicability, but when speed is needed, flash drives have a great advantage over HDDs.

Overall, the words for Tier 0 storage are *significantly enhanced responsiveness.* Sheer performance in the sense of IOPS (input/output operations per second) is one measure. However, the application response time overall is likely to improve even if the IOPS of a larger number of hard disks is equal to that of a smaller number of Tier 0 storage.

19.2.2   Tier1 FC and SAS

Although there are technical differences between using FC and SAS drives, from a data protection perspective they can be considered functionally equivalent. Tier 1 drives face some erosion of their place in the random-access storage firmament through some losses to Tier 0 for performance reasons when performance is paramount, and to Tier 2 drives which have good enough performance but lower cost per unit of storage. Note that for historical reasons, applications used Tier 1 storage even though there was no availability or performance justification for doing so.

However, businesses are likely to be reluctant to move mission-critical applications that are running well on Tier 1 storage to another tier. Performance may be important, but, even though the performance may be satisfactory on Tier 2, the savings in moving to Tier 2 may not be worth the risk.

Tier 1 storage is the proving ground for storage, data, and information management technologies, and the newest functionalities as well as the most mature ones are likely to reside on Tier 1 storage before becoming available on another tier.

The word for Tier 1 storage, then, is *solid*. Tier 1 storage has good performance and proven data protection preservation technologies.

19.2.3   Tier 2 SATA

SATA drives are becoming the workhorse HDDs for applications for which storage performance is not a gating factor. Surprisingly, this includes more mainstream applications than many people might have anticipated. More and more, active changeable production data is likely to reside on SATA disks. SATA disks are also likely to hold much, if not all, active archiving data as well. In addition, SATA is typically the target storage for disk-to-disk backup methods. In fact, Tier 0 SSD and Tier 2 SATA storage are likely to continue to reduce the need for Tier 1 storage—perhaps significantly.

However, there are two qualifiers to that assumption. The first is that each new generation of SATA storage tends to double in size, but the access speeds (in terms of revolutions per second) remains constant. At some point, if there is enough data, even relatively few accesses per some unit of storage is still going to run into performance constraints. This will mean that data that has not hit the performance wall will move to the newest generation and the other data will remain behind—sort of one SATA for performance and one SATA for capacity.

The other qualifier is availability. SATA drives are not seen as reliable as Tier 1 drives. While that is true, SATA drives are really quite reliable in an absolute sense. However, dual-parity RAID, such as RAID 6, is likely to become mandatory because the rebuild times will become longer and longer and there is too much capacity in a single disk to want to have to restore it from tape.

That provides for physical operational recovery. For disaster recovery purposes, dated-replication techniques are more likely to be used than either synchronous remote mirroring or asynchronous remote mirroring. Performance-critical data requirements tend to imply time-critical restore times as well—and both those mirroring methods are for time-critical information. Data on SATA drives is not as likely to be time-critical

Overall, SATA drives are designed to provide adequate responsiveness and satisfactory availability at the best price per unit of storage for random-access devices. Preservation is of course fine physically, but also logically, using snapshots on the drives themselves or working in conjunction with a continu-ous data protection (CDP) appliance (which is likely to use SATA drives).

19.2.4   Tier 3 Tape

Tape is a special example of a tier, because tape media uses a sequential-access rather than a random-access method to retrieve data. A principal use of tape is for making data protection copies of production data. Each piece of media stands physically on its own. If a tape is physically destroyed or becomes unreadable for any reason, an exact copy of the information is not likely to exist on another tape in its totality, but rather would have to be reconstructed from two or more other pieces of tape media.

Tape is useful in operational recovery for restoring from an unrecover-able disk system failure (if a disk-based system such as a virtual tape library is not used). Tape is useful in disaster recovery as individual cartridges can be transported manually to a disaster recovery site.

Tape has a limited role on the production side of the house, however, because it can only serve for archiving—not for active changeable data. But tape can serve a role in archiving. A deep archive is a tape copy of produc-tion data that is kept for historical or legal reasons and that one hopes will never again need to see the light of day. Regaining the ability to use the data requires not only restoring the data to a disk, but also ensuring that an application that can interact with (such as read) the data is available.

Tape can also play a role in some types of active archiving—say, where large bulk files (video or medical images) are rarely accessed. Disk needs to be used as cache in front of the tape in order to ensure that the files that are retrieved can be used in an online mode.

Overall, tape is not used when responsiveness is a concern. Availability has sometimes been raised as a possible concern, but for practical purposes, that concern is a chimera. The primary data protection objective that tape enables is preservation, from both a physical and a logical perspective.

19.3   The Impact of Server and Storage Virtualization on Data Protection

Here is a simple fact: The speed at which physical servers run has increased more rapidly than CPU cycle-devouring complexity in operat-ing system and application software. Of course, software has become more useful and powerful in terms of what are called functionality points. Also, smart planning on even the largest physical servers can ensure that CPU processing power is properly utilized. However, many organizations have found that they have a large number of physical servers for which CPU-utilization is very low, because the servers can manage most software with relatively few cycles of processing power.

19.3.1   An Overview of Server Virtualization

Server virtualization solves this problem of a very expensive IT infrastructure investment in physical servers that are severely underutilized. In server virtualization, a hypervisor, which is a control program called a virtual machine monitor, enables multiple "guest" operating systems to run on a host computer, i.e., physical server, concurrently, as what are called virtual machines. Server virtualization is "*déjà vu* all over again," as it has been available on mainframes for decades, but its use on open systems servers is of more recent origin.

The guest operating systems are called virtual operating systems because, although they seem to be in overall control, as is the prerogative of an operating system in normal circumstances, the hypervisor is actually controlling the software processes at the highest level. The fact that the guest operating systems are virtual rather than real (in an overall control sense) gives rise to the term *server virtualization*. This term is sometime shortened to simply "virtualization," but this is misleading because virtualization is a general concept that can be applied in many contexts, including network and storage as well as servers.

What the hypervisor does as a virtual operating system is create a layer of software abstraction between the workload (which are the guest operating systems and the software applications that run on each operating system) and the underlying physical server hardware. What that means is that, if the hypervisor can run on a piece of physical host server hardware and if the hypervisor can manage a guest operating system as a virtual machine, anywhere the hypervisor can run, so can the guest operating system. This decouples the virtual machine workload from the actual server hardware to create *hardware independence*. And hardware independence is important when virtual machines have to be migrated from one brand of physical server to another brand of physical server or, from a data protection perspective, a virtual machine on a different physical server has to retrieve data for data recovery purposes.

Server virtualization thus enables multiple operating systems to run on the same host server, which enables better use of CPU cycles. The result is that fewer physical servers are needed, with the attending economic benefits. In addition, hardware independence delivers greater flexibility in being able to use existing disparate physical servers more efficiently.

19.3.2   Server Virtualization and Data Protection

It is not surprising, then, that server virtualization has attracted a lot of attention. However, server virtualization also has some implications for data protection that have to be addressed.

- *High availability*—Packing more into each physical server raises the stakes as far as availability is concerned, because more applications are at risk.
- *Operational recovery*—Better CPU and IO bandwidth utilization in each physical server is great, but presents a resource challenge for backup/recovery processes.
- *Disaster recovery*—Virtualization enables hardware independence, and that can be a boon for disaster recovery if it is done correctly.

Server virtualization vendors distinguish themselves by how they deal with these issues. In addition, other vendors provide complementary software functionality that can extend or improve on the capabilities the server virtualization vendors offer to deal with each of these issues. The number of potential options for dealing with data protection issues is limited only by the imagination of the vendors (and many have been very creative in this area), but the basics of dealing with each issue can be addressed. First, however, storage virtualization, as a complement to server virtualization, needs to be introduced.

Introducing Storage Virtualization

Remember that data protection is about information, and that information resides on storage. When the three major data protection issues are addressed, storage has to be taken into account as well as servers, which process the information on behalf of users. And that can lead to the use of data management or storage management software that can complement the software on the server virtualization side of the house.

Storage virtualization can also play a role in dealing with that storage management and data management software. Storage virtualization masks the complexities of physical storage from an administrator's perspective. Storage virtualization may be used in a number of ways. Nondisruptive (i.e., no impact on running production applications) migration of data from one array to another is one example. Another form of storage virtualization is thin provisioning, sometimes called virtual provisioning, which enables more efficient space utilization in an array with less storage administrator overhead.

Storage virtualization may enable storage hardware independence. That seems quite impressive, because even though the underlying disk drives on different storage brands are the same, the storage architectures, including storage controllers and the use of different algorithms for the management of the front-end cache that enhances the performance of an array, are different. Moreover, storage vendors put their own stamp on their storage platforms with storage management software (for management functions, such as workload balancing) and data management software (for taking snapshots and managing replication and mirroring software). Storage virtualization can also enable better management of tiers of storage by providing better alignment between the different tiers of applications and the storage resources servicing those applications.

Storage virtualization should be kept in mind and examined, as appropriate, as a complement to server virtualization in attacking any one of three principal data protection issues—high availability, operational recovery, or disaster recovery.

19.3.3   How Virtualization and High Availability Go Together

When more application "eggs" are stored in one physical server "basket," the need to manage the "basket" more carefully becomes apparent. So high availability, at perhaps the five 9's level, (no more than a few minutes of unplanned downtime per year), is essential. One way of achieving this is to have a standby physical server that emulates a production physical server. In fact, provisioning other physical servers can also help with load balancing as well as providing a measure of protection against potential physical hardware failures.

However, restarting virtual machines from a standby server is only possible for physical problems, such as recovering from the loss of a server or disk storage. Logical problems—such as application, operating system, and database failures—cannot be addressed this way. These kinds of problems occur within the virtual machine itself and may result in the infamous "blue screen."

One way to reduce the risk of this problem is to use frequent snapshots or continuous data protection. These technologies provide the ability to recover more quickly.

Another possibility is to have software technology that monitors all of the critical components of the applications on each virtual machine. The software should be able to detect any failure in a server (either physical or virtual) and seamlessly failover to the alternative system. The software should be clever enough to identify problems or any form of performance degradation within an application that is running on a virtual machine. Moreover, all the hardware, network infrastructure, operating systems, and any software related to the server virtualization process should also be continuously monitored. Attempts should be made to resolve any problem that occurs. Only when all automatic preemptive solutions been exhausted should a switchover to the alternative system take place. That failover should be transparent to users—for example, they should not have to restart their client applications.

What is important about the process is that it is not just reactive; it is predictive and proactive. Some types of failure are not instantaneous but result from degradation that becomes progressively worse, so predictive software should be able to detect these situations. In some cases, software can take corrective action and thus be proactive. (Of course, there are situations where software cannot take action by itself, but then alerts can be issued to the parties responsible for maintenance.)

Since failover is automatic and transparent, why are these predictive and proactive capabilities important for improving availability? The answer is that if a problem is due to something like corruption in a database, failover only moves the problem to another machine. Do not forget that high availability is about more than solving physical problems.

Note that this solution may be useful at one physical site as a high-availability solution, but it could also be useful at a remote site as a disaster recovery solution.

19.3.4   How Virtualization and Operational Recovery Go Together

One of the keys to operational recovery is the effectiveness of the backup/restore process. A server virtualization environment presents extra challenge in terms of running the backup/restore process.

The good news about server virtualization is that the host physical CPU/IO bandwidth utilization is now high. This means that fewer dollars have to be spent on physical servers, which is a good thing. The flip side, however, is that there is not much CPU/IO bandwidth left for server-based applications. The available CPU cycles on a physical serer hosting a hypervisor and a number of virtual machines is limited and likely to be less than 20%. Consequently, there are simply not enough CPU cycles left to run any additional backup load on the server.

Typically, what should happen is that a backup agent accesses each of the virtual machines to determine what data needs to be backed up. The backup agent then sends data to a software-based backup server on either a virtual or a physical machine. The backup server writes the data to a tape library or virtual tape library.

That sounds fine in theory. In reality, the extra workload on the physical server would be high and could significantly degrade the response time of applications running on the virtual machines. Moreover, the virtual machines might have to be shut down during the backup process in order for the backup process to get all the data at a consistent point in time, which would affect the availability of the virtual machines. That might not be a problem if the virtual machines are not used 24 hours a day—the old nightly backup routine—but it becomes more difficult as 24/7 availability of applications on virtual machines becomes more and more of a requirement.

One common method of solving the overload problem is by installing the backup software on a host proxy server. Yes, that requires an additional physical server, but it can be sized to only what is necessary to run the backup processes. A software utility creates a virtual machine snapshot of the data on the storage that the virtual machines use. The backup software can use this snapshot as a consistent point in time from which to take a backup. The backup server can copy the data from disk storage to a tape library or virtual tape library without any impact on the virtual machines (with the possible exception of impact on the network). However, for the length of the backup, all new writes have to go to a redo log file rather writing on the files where the changes occur as is normally done. That is necessary to provide "crash consistency" (files should not be changed while a backup is occurring). When the backup is completed, the changes in the redo log file have to be written to the files to which changes need to be applied. Although this approach is crash-consistent, transactional integrity for applications themselves is not guaranteed. Also, the redo logs may cause significant performance overhead for the virtual machines.

One alternative is to use an application-aware snapshot. An application-aware snapshot knows what an application needs to ensure transaction integrity. And the way that an application-aware snapshot is taken eliminates the need for redo logs that a virtual machine snapshot requires. Thus the virtual machines can continue to write as normal while a backup is being taken, and there is no impact from redo logs. Thus the backup/restore process can continue to be done using virtual machines, but it needs to be thought through carefully.

19.3.5   How Virtualization and Disaster Recovery Go Together

Recall that, to provide disaster recovery (DR) capabilities, a business has to have both a primary local site as well as a remote secondary site, known as a disaster recovery site. In the event of a disaster, the disaster recovery site takes over the workload responsibilities from what had been the primary site. To do that, the DR site has to have a copy of data available on storage, but also the servers to run the necessary applications, and the networking capabilities to restore service to users.

For the most part, each site has to be a virtual replica of the other site. This means that not only do the servers in both locations have to be the same brand, but so does the storage (as well as the storage capacity). This is a serious limitation. If a company has two data centers and each acts as the DR site for the other, their hardware infrastructures must resemble each other closely, and that can be a planning challenge if the application workload of each is different. If a company uses a third-party service supplier, colocation is one answer, but it requires a lot of equipment. Using an on-demand subscription service is not a likely solution, because the third-party service supplier will be making its own server and storage hardware purchase decisions.

Virtualization has relaxed this constraint. A physical server or virtual machine running at the local site can be copied onto a virtual instance at the remote DR site. Although storage virtualization is not mandatory, storage virtualization improves flexibility in the creation, control, and nondisruptive migration of storage volumes from a local to a remote site (where heterogeneous storage can be used).

A technology refresh, where older servers and storage are replaced by newer ones, does not have to be disruptive either. The local site can go through the refresh, but there is no reason that a remote DR site would have to undergo the same transformation. If a colocation site is used, the older technology might be moved to the DR colocation site. If an on-demand third-party service provider is used, the technology refresh at the local site will not upset the arrangement.

High-availability strategies, such as the one discussed earlier, might also be applied to a DR solution.

19.4   Master Data Management and Data Protection

Managing risk, when data protection plays a demonstrated essential role, is a key mission-defending strategy of any business. For-profit businesses also have two key mission-enabling strategies: achieving and sustaining a competitive advantage; and managing costs efficiently and effectively. How well a business executes these latter two strategies in concert dictates its financial viability (also subject to managing the risk management strategy). All three strategies are dynamic—which means that continual improvement on all three strategic dimensions is a necessity.

19.4.1   Referencing a Couple of Key IT Initiatives

Since information systems are integral to all three strategies, information systems have to evolve and grow as well. New approaches to IT governance and software development are being applied in many organizations to deal with this evolution. For example, organizations are employing the concepts of the Information Technology Infrastructure Library (ITIL) and service-oriented architectures (SOAs) to deal with IT growth.

ITIL is a framework of best practices that facilitate the delivery of information technology as a service. Service support—such as incident management, change management, and configuration management—and service delivery—such as service-level management and capacity management—are among the many details covered in the ITIL framework. ITIL intersects with data protection in a number of ways, including availability management under service delivery and the separate topic of security management, where security means to be safe from risk. Recognizing that the ITIL framework (and the books that describe the framework) is the work of the government of the United Kingdom leads to an understanding of why the term "security management" is used instead of "data protection" (in the UK, data protection is the same as data privacy). Although ITIL was not designed to incorporate all the aspects of data protection that have been discussed, practitioners of ITIL should be able to apply the basic principles to data protection as well.

SOAs enable IT software and resources to be made available to participants in a network as independent services that are accessed in a standardized way without knowledge of the underlying platform implementation. The value proposition of SOAs is more rapid deployment of new IT-based business capabilities while using existing IT infrastructure wherever possible. SOAs are in keeping with the increasingly used IT strategy of being primarily a service provider. Even though SOAs are not directed specifically at data protection, SOA implementations should keep in mind data protection concerns, notably those relating to information security.

19.4.2   An Introduction to Master Data Management

Both of those initiatives have received a lot of attention. But there is another initiative that focuses on data. From a data perspective, a key focus is now on master data management (MDM). *Master data* is the authoritative copy of a data item or record. Because of the proliferation within a typical firm of systems recording vital data about customers, products, and resources, users often find that relevant copies of this data are inconsistent, incorrect, or unnecessarily unavailable. As a result, defining master data, managing it, and, if necessary, synchronizing the master with other data copies, is now important to the success of most medium- and large-scale organizations' strategies for mergers/acquisitions, using information for competitive advantage, and cutting storage costs associated with redundant data.

MDM sounds simple, but, in practice, it can be incredibly complex. For example, consider a customer purchase of a product. The transaction itself is stable; it does not change. However, the ways in which it is stored in various parts of the organization may vary widely, and the needs of each may diverge over time.

Consider the business functions of marketing, manufacturing, and sales. Marketing may classify the product in a product category that could change over time. Manufacturing may not use the same product categories that marketing uses (because it focuses on the bill of materials that are necessary to build a product, whereas marketing focuses on groupings that make sense from, say, an advertising perspective). Sales wants to know what sales region the transaction took place in, and sales regions may be reconfigured (such as a change of sales territories to take into account a new salesperson). Now add new data formats from organizations that have been acquired or merged, differing data formats implemented in existing systems by individual programmers and not documented, data input formats that fail to capture needed data about the transaction, and different language and cultural conventions embedded in the data across a global company. Recollect the compliance-related discussion of data quality, including consistency. Then the potential for a Tower of Babel inability to translate not only between functions—say, marketing and manufacturing—but also within functions, say, sales, is very real—and the result is lack of data accuracy and consistency.

MDM is sometimes divided into operational MDM and analytic MDM (as well as other variants such as collaborative MDM, which will not be discussed). Operational MDM includes the heartbeat systems of a business. For a manufacturing business, that might include enterprise resource planning, customer relationship management, supply chain management, and financial systems.

Analytic MDM includes the business intelligence (BI) and data warehousing systems of the enterprise—and, increasingly frequently, access to operational systems as well. Whereas operational MDM coordinates a loose collection of operational data, analytic MDM provides data consistency for an enterprise-wide consolidation or view of all data, operational, historical, or extraorganizational, that is used for data mining and decision making. Thus, while the overall database of analytic data does not change as frequently as an operational database, in order to maximize query performance, individual data items capture changes from more data copies, and therefore change more frequently than operational data master items.

Data warehousing can provide a nice starting point for both types of MDM. This is because data warehousing typically carries out "data cleansing" that creates a comprehensive, accurate, consistent master record. However, data warehousing is a one-way street; it does not enforce accuracy or consistency on the operational or other data sources from which it gets its data, nor does it typically record changes immediately. Thus, for operational MDM, synchronization and cleansing must still be done, and likewise for operational data accessed directly from BI.

Overall, biting off all of MDM at once may be more than a business can chew. A business might want to start off with customer data integration (CDI). CDI is the combination of process and technologies that is necessary to integrate and standardize the representation of customers as data entities across multiple systems, applications, and databases. CDI can feed into MDM.

MDM requires something else, too, and that is data governance.

19.4.3   MDM Architecture

Before we talk about the interplay between MDM and data governance, it is important to understand the nature of the information architecture in MDM. When an organization implements MDM, it is faced with a fundamental question: What do we do about all those data copies?

There are three general answers, each appropriate to a particular situation. The first is to insist that the master data record is the only data record, stored with other master data records and with metadata describing them in a master data repository. This often requires rewriting many applications to access the master data record, and means that transaction performance, and downtime or overload on the central repository's system, are real concerns.

The second answer is to leave the data copies where they are, but change them to a common format. Then, changes to local copies must be synchronized with changes to the central master record. Performance and downtime, both locally and at the central site, are a significant concern. The third answer is a "mixed" solution, where some copies are centralized and some left where they are.

This choice of information architecture means that MDM may "force the hand" of data governance in deciding the degree of centralization of data, say, for security purposes. However, as a result of implementing any of these three architectures in the ways described above, MDM offers several features useful to data governance:

1. An easily-accessible repository of information about all critical-data-item copies in the organization and their location

2. Full accuracy, consistency, and up-to-dateness of critical data items

3. A central data-security and data-compliance enforcement locus

4. A decrease in the need to back up local data

5. Enforcement mechanisms and data stewards to ensure ongoing common-format compliance

19.4.4   Master Data Management and Data Governance

Advocates of master data management tend to stress the need for data governance. Data governance has the same mantra as data protection. It consists of the people, process management, and technology required to manage and safeguard the data assets of a business.

Recognizing that data governance, as well as MDM, is a business issue and not a technical issue is paramount. Without the full and complete participation of data stewards of all stripes and varieties across all business functions in a cross-organizational collaborative effort that yields a coherent and structured policy-making process, data governance (and, by extension, MDM) is doomed to failure. Participation requires an executive commitment to populate the data governance stage with the necessary players and to keep them there for the requisite effort. Data governance then provides a superstructure on which MDM can be built, and vice versa.

Data governance, however, is more than just doing MDM (although MDM may be a core component of any successful data governance effort). Data governance is not only about improving the quality of data; it is also about data availability, data preservation, and data confidentiality. Note that MDM tends to be about business-critical data, which is mostly structured data that is in databases (relational or otherwise). Spreadsheets, semistructured information such as e-mails and word processing documents, and unstructured information such as graphics and images, are not likely to be covered. Recent surveys suggest that more than 50% of the data of the typical organization, even after MDM, has neither a single nor a master copy.

Still, MDM can play a key role in data protection issues, such as risk management and compliance. As noted in the previous section, implementation of MDM dictates the use of a repository where master data and the metadata that defines its common format is maintained. Having a single source of master data makes it easier to protect that data from both a preservation and a confidentiality perspective. Moreover, from a chain-of-custody perspective, tracing the provenance (i.e., origin) as well as the history of changes is easier.

The key takeaways therefore are simple. Although MDM can work in conjunction with and support some data protection efforts, the primary justification for MDM lies in its ability to aid in improving an enterprise's competitive position and in managing its costs better by decreasing the redundancy, inaccuracy, and inconsistency of data. MDM requires a strong data governance effort as a necessary condition for success, and data governance can leverage the features that MDM provides. MDM and data protection together reinforce the mandate for a strong data governance effort.

19.4.5   The Need for a Data Governance Maturity Model

The concept of maturity models was introduced in the discussion of third-party service providers, but the concept can easily be extended to data governance. The rationale for doing so is very simple: An organization needs to know where it is now and what it would take to improve its process maturity to each higher level in turn. Identifying resources—people, time, and money—as well as what can be expected as results at each level of the maturity model is essential not only for initial executive commitment to provide the initial resources, but also to ensure continued commitment over time. Any major effort—whether for MDM or compliance or anything else—can seem interminably slow with no results until the end (and perhaps not even immediately after the end).

A way to think about moving along the maturity model is from undisciplined (i.e., ungoverned) to fully disciplined (i.e., fully governed) in a number of stages. But, if an organization is currently in an undisciplined state, the organizational culture (which tends to reward certain types of behaviors) and the comfort-zone behaviors of individuals are likely to revolve about keeping the equilibrium state, which is one of a lack of discipline. This problem is not necessarily an intractable one, but it is one that requires careful planning and a lot of hard work to overcome. Old habits are hard to break, but without doing so, data governance (and any attendant activities such as MDM and data protection) are likely either to fail in total (MDM) or to fail to reach their full potential (data protection).

19.5   Green Computing and Data Protection

The law of unintended consequences does not mean that all of the consequences are bad. Consider "green" computing and data protection. Green computing (a.k.a., green IT) is about improving the energy efficiency of the IT infrastructure. Businesses do green computing not so much for the social benefits (although a little positive publicity is always helpful), but rather for the green as in the color-of-money benefits, i.e., cost savings. On the other hand, data protection is the mission-defending function of protecting against data loss in all its various forms. These two separate and distinct functions intersect, in some sense, only by accident, but the intersection is where actions related to data protection have an effect on green computing.

Since data protection is about data, and data is intangible, how can data affect something that results from tangible physical activity—the consumption of energy? The answer is that data resides on storage and takes up space. Online disk storage uses electricity in a double-edged approach: Electricity keeps the disks spinning so that information can be retrieved quickly, and electricity runs the air conditioning that keeps the heat that is caused by the disks spinning from building up and causing the disks to fail. The more data is stored, the more disks are needed, and the more energy is required.

In order of priority, there are five basic strategies for using data protection to go green, as listed in Table 19.2.

Simply deleting data is the most effective data protection-related green computing strategy. No copies of the data should exist, which means that there is not a production copy nor are there any data protection copies. However, the organization that has the most stake in the deletion of data is typically the IT organization. IT, as the data custodians, manages the storage infrastructure and receives the benefits of any energy savings. Yet IT is not the decision maker that can choose to delete the data. That responsibility lies with the data stewards—the mission-enabling data stewards, such as business users, who may think that there may still be business value in the data, or the mission-defending data stewards, such as the legal department

Table 19.2   Go Green with Data Protection

Action	What It Does	Example	Challenge
1. Delete unnecessary data	Reduces the number of HDDs that have to be kept spinning	Old e-mails that no longer serve any potential useful business purpose	Getting agreement on what can be deleted and then carrying out the deletion
2. Eliminate unnecessary data redundancy	Reduces the number of HDDs that have to be kept spinning as well as possibly improving performance and fast recovery	Data reduction (especially single instancing in an archive); master data management that eliminates multiple data copies	Finding the data and corralling it into a form (such as an archive) to which data reduction can be applied
3. Put data to sleep	Sleeping data uses no energy	Offline magnetic tape; MAID drives or drives that are spun down	If offline tape ever needs to be recovered, the time can be long; if quiescent drives need to be accessed more frequently than planned, that decreases the energy savings
4. Store more data per watt	Improves energy efficiency— fewer watts per unit of storage	SATA drives vs. FC drives	Make sure that the SATA drives can deliver satisfactory performance
5. Change technology mix	Improves energy efficiency— fewer watts per unit of storage	Use SSDs instead of HDDs	The additional SSD costs far outweigh any energy savings

or the compliance officer, who may feel that there is a legal risk in deleting the data. So deleting data is best but is not always possible.

Eliminating data redundancy, while keeping a production copy and any necessary data protection copies, is the next best strategy. IT does not have to get permission to get rid of redundancy as long as any changes are not apparent to users in their ability to access the data for business purposes. However, the first task that IT faces is data knowledge—what data is around and where is located. The second question is how to collect the data in as central a repository as possible without imposing an access burden on end users. For example, shared copies of attachments to e-mails may be scattered around the world. Putting the data in a form to which data reduction can be applied is another challenge. Once again the need for active archiving becomes apparent, although some form of federation rather than a single centralized archive may be necessary. The green computing benefits of redundancy elimination should give additional emphasis to finding ways to make it happen.

The third approach is to put data to sleep. Data that may have to be kept for legal or cautionary reasons, but for which it is reasonable to expect that it will never need to be seen again, can be written to magnetic tape. The magnetic tapes can be taken offline and stored as deep archives, where the data is really in suspended animation. An offline tape uses no energy. The downside is that if the data ever needs to be accessed, the time to retrieve and restore it may be measured in days at best.

For data that follow the long-tail paradigm (according to the long-tail statistical distribution that shows that data may be accessed, but very infrequently), storing on a MAID array or an individual RAID set of spun-down disks is a way of putting data to sleep. Disks that are asleep use no energy because they are not spinning around. The problem is that even one access requires that a drive be spun up to a working state, and with a large number of files involved, even a low number of average accesses may add up to a large number of energy uses. And that can dilute the energy savings. Preventing that from happening requires careful planning.

Another way of saving money is with energy-efficient drives. SATA drives use fewer watts per unit of storage than FC or SAS drives. That has been a secondary benefit, however, since the rise in popularity of SATA drives occurred because they give satisfactory performance for many applications while costing less.

Changing the technology mix is another alternative. In some instances, tape might be used for active archives to which access is infrequent. Disk as front-end cache for actual data-in-use enables that possibility. But the technology mix differentiator is SSD. For example, flash memory is more energy-efficient than a HDD of any variety. The problem is that the cost of flash memory is so much higher that the energy savings are lost.

All in all, going green with data protection is not a misnomer. It is possible to improve energy consumption while protecting the data, by using the opportunity to eliminate unneeded or redundant data or uptime. At the same time, users should note that data protection by keeping more recoverable copies of a data item, and the inexorable rise in the amount of data stored, moves energy consumption in the opposite direction—and wringing out unnecessary data is a one-shot, yielding diminishing returns as it gets more effective.

19.6   Key Takeaways

- Tiering separates storage into different physical classes by different physical characteristics. Tier 0 solid-state drives are best at meeting the responsiveness data protection objective, but they are the most expensive. Tier 1 Fibre Channel (FC) or serial SCSI (SAS) is the storage currently used for most mission-critical applications. Tier 2 serial ATA (SATA) drives have better cost per capacity than Tier 1 drives and are used for non-performance-intensive applications. Tier 3 tape focuses on its ability to provide long-term and, as necessary, offsite data protection.

- Server virtualization has great value in improving server utilization, but that putting more eggs in one basket raises the risk stakes for data protection. For high availability, having a failover strategy to standby servers is important, but that provides only a physical solution; High availability must also include monitoring software that helps deal with the logical data protection side as well. Doing the backup/restore process well is essential for operational recovery processes, and the process has to be thought through correctly. Application-aware snapshots is one approach that may be useful. The hardware independence that server virtualization provides gives greater flexibility in setting up disaster recovery sites, but the lessons learned on the high-availability side can be applied to the disaster recovery site as well.

- Master data management is essential for sharing structured information among multiple systems or business processes to yield competitive advantage. MDM cannot exist on its own; it has to be a by-product of a data governance effort. MDM therefore reinforces the need for data governance.

- Data protection can play a key role in green computing. Choices that enterprises make about their data, such as deletion or elimination of data redundancy, or about the storage technologies on which the data resides, can affect the green computing efficiency of an organization.

Chapter 20

Tying It All Together, Including the PRO-Tech Data Protection Model

20.1   What to Look for in This Chapter

- Why a comprehensive framework for data protection is useful
- What the PRO-Tech model for data protection is all about
- How moving to a deeper level of the PRO-Tech model facilitates understanding of what needs to be done to create a comprehensive data protection solution
- How the PRO-Tech model fits in with GRC business responsibilities
- Why formal data governance is important
- How organizations can synthesize a data protection framework
- What some general guidelines for data protection are

In order to meet enterprise responsibilities for compliance and governance, the scope of data protection has to be expanded greatly from its traditional focus on business continuity to include both data compliance and data governance. However, such a strategic change also requires a "sea change" in thinking. Although some businesses recognize that compliance should reside under the wing of data protection, only lately have they registered the barest inclination toward including governance in the framework.

All in all, the *breadth* of data protection has changed, yet in another sense, the *depth* of data protection has also changed. Note that the basic objectives of data protection—data preservation, data availability, data responsiveness, and data confidentiality—have not altered. However, to those four primary objectives, two secondary objectives (secondary only because they are not mandatory in business continuity-related data protection) must be added. Data auditability becomes crucial when data compliance is a recognized goal, and data knowledge becomes critical when data governance issues come to the forefront. Depth, as related to data protection, means that because of "24/7" requirements for applications (no tolerance for downtime or failure) and increased storage growth, an increasingly sophisticated technical challenge arises.

How to deal with both these increased breadth and depth requirements is not intuitively obvious. Existing frameworks, methodologies, and models may affect one or a few aspects of data protection, but not the whole. Why does this matter when organizations typically do not rip-and-replace existing data protection infrastructures but prefer to move in an evolutionary and incremental fashion? There are a number of reasons why putting together a comprehensive plan for data protection is a necessity and not an option. Two key reasons illustrate the benefits of a comprehensive approach:

- *To identify and close gaps in data protection*—using the framework in an extended fashion, IT organizations can identify where they have gaps in data protection coverage, determine what kind of capabilities are necessary to fill those gaps, and enable the exploration of the proper data protection technologies to fill those gaps.
- *To reduce or eliminate misallocation of data protection infrastructure resources*—not only is there a danger of doing too little in some areas of data protection, there is a danger of overkill in other areas. This means that an enterprise is paying too much for what data protection it gets while still not achieving all the data protection that it needs.

20.2   The PRO-Tech Model for Data Protection

The PRO-Tech model (Figure 20.1) provides a starting point for enterprises to drill down to and achieve their specific data protection requirements. The Level 0 framework is composed of four interrelated layers. The **P**rocess layer works with the **R**ules layer, which are business *policy* rules and are subject to the natural **O**rder or the physical and logical structure of the world in which an enterprise finds itself. The **TECH**nology Provisioning layer supplies the technologies that try to meet the rules within the "physics" within which an enterprise finds itself. "PRO-Tech" is a mnemonic to aid in remembering the layers of the model.

The **Process** layer represents the various courses of action that must be taken in parallel with policy issues to ensure that the technologies are doing the job to the best of their ability. Processes implement the business rules of an enterprise. A process consists of a number of steps that are fulfilled in some order—sequential, iterative, or branching. Practices are necessary to

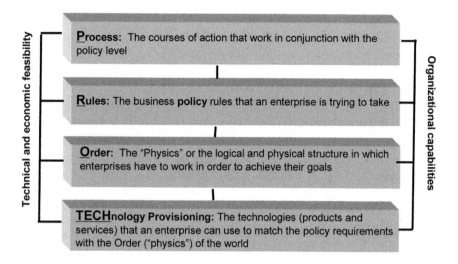

Figure 20.1   The PRO Tech Model for Data Protection Level 0

guarantee that the procedures are carried out. For example, a backup administrator might review a report to verify that a backup job was run successfully.

The **Rules** layer expresses what an enterprise does about data protection from a business rules perspective. Note that these are the actions that the enterprise actually takes—not necessarily the actions that the organization would like to take. For example, an IT organization might want a response time objective (RTO) of 99.999% for an application, but it may have to settle for 99.99% availability. What an organization wants and what it gets may be different because of various constraints.

These constraints are of two types—those external to the organizational structure, i.e., technical, legal, and economic constraints, and those internal to the organization itself, i.e., business/technical capabilities. An organization has greater control over organizational capabilities than over technical, legal, and economic constraints. For example, an organization can theoretically acquire the technical skill sets that it needs, but it may have to accept product limitations even if additional functionality is desired.

The **Order** layer represents the organization's physical and logical structure. Some of this structure is inherent in the nature of the data protection problem and is therefore not subject to change. For example, by definition, a problem can be only a logical or a physical problem. However, an organization can change the location of its physical sites and the structure of its IT infrastructure, such as the hardware components of networks, servers, and storage.

The **Technology Provisioning** layer represents the technologies and services that are applied to the structure of the data protection "universe" to attempt to get the results specified in the policies.

20.3   The PRO-Tech Model—Level 1

Level 0 is general enough that its structure applies to many IT-related projects, including application development projects. However, the moment that Level 0 is functionally decomposed into Level 1, the uniqueness of data protection alone becomes apparent.

20.3.1   Process Layer 1

A history lesson is relevant here. What we now call information technology (IT) was once called data processing, until the name changed to management information systems (MIS). That term lasted until somebody realized that the systems used at the time (accounts payable, accounts receivable, payroll, etc.) were really clerical information systems. However, no one wanted to be associated with that, so the word "management" was dropped and information systems (IS) came into vogue. And that term morphed into the current IT to reflect the ever-broadening perspective of what information is all about.

A return to the old term is not likely, but the term "data processing" is still important in the context of data protection. "Data processing" indicates that both data and process are important and that they are bolted together (as was shown in the movement toward object orientation). Process is still important, as can be seen in Figure 20.2.

For data protection to succeed, both the data (which is what needs to be protected) and the process (the protection mechanism) are critically important. The danger is that some see the process alone as the all-encompassing element (see Sarbanes-Oxley compliance) and stands as an example of what professional services organizations tend to be most comfortable with. Alternatively, starting with the data, specifying what has to be done, seeing what technologies are capable of doing that task, and then seeing what processes and practices have to be put in place to make sure that really happens is an approach that IT organizations should consider.

20.3.2   Rules Layer 1

The business rules layer describes the policies that an organization promulgates (Figure 20.3). The set of data to be managed has to be determined, after which the particular governance, risk management, and

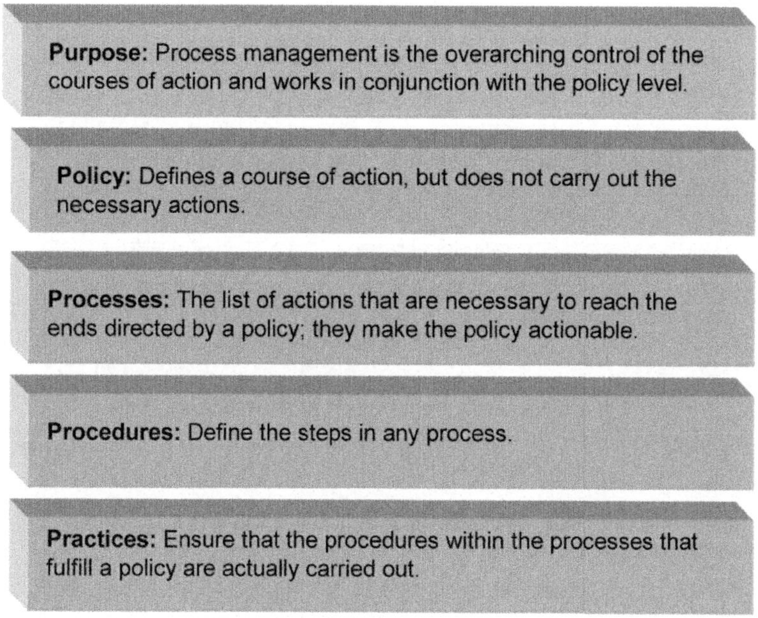

Purpose: Process management is the overarching control of the courses of action and works in conjunction with the policy level.

Policy: Defines a course of action, but does not carry out the necessary actions.

Processes: The list of actions that are necessary to reach the ends directed by a policy; they make the policy actionable.

Procedures: Define the steps in any process.

Practices: Ensure that the procedures within the processes that fulfill a policy are actually carried out.

Figure 20.2   Process Level 1

compliance (GRC) responsibilities that apply to that set of data has to be determined. Primary objectives apply to all GRC responsibilities, and secondary objectives apply as necessary. Recall that the basic objectives of data protection are preservation, responsiveness, availability, and confidentiality, and the secondary objectives are knowledge and auditability (the PRACtiKAl mnemonic).

The focus of the work, i.e., prevention, restart, recovery, or damage control, then has to be determined. Yes, everyone would like to meet service-level objectives, but that may not always be feasible. What are the fallback positions that may have to be invoked and under what conditions would invoking the fallback position be appropriate to minimize impact?

20.3.3   Order Layer 1

In Level 1 for Order (Figure 20.4), the type of problem (logical or physical) and the nature of the problem (logical or physical) are at the level of axioms that are simply basic elements in any data protection analysis.

Local and remote localities, while they appear to have similarities, are not quite so clearly associated. For example, equipment can be at a site, spread across a "campus," or spread over a WAN, which can be as wide-

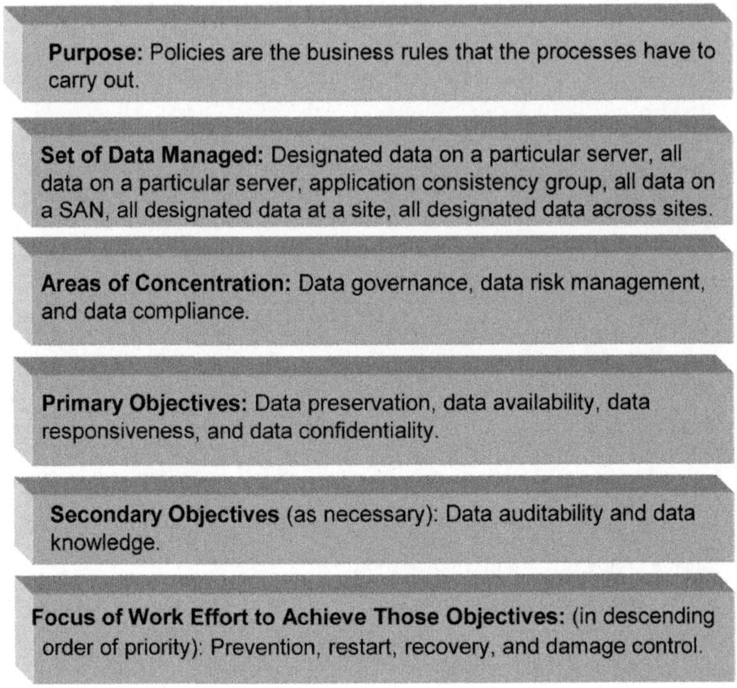

Purpose: Policies are the business rules that the processes have to carry out.

Set of Data Managed: Designated data on a particular server, all data on a particular server, application consistency group, all data on a SAN, all designated data at a site, all designated data across sites.

Areas of Concentration: Data governance, data risk management, and data compliance.

Primary Objectives: Data preservation, data availability, data responsiveness, and data confidentiality.

Secondary Objectives (as necessary): Data auditability and data knowledge.

Focus of Work Effort to Achieve Those Objectives: (in descending order of priority): Prevention, restart, recovery, and damage control.

Figure 20.3   Rules Level 1

spread as the earth itself. Organizations that require a finer granularity can refine the parameter of the locality variable.

Similarly, data is usually considered changeable (i.e., subject to I/O modifications) or fixed (not modified). However, slow changeability may be another choice, introducing the element of time, such as for an adjustable rate mortgage that changes very infrequently.

The elements of the IT infrastructure represent conditions under which the process of data protection has to operate. The hardware side includes servers, networks, and storage, while the software side includes applications, database management systems, file systems, and operating systems as well as all the necessary software "glue." However "physical" these elements are, the infrastructure is not necessarily fixed. For example, if a particular technology is absolutely required to protect a particular set of data in some way, but that technology does not run on the current operating system/hardware server combination, the underlying infrastructure might have to be changed to accommodate it. That is probably a last resort, but it illustrates that the infrastructure is not necessarily immutable.

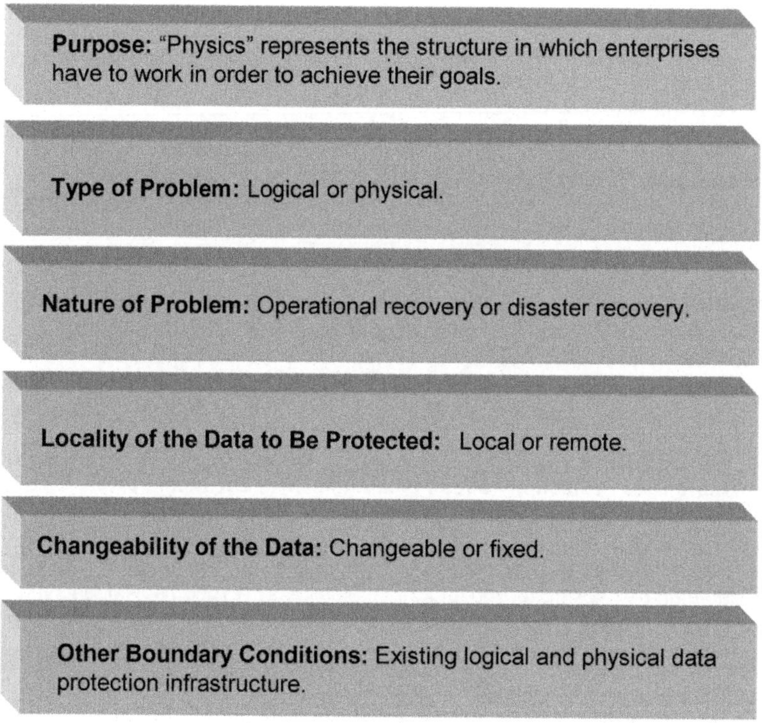

Purpose: "Physics" represents the structure in which enterprises have to work in order to achieve their goals.

Type of Problem: Logical or physical.

Nature of Problem: Operational recovery or disaster recovery.

Locality of the Data to Be Protected: Local or remote.

Changeability of the Data: Changeable or fixed.

Other Boundary Conditions: Existing logical and physical data protection infrastructure.

Figure 20.4   Order Level 1

20.3.4   TECHnology Provisioning Layer 1

Technology provisioning is the level of PRO-Tech that attracts the particular attention of IT organizations, data protection technology suppliers, and the media. Technologies work with existing (or possible) data protection infrastructures within the context of processes and practices to ensure that the policies are being met (Figure 20.5).

A taxonomy (or species "zoo") of data protection technologies reveals quite a range of products. The ones that are typically thought of are the *performers*—those technologies that actually *do* data protection. Recall the enabling, supporting, and facilitating technologies that play key roles in overall data protection. At first thought, enabling, supporting, and facilitating may all seem to be the same category, yet they all inhabit separate categories as well.

- *Enablers* make data protection feasible, either technically or economically. For example, an organization may not be able to afford

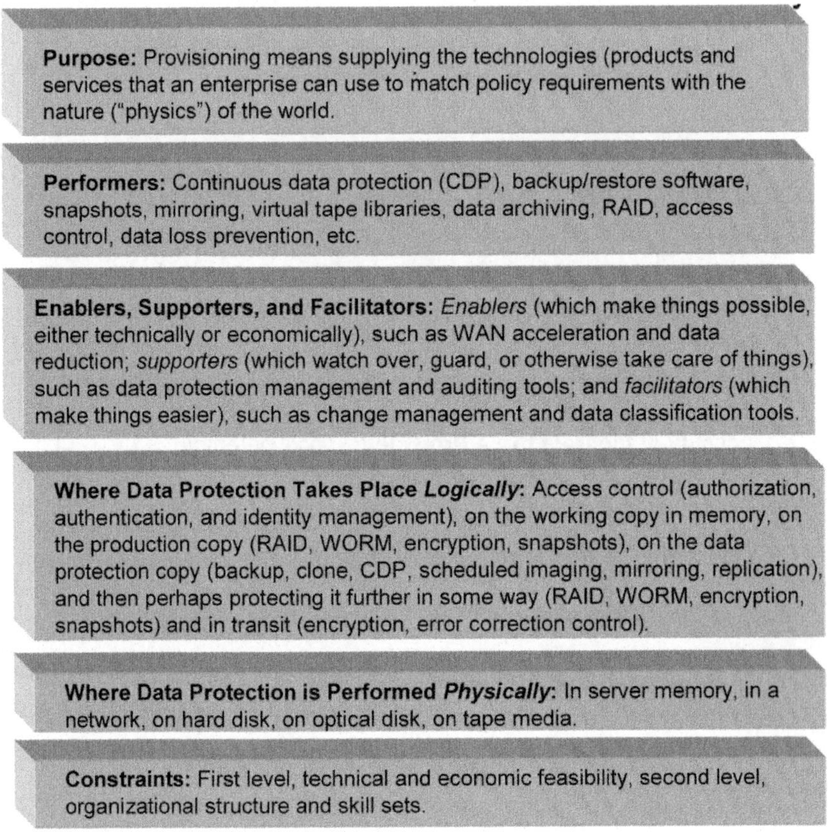

Purpose: Provisioning means supplying the technologies (products and services that an enterprise can use to match policy requirements with the nature ("physics") of the world.

Performers: Continuous data protection (CDP), backup/restore software, snapshots, mirroring, virtual tape libraries, data archiving, RAID, access control, data loss prevention, etc.

Enablers, Supporters, and Facilitators: *Enablers* (which make things possible, either technically or economically), such as WAN acceleration and data reduction; *supporters* (which watch over, guard, or otherwise take care of things), such as data protection management and auditing tools; and *facilitators* (which make things easier), such as change management and data classification tools.

Where Data Protection Takes Place *Logically*: Access control (authorization, authentication, and identity management), on the working copy in memory, on the production copy (RAID, WORM, encryption, snapshots), on the data protection copy (backup, clone, CDP, scheduled imaging, mirroring, replication), and then perhaps protecting it further in some way (RAID, WORM, encryption, snapshots) and in transit (encryption, error correction control).

Where Data Protection is Performed *Physically*: In server memory, in a network, on hard disk, on optical disk, on tape media.

Constraints: First level, technical and economic feasibility, second level, organizational structure and skill sets.

Figure 20.5   Technology Provisioning Level 1

to rip out the existing network infrastructure and upgrade (in which case the current network may not be able to handle the workload), so WAN acceleration (perhaps in conjunction with other technologies) may make remote office backup technically and economically feasible.

■ *Supporters* can be seen as technologies that stand off to the side and help with such things as making sure that policies work. A data protection management product does not have to be in-line to help improve the overall uptime by helping analyze data protection problems that are service-level-threatening (or actual) events.

■ *Facilitators* make some part (if not all) of the data protection process easier. For example, data classification processes help to sort data into piles that need to be protected and piles that do not need to be protected to the same extent. While such processes have little inherent effect on actual data protection, they play a significant role in facilitating the process.

20.4   Tying the PRO-Tech Layers to GRC Business Responsibilities

Since the data protection model is in at least some sense an abstraction, it has to be made real and tangible by functional decomposition into additional layers. For example, the four basic layers of the PRO-Tech model can be mapped to the three GRC business responsibilities—governance, risk management, and compliance—as shown in Table 20.1.

Note that even though all three general business responsibilities follow the PRO-Tech model, each should be treated separately and distinctly. For example, the key process issue in governance is eDiscovery, which is a knowledge issue, while for risk management the continuity of keeping busy processes running smoothly is paramount, and for compliance, proving compliance is the central theme.

Note also that the IT organization does not have the same degree of responsibility for IT governance and IT compliance as it does for IT risk management. IT can act as a service, but IT cannot assume a level of responsibility that is not appropriate. This shows up clearly in the policy rules, where governance focuses on evidence and compliance focuses on authentication, while risk management typically focuses on recovery (if prevention does not work).

Achieving order includes whether the data is retention-managed or not. Both governance and compliance *require* data to be retention-managed, which means that it must be fixed-content data, and the most appropriate home for fixed-content data is an active archive. Some (actually, much) risk management data is fixed-content and can be data retention-managed in an active archive. However, IT organizations have typically focused on active changeable data used with live production operational processes that are essential to the enterprise. Managing governance and compliance data thus may require a fundamental change in viewpoint by IT, since archiving data is typically viewed as an afterthought.

Other issues also arise. For example, the scope of governance also presents a concern for IT because the data for governance may be outside its traditional control, but IT is also likely to be asked to figure out a way to bring that data under IT's purview. In addition, IT will have to examine its data protection technology mix, because technologies that have served the

Table 20.1   Data Protection One Size Doesn't Fit All

		Governance	Risk Management	Compliance
Process	Value-added differentiator	Knowledge	Continuity	Auditability
	Primary responsibility	Shared	Information technology	Senior executives
Rule	Key policy goal for data	Evidence	Recovery	Authentication
Order	Primary type of data managed	Fixed	Changeable	Fixed
	First storage pool focus	Active archive	Active changeable	Active archive
	Data retention-focused	Yes	No	Yes
	Scope of data managed	Unbounded	Bounded	Targeted
TECH-nology Provisioning	First data protection mode focus	Replication	Copy	Replication
	Periodicity of requests	Ad hoc	Always on	On demand

test of time for the risk management responsibility may not serve as well (or at all) for the governance or compliance responsibilities.

Still, the PRO-Tech model enables organizations to start (in conjunction with the other material in this book) a comprehensive data protection architecture and infrastructure planning process. For each set of application data, an IT organization can examine the Order (structure) to which is can apply Rules which Process carries out using Technology. The PRO-Tech model does not provide all the answers, but it provides a starting point on which the organization can build.

Table 20.2 Data Coverance Leadership Requirements and Foundations

	What Needs to Be Done
Leadership	
Executive	Determine what ongoing commitment is required
Data stewardship/data custodianship	Determine the roles, responsibilities, and participation in data governance for individuals across the enterprise
Foundations	
Business continuity/disaster recovery (BC/DR)	Determine not only whether BC/DR is up to its traditional risk management responsibilities, but also whether BC/DR will be able to incorporate the new demands for compliance and governance
Information lifecycle management	Understand what events change the lifecycle stage for data and what that means for data protection
Data architecture	Institute programs for the management of data as appropriate, such as master data management
Retention management	Analyze the ongoing requirements for keeping and disposing of data
Data quality	Determine the appropriate data quality requirements across all applications
Security	Added focus on issues related to the confidentiality of information

20.5 Data Protection Is Everyone's Business—Last Call for Data Governance

The requirement for a formal data governance process has been a pervasive recurring theme throughout this book. Without such an integrating force, different aspects of data protection will continue to be treated as isolated islands. Although such an approach may work more or less well, it is unlikely to function as efficiently or effectively as when data governance is considered as an integrated whole.

Data governance can be divided into leadership and foundations (Table 20.2). Leadership is about organizational structure, and foundations are about the fundamental programs that should be part of a data governance program. Any particular data governance program may add other programs as necessary.

This does not mean that data governance controls every activity that can be associated with data protection. For example, a compliance effort to meet the requirements of a particular regulation or a particular eDiscovery effort needs to be coordinated with the data governance effort to ensure that efforts are consistent with the ongoing needs of the business, but the compliance effort is likely to run as an independent project on a day-to-day basis. And yet, without the big picture that data governance provides, the small pieces are not likely to be as efficient or effective as they could be.

Moreover, organizations should take advantage of already ongoing activities and leverage them as much as possible. These might include the Information Technology Infrastructure Library, information assurance, information risk management, and any other ongoing efforts that might be relevant.

20.6   Synthesizing a Data Protection Framework

Assimilating all the concepts presented in this book is likely to be a challenge, so considering some suggested basic actions may help provide a little final grounding. Although the actual work may be time-consuming, the overall actions can be easily specified:

1. *Separate active archive data from active changeable data.* Start with the reordered and revised matrix (Table 11.1). For each application, determine the mix of active changeable data versus fixed-content data. Can a "distillation" process be put in place to move the fixed content into an active archive? Does it make sense to do so? What does it take to put an active archive in place? Can the active archive serve the needs of multiple applications, or do you need to create appliances, such as for a compliance application?

Table 20.3   Data Protection Requirements for Application n

	Active Changeable		Active Archive	
	Operational Continuity	Disaster Recovery	Operational Continuity	Business Continuity
Physical				
Logical				

(The analysis devolves to the left side of Table 20.3 for those applications for which an active archive is not a consideration.)

2. *Determine the minimum acceptable requirements for both the left side (Active Changeable) and right side (Active Archive) for all data protection objectives.* There is no easy way to set requirements. What an organization might like (say, 100% availability) may not be affordable, and what an organization can afford to budget (say, 95% availability) may not be acceptable to the business. Start with a realistic number. When the time comes later for analysis, determine the cost. If the cost is too high, opt for a solution that is close to the desired goal but still meets budget requirements. Determine the impact on the business of the gap between the two choices. Perhaps a business case can be put together to justify additional funding. Remember that, in this whole process, all objectives—data preservation, data availability, data responsiveness, and data confidentiality—have to be met. Do not get locked into defining a requirement that is not comfortable for you. For example, as discussed earlier, recover-point objectives for operational continuity and for disaster continuity may be different.

3. *Determine the degrees of data protection (including both high- and low-availability alternatives) that can help meet selected objectives.* This book focuses strongly on data preservation and data availability objectives, which is where the degrees of protection come in. Data responsiveness and some aspects of availability are over-all IT infrastructure issues. The confidentiality objective must be worked through with the security officer.

4. *Determine whether current data protection processes and technologies meet the requirements of data protection to the required degree.* This is a gap analysis to see if there are any differences between what is "required" and what is being delivered today.

5. *If there are any deficiencies (or excesses) in data protection, determine what classes of data protection technology might close the gap and then evaluate those technologies for suitability.* The first goal is to determine the feasibility of the technology from a general perspective. The second goal is to examine the particulars and costs of specific vendor implementations of those technologies that can work in conjunction with an IT infrastructure.

Although the steps have been discussed in linear fashion, the actual process is likely to be more iterative, may branch in different directions, and may drill down to finer levels of granularity.

20.7   Guidelines for Data Protection

The preceding section discussed how to go about using the frameworks. Some general guidelines (or rules of thumb) may be useful for an overall perspective (fully recognizing that prescribing bromides is a lot easier than taking them).

1.   Make sure that the necessary layers of both physical and logical data protection strategies are in place. Organizations do not want to leave gaps in their protection coverage.

2.   Take the complexity out of the process wherever possible. One way of doing this is to minimize the number of things that can go wrong (which is why using dated replication instead of backup/restore software for fixed-content information is important).

3.   Remember that an information lifecycle management plan that creates a strategy for active archiving requires data classification, a pooling and tiering plan, and data retention policies as part of the process.

4.   Have a triage plan in place in case of emergency; but remember that such a plan first requires being able to isolate the interactions among applications (if everything is interrelated, that may be a problem).

5.   Remember that physical data protection is often a simple matter of "dialing up" the level of protection that you need, but that logical data protection has to be thought through very carefully to determine the level of protection that is provided.

6.   Know who is going to address a general class of problems, and how, before it occurs. Make sure that you have at least two people (preferably at different sites) who can take action in case one person, for whatever reason, is not able to deal with the problem.

7.   Remember that tasks can be delegated, but responsibility cannot be. If a third party is involved, such as for eDiscovery, compliance, or storage as a service, the enterprise can delegate work, but it is still responsible for the results.

20.8   The Challenge Ahead and a Call to Action

Organizations face a dilemma regarding data protection. If they maintain the status quo and try to do only what they are now doing, they face the prospect of increased unmanageability, with the prospect of not protecting all the data all the time as it should be protected. If they make changes in their data protection processes and infrastructure, they run the risks inherent in introducing new technologies, including management of the organizational change processes.

This book should help organizations think about preserving what they can preserve, but also help organizations move forward to adapt to the ongoing sea change. This means that the status quo is not acceptable. Organizations have to move forward—and they have to do it now.

The sea change in data protection is here. Here's hoping that what you have learned from this book can help you and your organization ride the waves of the sea change successfully.

20.9   Key Takeaways

- If they are all considered independently, the concepts and technology of data protection can be overwhelming. Using a planning framework can help identify and close gaps in data protection as well as reduce or eliminate the misallocation of data protection infrastructure resources.

- The PRO-Tech model is a memory aid to remember four interrelated layers—**P**rocess, **R**ules, **O**rder, and **T**echnology—that all have to be examined to put together a workable data protection plan. The Process layer describes the courses of action that have to be carried out in accordance with the policies specified in the Rules layer. These can only be performed within the logical and physical infrastructure constraints of the Order layer. The Technology provisioning layer must provide solutions that are feasible in the Order layer and can actually be carried out through policy and process.

- The high level (Level 0) of the PRO-Tech model is very conceptual. In order to start thinking about planning, a deeper level (Level 1) needs to be understood. While this level is still very general, it provides a starting point where organizations can think about what they will need to think about when drilling down to a Level 2 that is specific to their organization's requirements.

- When starting the data protection planning process, organizations have to keep in mind each of the GRC responsibilities (governance, risk management, and compliance), because each has different requirements when applied to the PRO-Tech model. One-size data protection does not fit all three responsibilities.
- To be successful, data governance requires leadership in terms of both executive commitment and day-to-day work. Active projects need to be established to build the foundations of data governance.
- Synthesizing a data protection framework is not as easy as painting by the numbers, but some rules can be followed to simplify the process.
- Even though data protection is complex, following some simple guidelines can help organizations manage the process better.

Glossary

Active archiving   Data for which frequency of access is active rather than inactive, while frequency of updating is nonexistent so the data is fixed (i.e., unchanging) and not subject to I/O writes that would change the data.

Active changeable   Data for which frequency of access is active rather than inactive, while frequency of updating leads to changes in the data so that the data is not fixed (i.e., unchanging).

Advanced authentication   Authentication that goes beyond username and password, such as two-factor authentication.

Advanced encryption management   Sophisticated management of the encryption process, especially key management that includes the ability to restore at any location, key sharing among more than one individual, and a secure key repository.

Appliance   A storage system that is dedicated to a specific function, e.g., data protection or compliance.

Archive   A long-term collection of data that typically is fixed-content data; i.e., no I/O writes are allowed to change the data.

Asynchronous remote mirroring   Remote mirroring in which the source and the target may not necessarily be identical because of a delay from the target in acknowledging a write.

Auditability   The level of transparency to which transactions in a system can be traced, examined, and verified with regard to an external audit. Auditability refers to all the data in a system taken as a whole, whereas authentication applies to individual pieces of data.

Auditing   A security function that requires the capture and retention of logs that detail attempts to obtain access as well as attempts to make unauthorized modifications to data of any type.

Authentication	(1) A legal evidentiary standard that, in the case of electronically stored information, ensures that the data and its associated metadata is accurate, complete, and has not been altered. Without authentication, data cannot be used as evidence. (2) A security function that defines the rules and responsibilities of individuals, applications, and devices for creating, reading, updating, and deleting data.
Authorization	A security process that verifies the claims of an individual, application, or device to be the entity that it purports to be.
Backup/restore	Backup is a dated (i.e., specified-time) duplication of a designated set of data from a data source on one set of media (typically disk) to a backup set of media (either disk or tape); restore takes the data from a previously created set of data on backup media and copies it to a set of media from which an application that uses the data can access it.
Business continuity	A business function that attempts to prevent any major disruptions to business processes, both through planning, to avoid unplanned outages in the first place, and then through implementing solutions that minimize the effects of unplanned outages if they do occur.
Capacity disk	A disk drive designed to give a more effective cost ($/GB) than drives that are considered performance disks; capacity disks are suitable for applications that are not I/O-bound.
Chain of custody	A jurisprudential process for validating how electronic records that may need to serve as evidence have been gathered, tracked, and protected over time; preserving the chain of custody for data is key to the authentication process and involves system audit logs and access controls.
Clone copy	A point-in-time copy that also creates an additional physical copy.
Cloud computing	The service delivery of any IT resource as a networked resource.
Colocation	A third party provides only physical plant services, such as space and power, to a customer, which provides its own hardware and software.

Compliance	(1) Conforming or acquiescing to requirements from a third party. (2) A subset of data retention policies and procedures that must adhere to more rigid and rigorous conditions.
Compliance appliance	An active archive appliance that serves the dual purposes of storing compliant data that can be accessed online by authorized users and of enforcing data retention policies on that compliant data.
Compliance software	Software that electronically enables the carrying out of compliance management functions, such as chain-of-custody management, or enables the enforcement of regulations, such as for privacy and confidentiality.
Compression	Removing the redundancy found in a stream of bits within a single file in order to condense the file.
Continuous data protection (CDP)	The ability to create a copy of data that can be restored to any point in time.
Copy	An imitation or reproduction of an original.
Customer data integration (CDI)	The combination of process and technologies that is necessary to integrate and standardize the representation of customer as a data entity across multiple systems, applications, and databases.
Data auditability	The ability to verify that data is always correct.
Data availability	The ability of I/O requests to reach a storage device and take the appropriate action.
Data breach	The unauthorized disclosure of confidential information, notably that of identifying information about individuals.
Data classification	The process of separating data into separate piles (i.e., categories to which different policies—say, different data protection policies—apply).
Data confidentiality	Data is available only to those authorized.
Data deduplication	A data reduction approach that determines common sequences of data at a subfile level across a large volume of data and then eliminates all the redundant copies of the common data sequences.
Data destruction	An alternative term for data shredding.
Data disposition	An alternative term for data shredding.
Data governance (a.k.a. information governance)	A subset of IT governance that includes the people, processes, and technologies necessary to ensure the preservation, availability, confidentiality, and usability of an enterprise's data.

Data integrity   The bits of data that are put in storage (via I/O writes) are the same bits of data—order and completeness—that come out (via I/O reads).

Data knowledge   A secondary objective of data protection that requires being able to look at content itself, i.e., content-aware.

Data leak   Same as a data breach.

Data lifecycle management (DLM)   Managing data as blocks without underlying knowledge of the content of the blocks, based on limited metadata (e.g., creation date, last accessed).

Data loss   Deprivation of something useful or valuable about a set of data, such as unplanned physical destruction of data or failure to preserve the confidentiality of data.

Data loss prevention   Attempts to prevent the loss of confidentiality of sensitive information by limiting the use of confidential information only for authorized purposes.

Data management   The non-data-path control and use of data itself from creation to deletion, such as migration, replication, and backup/restore processes.

Data migration   Form- and function-preserving movement of data between locations or formats, which can take one of three forms: (1) from one physical system or location to another; (2) from one physical format to another; or (3) from one logical format to another.

Data preservation   Data must be consistent and accurate all the time, and also must be complete within acceptable limits.

Data privacy   The right to have personally identifiable information not disclosed in any unauthorized manner.

Data protection   Mitigation of the risk or loss of or damage to an enterprise's data on either a temporary or permanent basis.

Data protection appliance   A dedicated, self-contained bundle of software and hardware that serves a specific data protection function.

Data protection change management   Detailed software that enables data-protection-related configurations to be kept up to date and/or tested regularly.

Data protection management   Enables the management of data protection processes that actually perform data protection, but does not itself do data protection.

Data protection services Professional services, such as consulting, integration, project management, and knowledge transfer, that are specific to helping organizations with their data protection requirements.

Data quality Assurance that data is accurate, complete, and consistent, to ensure that a particular business purpose can be carried out correctly.

Data responsiveness The ability of I/Os to deliver data to an authorized user according to measures of timeliness that are deemed appropriate for an application.

Data retention Policies and practices concerning when specific data should be kept and when it should be disposed of.

Data reduction Removing redundancy in data across a pool of storage at a low level of granularity, for example, at the subfile level

Data security Secures the data assets of an organization.

Dated replication A time-stamped new physical copy of data.

Data shredding The process of legally destroying all copies of electronic information on or after the appropriate expiration of the designated retention period for the information.

Deduplication May refer to data reduction in general or to specific approaches to data reduction in particular.

Deep archiving The original definition of archiving, whereby production data is written to another set of storage media (typically tape) and moved offsite while the original version is deleted (typically from disk).

Degree of data protection Each degree of data protection is a layer that can tolerate one point of failure.

Digital rights management (DRM) Manages the storage and delivery of confidential content to authorized users, such as within an organization and its partners or to customers in an e-commerce context.

Direct-attached storage (DAS) One or more storage devices that connect to a server on a dedicated basis.

Disaster continuity Proactive planning, provisioning, monitoring, and preventive maintenance to minimize the impact of a devastating event on an enterprise if one should occur.

Disaster recovery (DR) The attempt to minimize the impact of a disaster on business processes if a disaster should occur.

Disk-based backup	Using a disk array rather than a tape automation system as the target of a backup process.
DRAM-based drives	Solid-state drives that use dynamic random-access memory (DRAM) devices.
eDiscovery	Electronic discovery, the process of making electronic records (eRecords) available.
eDiscovery software	Software that is specifically designed to aid in the legal discovery process for electronic documents.
Electronic Discovery Reference Model (EDRM)	A model that describes all the stages of the electronic discovery process.
Electronic locking	Through the use of software, "lock" data from being modified.
Electronically stored information (ESI)	Information that is stored as a result of the use of electronic information systems.
Electronic vaulting	Moving data for data protection purposes from a source site to a target site over a network.
Encryption	Reordering of bits of data to make it unintelligible (and therefore useless) to an unauthorized third party, while still enabling the authorized user to use the data after the reverse process of decryption.
eRecords	Electronic records, data that is part of overall electronically stored information.
Fibre Channel (FC)	A set of standards for a serial I/O bus.
File differencing	Sending only the small changes in a file detected via a byte-level scan over a network from a target to a source repository.
Fixed content	Data that is highly unlikely (or impossible) to change via I/O writes.
Flash drives	Solid-state drives that use NAND technology.
Governance	(1) Planning, influencing, and conducting the decision-making affairs of an enterprise. (2) The processes and systems that ensure proper accountability for the conduct of an enterprise's business.
Governance, risk management, and compliance (GRC)	Three independent but closely interrelated, major responsibilities of any organization.

Governance, risk management, and compliance (GRC) software
Software that is specifically designed to aid a formal GRC program in an enterprise.

Green computing
Improving the energy efficiency of the IT infrastructure; also known as green IT.

High availability (HA)
A relative term to indicate that the unavailability of an IT application to users is measured in terms of seconds or minutes per year.

Hypervisor
A control program called a virtual machine monitor that enables multiple operating systems to run on a host computer.

Identity management
The process of identifying individuals so that their access to resources is restricted to the established identity.

Information assurance
All the actions that protect and defend information and information systems to ensure their availability, integrity, authentication, confidentiality, and nonrepudiation.

Information lifecycle management (ILM)
Policy-driven management of information as it changes value throughout the full range of its lifecycle, from conception to disposition.

Information governance
See Data governance.

Information management
Manages the content and decision-making relationships of information as it moves through the lifecycle of a business process, such as records management and content management.

Information risk management
An approach that deals with the management of risk for an information portfolio.

Information security
Secures the information assets of an organization.

Information Technology Infrastructure Library (ITIL)
A framework of "best practices" that facilitate the delivery of information technology as a service.

I/O
Input/output; the process of moving data between the main memory of a computer and some other device, such as a piece of storage media.

IOPS
Input/output operations per second; indicates the number of operations that can be executed in 1 second and is a measure of performance for storage.

IT governance	The structure of relationships and processes that govern IT decision making in investment decisions, infrastructure management, client relationships, and all other aspects of the IT business function.
Logical data protection	Protection of the data itself from change through unauthorized or erroneous I/O requests.
Long tail	For data, a statistical distribution that contains a large amount of data in which the value of individual files, streams, or records is relatively low, but the value of the long tail as a whole is high.
Long-term archiving	Active archived data for which the frequency of access has fallen so low that a tier of more cost-effective storage may be a more appropriate place to house the data.
Low availability	A relative term to indicate that the unavailability of an IT application to users is measured in terms of hours or days per year.
MAID (Massive Array of Idle Disks)	Spinning down disks when they are not accessed increases lifetime and lowers cooling and electricity costs while at the same time preserving online accessibility as required.
Managed hosting	The highest level of off-premises service provision, in which the service provider may take over all tasks having to do with the service, as well as providing the software that carries out the service.
Managed services	The service supplier provides support and administration services and sometimes the hardware to run the software on (as well as specialized services), while the customer provides the software.
Master data	Data that needs to be shared by multiple systems or business processes.
Master data management (MDM)	The process of governing master data as well as supporting information technologies that is responsible for defining, managing, and synchronizing the use of master data across disparate systems and business processes.
Media sanitization	A technical term that can be used in place of data shredding, but it applies to all of a piece of media, whereas data shredding may be more selective.
Mirroring	Duplicating the data in an array on another array.
Multitenancy	Applications and resources may be shared among multiple customers while maintaining confidentiality.

Multiple-parity RAID RAID (redundant array of independent disks) configurations that can sustain the loss of at least two drives without data loss; for example, RAID 6.

Nearline Data protection data that can be accessed "online," typically only by authorized specialists.

Offline Data protection data that requires a manual process to put it back in a network-accessible state (such as inserting into a tape library).

Online Production data that can be accessed directly by a user over a network; typically considered to be stored on high-performance disks, but that is not a necessity.

Operational continuity Proactive planning, provisioning, monitoring, and preventive maintenance to prevent a service-level-impacting event for specific applications from occurring in the first place, or to minimize the impact of such an event if it does occur.

Operational recovery (OR) Minimizing the impact of a service-level-impacting event for specific applications when one occurs.

Performance disk FC- or SAS-based hard disk drives or DRAM or flash-memory-based solid-state disks for which capacity disk drives do not have adequate performance characteristics; the trade-off is typically a higher price ($/GB).

Physical data protection Protection of data by preserving the physical integrity and functionality of the physical substrate on which the data resides, travels, or is processed.

Point-in-time copy A "copy" of a pool of data, "frozen" (i.e., made unchangeable) at a chosen instant of time.

Pooling A collection of information that is managed as a homogeneous whole for quality-of-service (QoS) purposes.

RAID (redundant array of independent disks) Using more disks than is necessary for the actual data itself, as a buffer against failure of one (or possibly more) disks.

Recovery management Combines data protection technologies and supporting software services to deliver a broader and more integrated focus on data recovery than any targeted data protection software product can achieve on its own.

Recovery-point objective (RPO)	The difference between the time when a failure occurs and the previous time when a set of data was available (such as a tape from the previous day) to which a recovery is made. Such a recovery results in a potential permanent loss of all changes to data for the intervening time.
Recovery-time objective (RTO)	The time required to return an application to a working state after a downtime situation occurs.
Removable disk	The ability to remove a RAID group of disk drives (which also contain the disk media) as a whole, or the ability to separate the disk platters themselves from the disk drives.
Replication	Carrying out an identical transaction on two copies of the data in sequence.
Risk management	A structured process for managing risk.
SAS (Serial Attached SCSI)	Serial Storage Small Computer System Interface; an evolution of SCSI that has a common electrical and physical interface with SATA.
SATA (Serial ATA)	Serial Advanced Technology Attachment; a serial signal processing standard for connecting hard drives to computer systems.
Scheduled-image data protection	A low-RTO/RPO solution that can restore data to an application-marked event that yields a consistent durable recovery point (sometimes called near-CDP); typically-based on using tight-interval snapshots.
Sea change	A marked transformation over time.
Semistructured data	"Text" documents, such as e-mail, word processing, presentations, and spreadsheets, whose content can be searched.
Semisynchronous remote mirroring	Remote mirroring in which a limited number (greater than one) of I/O operations at the source site are allowed to complete before requiring acknowledgement from the target site.
Server virtualization	Enables multiple instances of operating systems operating as virtual machines under the control of a Hypervisor to run on the same physical server.
Service-level agreement (SLA)	An agreement between a service provider and a service recipient that formally defines the levels of service that are to be provided.

Service-oriented architecture (SOA)	An architecture that enables IT resources to be made available to other participants in a network as independent services that are accessed in a standardized way without knowledge of the underlying platform implementation.
Single instancing	Storing only a single copy of a file in a pool of storage.
Snapshot copy	A point-in-time copy.
Software-as-a-Service (SaaS)	A client business uses a software application that is designed to be accessed over the Web at a third-party site
Solid-state drive (SSD)	A device that has no moving parts and is assigned the role of storage drive.
STorage-as-a-Service (STaaS)	A third-party-hosted services model for storage services and storage capacity.
Spoliation	The ruination of data as evidence due to alteration, mutilation, or destruction.
Storage area network (SAN)	A network dedicated for transferring data between a computer and storage elements as well as between storage elements themselves.
Storage management	Discovers, monitors, and controls physical storage assets.
Storage pool	A mapping of a pool of information to a storage tier.
Storage security	Security that focuses on preventing unauthorized access to, and modification/deletion of, data on storage devices.
Storage virtualization	The process of taking physical storage and making it appear as one virtual entity for management purposes.
Structured data	Database data, such as OLTP (Online Transaction Processing System) data, which can be sorted.
Synchronous remote mirroring	Remote mirroring in which the source and target pools of information are identical.
Tape automation	Combines pieces of tape media, tape drives, and tape robotics into a unified system for the movement, processing, and storage of tape-related information.
Tape library virtualization	The ability to allocate tape drives and tape slots dynamically rather than having fixed assignments.
Thin provisioning	A means of overbooking physical capacity on a virtual basis while actually releasing capacity only on an as-required basis until real physical capacity is exhausted.

Tiering   Separation of storage into classes by the characteristics of the storage itself.

Tier 0 storage   Use of high-speed SSDs for added storage performance.

Tier 1 storage   Often referred to as primary storage; typically uses FC or SAS drives.

Tier 2 storage   Offers good price per unit of capacity compared to Tier 1 storage, but with not as good performance; typically uses SATA drives.

Tier 3 storage   Tape system infrastructure.

Two-factor authentication   An authentication protocol that requires two forms of authentication for access to data, such as something a user knows (factor one) as well as something that the user has (factor two).

Unstructured data   Natively bitmapped data, such as video, audio, pictures, and MRI scans, that can be sensed either visually, audibly, or both.

Vaulting   Typically, the movement of data on tapes from a target site to a protected remote site.

Virtualization   Creation of a virtual, as opposed to a real, instance of an entity, such as an operating system, server, storage, or network.

Virtual machine   Everything under the control of a guest operating system that is managed by a Hypervisor.

Virtual tape   Making disk appear as a piece of virtual tape media (not a tape library) so that data can be more efficiently written to tape media.

Virtual tape library   Use of disk as if it were a tape library through a process of creating virtual tape drives on disk.

WAFS (wide-area file services)   Deals with bandwidth and application performance issues associated with accessing files from a central site at a remote location.

WAN acceleration   Speed-up of transmission rates over a wide-area network (WAN). This accelerates the data transfer process over the WAN.

WORM (write once, read many)   The ability to write only once to a piece of media, but read that media as often as necessary.

WORM disk   Disk media that appear to be write-once, read-many to any user application.

WORM tape   Tape media that are nonerasable and unalterable after the first writing, but that may be read many times.

Index